Institutions and Development

ADVANCES IN NEW INSTITUTIONAL ANALYSIS

Series Editor: Claude Ménard, *Professor of Economics and Director, ATOM (Center for Analytical Theory of Organizations and Markets), University of Paris Pantheón-Sorbonne, France*

Understanding the nature and role of institutions in the dynamics and failures of modern economies is an increasing concern among scholars and policymakers. Substantial progress has been made in economics as well as in other social sciences, particularly political science, history, sociology and the managerial sciences. New institutional scholars have been, and remain, at the forefront of this movement. Alternative views have also been proposed that deserve consideration. This series intends to promote the development and diffusion of these analyses with books from leading contributors as well as younger up-and-coming scholars.

The series will include topics such as:

- Institutions and growth
- Transaction cost economics
- The role of formal rules and legal institutions
- Regulation and deregulation
- Political institutions and the state
- Institutions and modes of governance
- Contracting issues
- Customs, beliefs and institutional changes.

The series will be essential reading for researchers in economics, the social and managerial sciences, as well as policymakers.
    Titles in the series include:

Institutions and Development
Mary M. Shirley

Institutions and Development

Mary M. Shirley

President, the Ronald Coase Institute, USA

ADVANCES IN NEW INSTITUTIONAL ANALYSIS

Edward Elgar

Cheltenham, UK • Northampton, MA, USA

Published by
Edward Elgar Publishing Limited
The Lypiatts
15 Lansdown Road
Cheltenham
Glos GL50 2JA
UK

Edward Elgar Publishing, Inc.
William Pratt House
9 Dewey Court
Northampton
Massachusetts 01060
USA

A catalogue record for this book
is available from the British Library

Library of Congress Control Number: 2008932902

ISBN 978 1 84542 968 3

Printed and bound in Great Britain by MPG Books Ltd, Bodmin, Cornwall

Contents

Figures

Tables

Abbreviations

AA	Aguas Argentinas
CPIA	Country policy and institutional assessment
CCP	Chinese Communist Party
EC	European Commission
EMOS	Empresa Metropolitana de Obras Sanitarias
ETOSS	Ente Tripartito de Obras de Servicios de Saneamiento
GNI	Gross national income
GNP	Gross national product
IBRD	International Bank for Reconstruction and Development, i.e. the World Bank
ICRG	International Country Risk Guide
IDA	International Development Association
IDB	Inter-American Development Bank
IFC	International Finance Corporation
IMF	International Monetary Fund
IRI	Istituto per la Recostruzione Industriale (Institute for Industrial Reconstruction)
IRR	Internal rate of return
KMT	Kuomintang Party
MCA	Millennium Challenge Account
NGO	Non-governmental organization
NIE	New institutional economics
NPV	Net present value
NYSE	New York Stock Exchange
PIU	Project implementation unit
PPP	Purchasing power parity
RPI	Retail price index
SEC	Securities and Exchange Commission
SIDA	Swedish International Development Agency
SOE	State-owned enterprise
SSS	Superintendencia de Servicos Sanitarios
TA	Technical assistance
TVE	Township and village enterprise

UAW	Unaccounted for water
UN	United Nations
USAID	US Agency for International Development
WTO	World Trade Organization

Preface

WHY THIS BOOK?

So much is written on institutions and economic development that a reader may wonder, why this book? This book is different because it peers inside the black box of institutions. Most of the literature treats institutions as gross abstractions, such as "rule of law," or as outcomes, such as "secure property rights." We lose sight of the host of specific norms and rules that make up societies' institutional frameworks. Thus, property rights are secure in one country and not in another because of specific constitutional clauses, laws, regulations, traditions, norms, and enforcement characteristics. Real-world institutions are complex, and this volume tries to convey this complexity without getting bogged down in a quagmire of details. It shows the forest, illustrates some of the trees, and relates both to the problem of poverty.

This book also differs in its approach to aid and development. The fundamental premise of this book is that development depends on wrenching changes in deeply-rooted institutional frameworks, changes that only happen when people transform their shared beliefs and overturn their power structures. Fundamental changes in shared beliefs and power structures do not happen because of outsiders' money, advice, pressure, or even physical force. Powerful elites oppose reforms they believe will seriously undermine their power and position in society. Non-elites fear reforms they believe will cause instability and violence. Opposition and fear cannot be overcome by more money, better advice, greater reliance on NGOs, more participation of civil society, or other oft-proposed reforms to aid. Aid provides useful humanitarian assistance, but it is ineffective in promoting development because of damaging institutions; damaging institutions that are not changed by aid. To the contrary, because aid must work within a country's power structure, aid often supports the very institutions that render it ineffective.

If aid has not worked, what *has* worked to change societies' beliefs and institutions? We need to know more to answer that question fully. In the last chapter of this book I suggest one force for progress – local scholars who designed new policies and advocated new paradigms that eventually transformed their economies.

WHENCE THIS BOOK?

This book reflects my 35 years as a development practitioner and researcher, 21 at the World Bank. During those years I lived and taught economics in Bogotá, Colombia; worked as a senior economist at the Organization of American States; managed and did economic research at the World Bank; and worked intensively on 34 countries around the world. My perspective on institutions has also been shaped by reading and talking to institutionalists, especially members of the International Society for New Institutional Economics (ISNIE). Not only have I learned a great deal from talking with like-minded scholars at ISNIE, I have also learned from ISNIE's history. I co-founded ISNIE with Alexandra Benham, Lee Benham, John Drobak, Claude Ménard, and Douglass North in 1997, and in ISNIE's evolution I saw how an iconoclastic economic paradigm like new institutional economics could be nurtured and spread by scholars who could organize and communicate at low transaction costs. My perspective has also been shaped by my experience as President of the Ronald Coase Institute since its founding in 2000, working with young researchers from all over the world to promote research on the institutions that govern real economic systems. I have met almost 200 scholars from 50 different countries, participants in the institute's workshops on institutional research. The research and aspirations of these excellent researchers taught me that young scholars are a force to change the world.

Acknowledgements

I have been inspired by two scholars in particular that I am privileged to know. Ronald Coase's brilliant analyses have motivated me, as they have so many others, to strive always to describe accurately how the real world works, never to sacrifice facts to grand ideas or abstract models, never to cite works I have not read. In his conversations as well as in his writings, Ronald Coase challenged economists to make economics useful by grounding it in the world around us, rather than shaping our science to fit the worlds we create on our blackboards or our computers.

Douglass North's wonderful ideas have spurred me to try to draw parallels from his analysis of history to what I know about underdeveloped economies today. I have made extensive use of his writings in this book, and I owe him a large debt of gratitude for allowing me to draw on his most recent manuscript, for his valuable comments on an earlier draft of this book, and for our countless conversations on many of these ideas.

There are many others to thank, in particular Claude Ménard, the editor of this series, for prompting me to write this book to begin with, and for his invaluable and extensive comments. Chapter 7 draws on joint work with Jessica Soto, currently with Instituto Invertir in Lima, Peru, and I thank her for being such an excellent co-author. I thank Colin Xu for his suggestions on China, and Sebastian Galiani for his comments on an earlier version of the chapter on water. I benefited greatly from discussions about some of the ideas in this book with Manuel Abdala, Alexandra Benham, Lee Benham, Avner Greif, Philip Keefer, Roger Noll, John Nye, John Wallis, and Barry Weingast. Parts of this book have been presented to different audiences in seminars at George Mason University, the International Food Policy Research Institute, Stanford University, the Swedish Institute for International Development, and Washington University in St Louis; at conferences organized by the International Society for New Institutional Economics, the Technical University Delft, the Netherlands, and the Western Economic Association; and at workshops of the European School for New Institutional Economics, the Institute for Humane Studies, and the Ronald Coase Institute, and I thank them all for their comments and suggestions. Finally I thank Frans J. Kok for his insightful comments and suggestions and his invaluable moral support.

1. Introduction

Our first evening in Bogotá, Colombia, my husband and I happened upon two small, dirty little boys on the hard cement stoop of a shop, asleep. Very concerned for these poor little boys, we rushed home and asked our landlady to alert the police and social services. She was amazed by our attitude. "It's useless to call." she said, "They will just laugh. Over 50,000 such gamines live on Bogotá's streets, robbing and begging."

Poverty is the rule, not the exception. Most of humanity lives in underdeveloped countries, vast numbers in appalling circumstances. This misery continues despite a fall in extreme poverty from one-third of the world's population in 1981 to 18 percent in 2001 (Chen and Ravallion 2004, p. 14). This drop is welcome indeed, but it does not mean that poor countries are developed now, or will be developed any time soon. Extreme poverty is just that, extreme. The extremely poor live on less than about $1 a day adjusted for difference in the purchasing power of the dollar. If, instead of extreme poverty, we measure poverty as most middle-income countries do – incomes below about $2 a day – then the number of poor increased between 1981 and 2001 and is still 45 percent of the world's population. China does well even on this measure. Poverty in China fell from 85 percent of the population in 1981 to 47 percent in 2001. That is an extraordinary achievement – but not the same as development. Very few people in developed countries live as poorly as the bottom 45 percent of China's population. Moreover, development means more than just fewer poor people. Citizens of developed countries enjoy freer access to political and economic markets, and to ideas, information, and knowledge. They can start businesses, form civil organizations, or create political movements with much greater ease and lower cost. They also benefit from stability and order and from laws that are enforced for most residents, not just for the privileged few.

Why are poor countries poor? At one time development experts believed poverty was caused by too little investment – a problem that could be solved with foreign aid. Yet when investment went up in some poor countries, it did not trigger sustained growth. As Chapter 2 describes, new investment did not spur growth in countries with high transaction costs, powerful business groups, and large informal sectors. When investment did not work, bad macroeconomic policies were blamed. Macroeconomic policies in poor countries were often bad, and development economists preached to poor countries: "Get your prices right." But this advice begged the question: why were governments able to sustain such blatantly damaging policies? Even when countries reformed their macroeconomic policies, they still did not always grow. A new explanation was needed, and education became the development mantra. Yet when workers in poor countries increased their average years in school, labor force productivity did not improve. The benefits of increased education were undermined by poor quality and low returns. Underinvestment, bad policies, and lack of education are proximate, not ultimate, causes of poverty. Ultimately development rests on choices made by societies' members, and those choices are constrained by institutions, the rules and norms that structure human interaction (North 1990).

Every society has a set of fundamental institutions that provide the basic scaffolding for human interactions, what North calls an institutional framework (ibid.). In modern developed societies, institutional frameworks nurture market exchange by lowering the cost of transacting, encouraging trust, and motivating the powerful to protect the property and individual rights of the weak. Institutional frameworks that encourage modern markets only developed in the last 300 years. For millennia people relied on eyeball-to-eyeball barter, and used family ties, religious affiliations, business networks, or social groups to learn the reputations of their trading partners. Traders enforced their bargains by threatening to ostracize cheats. In the late Middle Ages new, more impersonal institutions began to emerge in Europe. Traders began to write bills of lading and contracts and to codify merchants' rules; they began to enforce their agreements through laws, courts, police, and similar third-party mechanisms. Thanks to these new institutions traders were able to contract with people they did not know, who were outside their networks, even outside their country.

How did these impersonal institutions emerge in Europe? Why are such market-supportive institutions weak or absent in many poor countries? Chapter 3 addresses these questions, drawing on recent research by institutional economists and historians. Despite this research, our understanding is incomplete. Academics debate the relative importance of Enlightenment ideas, nation-states, limits on government powers, border conflicts, and other explanations for the industrial revolution. Similar debates rage over the causes of poverty today. Some scholars emphasize the institutions inherited from colonialism. Settlers from England, with its limited state and more competitive economy, brought very different rules and traditions compared to colonists from Spain, with its powerful, centralized state serving a narrow elite. Other scholars emphasize factor endowments, land and labor. Regions such as South America had rich lands suited for plantations or large native populations suited to be a cheap source of labor. Small numbers of colonizers settled in these regions and designed institutions to extract wealth and to suppress the native population or imported slaves. Large numbers of settlers immigrated to places like the US and Canada that had lands ill-suited for plantations and few or hostile native occupants. Where colonists settled in large numbers they behaved differently, expanding the franchise, investing in schooling, encouraging immigration, promoting secure land rights, protecting intellectual property, and generally establishing rules that favored equality.

Colonialism is not the only explanation for underdevelopment; some scholars focus instead on how poor countries today differ from Europe in the late Middle Ages. Border wars raged in medieval Europe, and kings needed nobles to provide armies, and merchants and creditors to provide the funds to pay the armies. Leaders of poor countries today rely far less on their citizens for self-defense. Instead they depend on great power détente to protect their borders and outside aid to fund their military. They use their armed forces predominantly to suppress internal rebellion. Such states are less responsive to citizens' demands and less concerned about growth; they impede institutions that might increase access to markets or politics because greater access threatens their survival.

Another group of scholars stresses beliefs and norms. In their view, societies whose beliefs and norms centered on individualism were quick to develop organizations, such as corporations, that exploit mutual interests. Societies dominated by collectivist beliefs and norms retained social structures based on family, clan, religion, or ethnic ties, group-based social structures that were less conducive to modern, impersonal markets.

North et al. (forthcoming) have a different explanation. They argue that underdeveloped institutions are a "natural" state, the dominant social order for most of human history. Natural states arose from primitive societies when powerful groups formed coalitions to reduce costly violence. In the natural state an elite group controls the military, the political system, and the economy, and creates institutions that make entry by non-elites prohibitively costly. Laws are enforced only for elites; non-elites must seek elite protection and patronage. Natural states evolved into modern democracies in Europe through incremental changes that slowly opened access to markets and trade. Freer economic access was sustained by freer access to politics and civil society more generally. Open access states are the exception, however. Most states today are natural states; even in those that appear to be democracies, access has remained largely limited to elites. Over time the personalities of these elites may change and new groups, such as leaders of labor unions or ethnic minorities, may become elites, but the exclusionary power structure persists.

All of these explanations for underdevelopment have one thing in common: they are bad news for foreign aid, something I explore in detail in Chapter 4. The amount of aid and the size of the aid community are burgeoning, yet there is *no* evidence that aid promotes development and *no* evidence that aid can improve institutions. Foreign aid can play a vital humanitarian role and improve the lives of direct beneficiaries by, for example, vaccinating children against dangerous diseases. But aid has been ineffective in fostering the market-supportive institutions that distinguish today's developed countries from the rest of the world. Indeed the nature of aid makes it impossible for aid-givers to improve damaging rules and norms. Institutional frameworks usually endure for centuries; aid is focused on the short term. Institutional frameworks endure because they are congruent with society's underlying power structure; aid-givers necessarily work within this power structure. Changes in power structures, rules, and norms do occur, but they occur through heterodox experiments adapted to local conditions; aid agencies seldom support these experiments. Aid-givers focus their support on what their staff and consultants know best, what they can best defend to sponsoring governments, and this usually turns out to be Western best practice. Aid cannot repair broken institutions; it has tried to bypass them by creating special units to implement projects, by operating through non-governmental organizations (NGOs), or by working directly with groups of beneficiaries. These efforts leave harmful institutions intact, so they do little to promote development, and they sometimes hurt the sustainability of aid projects.

If aid cannot improve or avoid damaging institutions, it makes sense to assist only those countries that are already improving their institutional frameworks. This is theoretically possible, but unlikely. How will we identify institutional progress? An institutional framework is a large and intricate network of interrelated rules and habits embedded in a broad social order. Institutional frameworks are self-enforcing because they fit with people's beliefs about proper behavior, their expectations of how others will behave, and their assumptions about how others expect them to behave. Current measures of institutions were designed for cross-country statistical analysis and reflect little of this complexity. These measures serve econometrics well since they aggregate a multitude of rules, norms, and enforcement characteristics into a single variable, such as rule of law or democracy. But an aggregate measure like rule of law does not give local reformers or foreign aid-givers the precision they need to determine progress or aid effectiveness. I analyze common measures of institutions in Chapter 5, looking specifically at measures used: (1) to describe democracy, (2) to qualify countries to receive US aid money, and (3) to qualify countries to receive World Bank soft loans. These measures have many weaknesses typical of most institutional indicators, yet in some ways they represent progress. Previously, economists used to assume away institutions entirely. Adding institutions adds realism to economic models, but it also necessarily adds complexity, because reality is messily complex.

Reform in water and sanitation (Chapter 6) illustrates this complexity and also shows how critical it is to improve our understanding of institutions. Many countries reformed their urban water and sanitation systems in the 1990s, and we have a woefully inadequate understanding of the outcomes of these experiments. Most cross-country analyses of water system reforms fail to account adequately for local circumstances, politics, and beliefs. Beliefs and institutions affect the demand for and design of water system reforms as well as the willingness of investors to supply the requisite capital and skills. Water and sanitation reform is a politically charged issue subject to powerful competing interests. People without connections will favor reforms that add connections, so too will developers, builders, contractors, and property owners seeking lucrative business opportunities or higher property values. Often overlooked, however, are people who are already connected to the system who often oppose expansion for fear that their water tariffs will increase and farmers who fear urban expansion will reduce their water supply. These different interest groups influence the design of reforms differently depending on how well they can act collectively and on how much political institutions encourage politicians and bureaucrats to respond to their demands. The motives of private investors matter if the reform privatizes operation of the water and sanitation system. Private investors will only be willing to bid on water contracts if they can earn reasonable returns, and then only if they believe government will honor its bargain. Such credible commitment is demanding because it depends on how well institutions bind future politicians, regulators, and judges.

To illustrate how such institutions work in practice, Chapter 6 analyzes water reform in Buenos Aires and Santiago. These two cities experienced notionally similar reforms with very different outcomes. These differences were largely determined by the countries' different economic and political institutions, some specific to the water sector, others fundamental to the governance of the country. Their networks of institutions are themselves the outcome of long histories of jockeying between powerful elite groups.

This book argues that progress in a sector such as water or in the broader economy is determined by durable institutions and deeply-rooted power structures. This argument does not mean that development is impossibly difficult. Development is rare, but progress does occur and deeply-rooted institutions do change, sometimes dramatically. This happens when new ideas profoundly alter a society's assumptions about the world, opening the way for incremental reforms that ultimately transform its institutions. We have only a very partial understanding of how this happens, which I summarize in Chapter 7.

Based on work with Jessica Soto, Chapter 7 explores some hypotheses about when local scholars act as institutional entrepreneurs devising and disseminating a new economic paradigm, a new conceptual model of how the world works. When elites feel their present policies and paradigms cannot cope with an economic shock or an external threat, they are ready to consider new policies and even a new set of economic assumptions. Policymakers and the wider public will be influenced by local scholars only if they are organized and persuasive and if they are believed to be credible, disinterested, and truthful experts. Change follows if the elites accept the new policies and paradigm and are powerful enough to overcome or ignore opposition. Under the right circumstances, the new policies cause beneficial changes, triggering incremental transformations that gradually move societies well beyond the elites' original intentions. In this way, intellectuals promoted new ideas and institutional change in Enlightenment Europe and in today's newly developed countries.

Chapter 7 explores these hypotheses in six case studies. Two of the cases, Taiwan and, to a lesser extent, South Korea, were transformed into open access societies, both politically and economically. Chile may be on a similar path, although there is a worrying level of public skepticism about Chile's development model. The fourth case, China, is harder to assess. China has increasingly opened access to the economy, generating great growth, but its open markets are out of equilibrium with its closed political system. Argentina is a counterfactual case: reforms were not sustained despite the influence of prominent scholars. Indonesia is another counterfactual case: scholarly influence was limited to devising macroeconomic policies in response to economic downturns; despite two decades of growth, the Indonesian economy and polity remained closed.

Although there is much we do not understand about institutional change, these preliminary case studies suggest that damaging institutions are not destiny. Since the Second World War, a few countries have transformed themselves into developed market economies and open access societies, despite the challenge of an increasingly competitive global market. Although fortuitous circumstances played a part, foreign aid was usually not important; except for the impetus it gave South Korea and Taiwan to reduce their dependence on US aid. Local intellectual capital was important. Local scholars devised new paradigms, argued the case for their ideas, advised and directed economic policy. Local scholars are not sufficient to promote institutional transformations, but they are beneficial and quite possibly necessary. Yet there are few efforts to foster this sort of scholarship. Most large-scale support tends to stifle self-directed research by offering funds for topics favored by donors or by hiring local scholars as consultants or staff. What is needed is scholar-by-scholar support and mentoring, such as that provided by the Ronald Coase Institute, which nurtures local researchers without stifling them.

2. Why are poor countries poor?

MOST PEOPLE LIVE IN POOR COUNTRIES

Most of humanity – over 84 percent – lives in countries that the World Bank defines as underdeveloped (Figure 2.1), and this proportion has changed little over the last 25 years (Figure 2.2). Few underdeveloped economies are growing fast enough to become developed anytime soon; quite the contrary, in one-third of poor countries gross domestic product (GDP) per person in constant dollars has not grown at all since 1980 (Easterly 2002b).

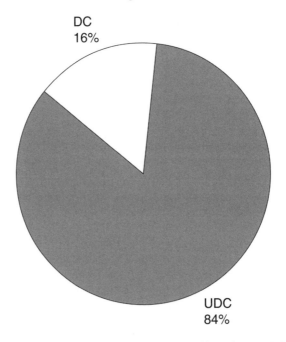

DC
16%

UDC
84%

Source: Author's calculations based on World Bank, *World Development Indicators.*
Underdeveloped countries (UDC) in 2004 are those defined by the World Bank as upper middle income, lower middle income, and low income (World Bank 2006g, pp. 292–3) that were eligible to borrow from the World Bank in 2005 (World Bank 2005a).

Figure 2.1   *World's population living in developed and underdeveloped countries, 2004*

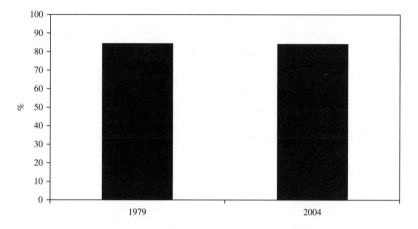

Source: Author's calculations based on World Bank, *World Development Indicators.*
Underdeveloped countries in 1979 are those defined by the World Bank as middle income,
low income, and non-market industrial economies (World Bank 1981, pp. 134–5).
Underdeveloped countries in 2004, as defined in sources for Figure 2.1.

*Figure 2.2   World's population living in underdeveloped countries, 1979
and 2004*

Assessing trends in global poverty by looking only at income by country
may be unduly depressing. After all, most of the world's population lives in
a few, very big countries and two of the biggest – China and India – have
been growing fast. Between 1980 and 2000 China's GDP per person grew
by an average of 8.3 percent after correcting for inflation, and India's grew
by 3.6 percent (World Bank various years, *World Development Reports*).
Since together these two countries represent almost 2.3 billion people, that
is a welcome improvement for a large number of poor people. Rapid economic growth in China, India, and the rest of Asia has reduced the percentage of humanity living in "extreme poverty." The proportion of those
living on less than about $1 a day (in purchasing power parity, that is,
adjusted to take account of differences in what a dollar will buy) fell from
over 40 percent of the total population in underdeveloped countries in 1981
to 21 percent by 2001 as shown in Figure 2.3 (Chen and Ravallion 2004,
table 4).[1] This improvement was heavily concentrated in Asia; elsewhere
extreme poverty stayed the same, or even rose, as it did in Sub-Saharan
Africa (Figure 2.4).

Moving people out of extreme poverty is an important step, but it does
not constitute development. The extreme poverty threshold approximates
what a sample of underdeveloped countries define as their poverty line, but
people living on less than $1 a day are still leading lives of appalling misery.

Extreme poverty (<$1.08/day)

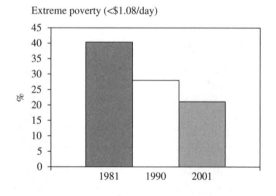

Below the poverty line (<$2.15/day)

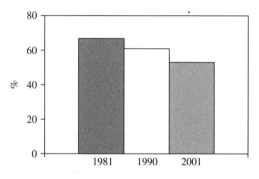

Note: * Percentage of the population in underdeveloped countries living in households where the average per capita consumption is less than $1.08 per day (extreme poverty) or less than $2.15 per day (below the poverty line) using 1993 dollars in purchasing power parity (PPP).

Source: Author's calculation based on data in Chen and Ravallion (2004, table 3).

Figure 2.3   *Proportion of the population of poor countries living in poverty, 1981, 1990, and 2001**

The picture is much grimmer if we raise the bar and calculate the percentage of people in poorer countries who are living below about $2 a day, which is closer to what most middle-income countries would define as their poverty line. True, China sharply reduced the percentage of its population living below $2 a day from 85 percent in 1981 to 47 percent in 2001. But 80 percent of India's population still lives on less than $2 a day, despite its rapid growth, and in Sub-Saharan Africa the percentage went up, from 73.3 percent in 1981 to 76.6 percent in 2001 (Chen and Ravallion 2004, table 3).

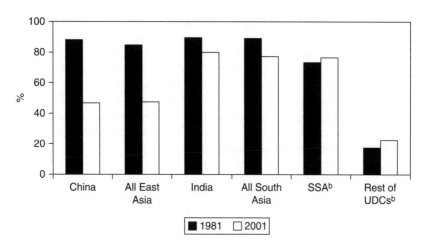

Notes:
a. Percentage of the population in underdeveloped countries living in households where the average per capita consumption is less than $2.15 per day using 1993 dollars in purchasing power parity (PPP).
b. SSA = Sub-Saharan Africa. Rest of UDCs = Eastern Europe and Central Asia, Latin America and Caribbean, and Middle East and North Africa.

Source: Author's calculation based on data in Chen and Ravallion (2004, table 3).

Figure 2.4 Proportion of the population living below the poverty line in China, India, rest of Asia, Sub-Saharan Africa and rest of underdeveloped countries (UDCs), 1981 and 2001[a]

Worldwide, the total number of people living below $2 a day increased by 285.4 million (Chen and Ravallion 2004, table 4). Even by this higher standard, 45 percent of humanity was living in poverty in 2001.

The sad fact is that very few non-oil exporting countries that were poor at the end of the Second World War have per capita incomes approximating those of developed countries today. Some Central European countries are beginning to approach European income levels (about $29,000 per capita in 2005), including the Czech Republic, Hungary, the Slovak Republic, and Slovenia.[2] But few others have made the transition to economic wealth. The few that have are in Europe (Ireland, Greece, Spain) or East Asia, specifically Japan, Hong Kong, Singapore, South Korea, and Taiwan.[3] South Korea's status is particularly striking. In 1960 South Korea's gross national income per person was the same as Ghana's; by 2005 South Korea's GNI per capita in purchasing power parity terms exceeded Ghana's GNI by eight times. Elsewhere, however, the picture is far bleaker. Despite trillions of dollars in foreign aid and advice, few underdeveloped countries are poised to join the ranks of the rich. Even once wealthy Argentina has about half the average per capita income of European Union countries; the rest of Latin America has even less.

I have been discussing development in purely economic terms, but the countries we consider developed today differ from poorer countries on many margins besides wealth. As North et al. describe in their forthcoming book, today's developed countries have open access markets characterized by a creative stream of entrepreneurship. They also have open access political systems characterized by a rich array of political, economic, social, and religious organizations. North and co-authors argue that a thriving modern market cannot exist outside an open access political, economic, social, and intellectual infrastructure that supports competition between a host of sophisticated and complicated organizations and creates a sustainable equilibrium.

Why is this transition to modern markets, thriving civil societies, and responsive and stable polities so rare? Why is misery so prevalent? Why do poor countries stay poor? Progress in answering such questions has been frustratingly slow, in part because past explanations failed to consider institutions.

EXPLANATIONS THAT IGNORE INSTITUTIONS ARE INADEQUATE

In the 60 years since the Second World War ended scholars have embraced and discarded a number of different explanations for underdevelopment, nicely summarized by William Easterly (2002b). Easterly shows how foreign aid agencies in poorer countries tried to ignite a succession of "engines of growth." Among the most prominent "engines" were: (1) investment and technological innovation; (2) market-friendly macroeconomic policies; and (3) education. Yet despite the support of foreign aid, each of these "growth engines" failed in turn.

Growth Engine 1: Investment

Investment is not correlated with growth in many specifications, which seems surprising until we consider that investment only stimulates growth where there are economic opportunities and incentives to run businesses productively. But poor countries are crippled by non-economic limits on business entry and non-market threats to business survival, except for a privileged few. For all others, the transaction costs of starting, operating, or liquidating a business are inflated by corrupt and inefficient bureaucracies, weak enforcement of laws against crime and expropriation, lax enforcement of contracts, uncooperative and exclusionary business norms, the absence of political mechanisms to hold bureaucrats and politicians accountable for their actions, and a general lack of credible protection of property. As a consequence: (i) business success is determined more by who you know than by what you do, and (ii) a large number of businesses operate informally.

Poor countries are governed by a coalition of powerful elites who limit non-elite access to politics, education, organizations, and the economy. This situation has prevailed for so long that North et al. (forthcoming) call it the "natural state," the default option for most societies throughout recorded human history. Even so-called democracies have constitutional, electoral, and party rules that allocate power to a narrow elite group. In these societies firms whose owners have political influence face fewer constraints from taxation, corruption, and government regulation than less influential firms; they also have easier access to finance (World Bank 2005f, figure 2.3, p. 44).

Governments of poor countries typically impose large administrative costs on firms, costs that are especially burdensome for non-elite firms. Red tape, bribes, and delays raise the costs of registering a new firm, getting a license to operate, or paying taxes. Where property rights are weak and bureaucracies are corrupt and inefficient, the cost of doing business will be high. Firms in Bolivia, for example, reported that tax authorities visited them four times a year on average and they had to go to La Paz to see government authorities on tax matters nine times a year on average. More than one in five Bolivian firms had had their tax returns challenged in the three years before they were surveyed, and half of these firms reported that tax authorities had offered to reverse the challenge for payment of a bribe (World Bank 2001). Eighty percent of firms surveyed in Uganda reported that they had to pay bribes that were, on average, three times larger than their income taxes. These firms received no benefits for their payments; rather the bribes were extorted by bureaucrats as the "price" of public services based on what they thought the firm could afford to pay (Svensson 2000). Government-imposed costs are not only high; they often vary widely, even from one individual bureaucrat to another, adding to the risk and uncertainty of starting or operating a business. For example, in 2003 the average cost to register a small garment firm in Sao Paulo, Brazil was $282, including fees and the opportunity cost of the entrepreneur's time valued at the entrepreneur's reported salary (Zylbesztajn et al. 2004). The cost for one-third of new enterprises was less than $150, while the cost for 17 percent was more than $400. The variance was large even though these firms were all of similar size and condition, operating in the same sector in the same city. Politically influential firms can bypass these restrictions, but non-elite entrepreneurs must pay these costs.

Influential firms also have less detectable advantages, such as privileged access to lucrative government contracts or protection from competition through special tariffs and restrictions tailor-made for their benefit. Politically influential firms are unfair competitors, using their access and economic advantages to dominate markets and keep their rivals small and few. Their influence is costly to their societies. Politically influential firms innovate less: they are less likely to introduce new technology or new products, upgrade their product lines, or build new facilities (World Bank 2005f, figure 2.4, p. 45).[4] Politically influential firms also have negative effects on innovation by non-elite firms. Non-elite firms are less innovative in markets dominated by politically influential firms because innovation does not benefit them much, and their growth is restricted by limits on their access to credit, markets, and contracts.

Informality is another reason why new investment and new technology do not always stimulate growth. When non-elite firms face high costs and unfair competition, many potentially successful firms do not enter the market or if, they do choose to enter, do not survive or prosper. Instead they often choose to operate in the informal sector. As a consequence large parts of some underdeveloped economies are informal, more than half in countries as diverse as Georgia, Nigeria, Peru, Tanzania, or Thailand (World Bank 2005f). This means that half of all businesses in these countries are committing a crime by their very existence. Informality is costly to firms: they live in continual uncertainty, they cannot do business with the government or with larger firms; they cannot export through formal channels or raise funds through the banking system; they are more vulnerable to police harassment and bribery; they cannot enforce contracts through courts or other formal means. To avoid detection, informal businesses usually stay small and seldom advertise. Not surprisingly, informality is inversely correlated with development: informal firms represent about 47 percent of GDP in low-income countries compared to 15 percent in high-income countries (Ayyagari et al. 2003, p. 10).

Such institutional failures illustrate why an increase in investment does not necessarily lead to innovation or growth. Political connections and administrative burdens distort the market. The business sector is dominated by influential firms that have neither the incentive nor the capacity to make the best use of funds or opportunities to innovate, and by informal firms that have neither the capital nor the legal means to expand.

Growth Engine 2: Macroeconomic Policy

When investment failed to spur growth, poverty was blamed on macroeconomic policy failures – large fiscal deficits, inflationary monetary policy, overvalued exchange rates, high trade barriers. During the 1980s much foreign aid was made conditional on reform of bad macroeconomic policies but in most cases conditionality failed to produce sustainable improvements. Policy choice turned out to be endogenous to organizational and institutional frameworks. In democracies, policy choices are endogenous to political rules and norms that determine, among other things, how candidates are selected and who selects them, how powerful they become, how long they are likely to stay in power, and how accountable they are and to whom. In other words, political rules and norms affect which issues and which interest groups politicians care about, and that in turn affects whether they will support policies with short-run political benefits, such as subsidizing food for their supporters and monopoly privileges for powerful elites, or long-run economic gains, such as cutting spending to reduce budget deficits and opening markets to competition. Institutional frameworks affect policy in dictatorships too, although these effects may be harder to gauge. We can see evidence of this in dictatorships that attempted to broaden their base of support by allowing political parties and legislatures, such as Brazil's military dictatorship in the 1960s. Parties and legislatures may appear to be window-dressing, but they have real effects on policy. Dictatorships that allow parties and legislatures spend more on education and less on the military than dictatorships that dispense with these organizations (Gandhi 2003).

Until recently most development economists viewed bad policies as the simple result of sick politics, a product of corruption, state capture, lack of democratic competition, and the like. But North et al. (forthcoming) argue that such policies are not a disease. In the typical, "natural" state, macro policies are designed to generate rents and protections that keep the dominant ruling coalition stable, something I describe in more detail later. The important point for this discussion is that macroeconomic policies are outcomes, the products of economic systems, political systems, and belief systems. Attempts to change policies without changing the systems that produced them are doomed to failure.

Growth Engine 3: Education

Human capital is clearly vital to development, so education seemed like a logical growth engine. Many studies establish the centrality of human capital. For example, initial levels of secondary education in 1900 are correlated with current levels of GDP per capita, leading some analysts to argue that initial endowments of human capital are more important to growth than institutions (Glaeser et al. 2004). But investment in education in poorer countries turned out *not* to increase human capital in measurable ways. Increased years of labor force schooling are *not* correlated with growth in GDP per worker in underdeveloped countries, except perhaps negatively (see Easterly 2002b, chapter 4; Prichett 1996). From 1990 to 2005 the World Bank lent $12.3 billion for primary education, and enrollment increased by 19 percent in a sample of 12 recipient countries (World Bank, Independent Evaluation Group 2006). Yet the World Bank concluded that most of these primary education projects were ineffective at improving educational quality (ibid.). In those few countries where student learning was tested, achievements were shockingly low. For example, in Ghana only 5 percent of students had mastery in English and only 10 percent in math; in Niger 13 percent had mastery of French and 11 percent of math; in Peru 8 percent had mastered Spanish and 7 percent math; in Yemen 19 percent had mastered Arabic and 9 percent math (ibid., p. 34). An independent assessment of literacy among 7 to 10 year olds in India found that half could not read fluently at the first grade level (Pratham 2006, cited in ibid.). Seventy percent of students who completed grade five in Bangladesh were not minimally competent in writing (World Bank 2004b, p. 112). The 1994 Tanzania Primary School Leavers Examination found that four-fifths of students scored less than 13 percent in language or mathematics after seven years of schooling (ibid.).

Why has education not improved learning and raised productivity in poor countries? One reason is that the broader environment does not reward those who invest time, study, and money in getting an education. Returns to education are low in countries where incentives to invest in the future are low. Another reason why spending on education does not pay off economically is poor educational quality. Conditions in many schools are dreadful. Enumerators who made unannounced visits to primary schools in Bangladesh, Ecuador, India, Indonesia, Peru, and Uganda found that on average 19 percent of teachers were absent (27 percent in Uganda), and many teachers who were present were not working (Chaudhury et al. 2006, p. 92, table 1). Only 45 percent of the teachers present were engaged in teaching activities, broadly defined to include cases where the teacher was just keeping the class in order (Chaudhury et al. 2006, p. 96). Another problem is overcrowding; for example there are 67 pupils to a teacher in Mali and from 2 to 12 students per book (World Bank, Independent Evaluation Group 2006, p. 36).

Such poor educational outcomes result not from lack of funding but from wrong incentives and weak institutions. As Prichett argues, the failures of schooling to produce educated citizens "are almost entirely the endogenous outcome of the existing incentives of the public sector (which is unconcerned about quality and unresponsive to citizen demands for higher-quality schooling) and of public sector producers who are given no support in increasing quality" (Prichett 2004, p. 216). He asserts that change will only occur when the institutional conditions lead to a public sector that is "*motivated to* and *capable of* implementing the required actions" (ibid., italics in original). The political systems in many poor countries reward policymakers who generate lucrative contracts to construct schools or who distribute patronage jobs in teaching or school administration, and punish those who fire non-performing teachers and administrators.

Poor countries also lack the institutions and organizations that hold politicians accountable for their actions, such as independent media to report on school spending and achievement, parent groups to demand improvements, or elections and political parties to force politicians to compete on their record in education. Without accountability much educational assistance is simply diverted or stolen. A survey of public schools in Uganda found that on average only 13 percent of the grants disbursed from the central government actually reached the schools; most schools received nothing because most of the funds were siphoned off by local officials and politicians as political patronage (Reinikka and Svensson 2004).

Summary

It was reasonable to assume that investment and innovation, sound macroeconomic policies, and education could stimulate growth, since they do promote growth in developed countries. But it was wrong to assume that these growth engines would function the same way in every economy. In developed countries, increases in investment and innovation, improvement in policies, and expansion of education set off a virtuous circle of changes that reinforced one another. But that failed to occur in underdeveloped countries. It turned out that underinvestment, bad policies, and lack of good education are proximate causes of underdevelopment, but they are not ultimate causes. Ultimately, an economy's future rests on choices made by economic, political, and social actors, choices that are largely motivated by institutions.

INSTITUTIONAL EXPLANATIONS FOR UNDERDEVELOPMENT

Institutions are the "humanly devised constraints that structure human interaction" (North 1990, p. 3). They include written, formalized constraints such as constitutions and laws, and tacit, informal constraints such as norms, conventions and self-imposed codes of conduct (ibid, p. 3).[5] In Douglass North's view, institutions are the product of intentional human efforts to provide structure in an uncertain world. They reduce uncertainty and risk by making others' actions more predictable. (Greif (2006) has a broader definition of institutions as a system of shared beliefs, internalized norms, rules, and organizations that motivate, enable, and guide individuals to follow one rule of behavior thereby generating regularities of behavior. In Greif's view an institution is by definition self-enforcing; a rule imposed by the state would not constitute an institution unless it affected behavior.)

Consider a very simple institution: the rule that cars should drive within painted lines and cross the line only when the driver can see that the adjacent lane is empty. This is not just the law; it is an internalized norm in many cities, such as Washington, DC in the United States. But in other cities, such as Cairo, Egypt, drivers straddle the lanes, and often move from lane to lane without looking behind them. Drivers in lanes that are being encroached upon respond with the "son et lumière" driving technique, honking their horns and flashing their lights when a motorist tries to weave in front of them. In Washington, DC, the idea of straddling the lanes is inconceivable to most drivers and would likely result in collision, arrest, or risk of attack from outraged fellow motorists. It would be just as dangerous in Cairo to fail to anticipate lane straddling or respond with outrage. A driver from Cairo would quickly adapt to the dominant norm when driving in Washington rather than suffer the nasty consequences, and vice versa. This simple example illustrates that it is not just the written rules that constitute institutions, but also the norms of behavior that people internalize over time, and the extent to which state-devised rules and internalized norms are enforced.

Every society has a set of fundamental institutions that provide the basic scaffolding for human interactions, such as constitutions or widely held norms. Although many rules and habits change frequently, these fundamental institutions are more persistent and deeply rooted. North calls this set of fundamental institutions the institutional environment or institutional framework. A society's institutional framework is the product of its history. Powerful groups and individuals shape fundamental institutions to perpetuate their power, and some of these structures persist. They endure, and not just because powerful elites enforce them. Over time they become part of society's shared beliefs about how the world works, or should work, beliefs about how others will behave, or should behave; they become internalized norms and can be difficult to change and impossible to ignore (North 2005b).

Internalized norms can persist even when they conflict with what outsiders perceive to be self-interest, as we can see in the history of the water supply lease in Conakry, Guinea. In the late 1980s Conakry's water system was in disastrous shape, with over 40 percent of the population not connected, poor water quality, frequent interruptions in service, no funds for repairs or expansion, and 60 percent of water lost through leaks, theft, and the failure to bill or collect. In 1989 the government of Guinea signed a lease with a private consortium to operate the water system in its capital and several other major cities. The lease introduced cost recovery pricing, more efficient billing and collection, and curbs on illegal connections, and as a result, most customers faced higher water costs. Government's failure to pay its water bills drove prices even higher than originally forecast (Ménard and Clarke 2002b). Rates were lower for low volume users, but most household connections were high volume because an individual connection, which was a standpipe in the yard, was often shared by many families (ibid., p. 279). The average number of consumers per connection in Conakry was estimated to be as high as 27. Many of Conakry's poorer residents could not afford to pay so about half the city remained without piped water (Ménard and Clarke 2002b, p. 295). Abidjan, Côte d'Ivoire, had a similar lease and similarly high prices, but affordability was not a problem there. Abidjan was wealthier, and more importantly groups of neighbors who shared water from one standpipe split the water bill (Ménard and Clarke 2002a). In Conakry the family paying for the water connection did not charge their neighbors, but allowed them to take water freely. Household surveys suggest that there are strong social mores against charging neighbors in Conakry perhaps as a result of its recent rural culture (Shirley and Ménard 2002, p. 33). This norm may have been advantageous when a water connection signaled influence with the ruling powers, water rates were very low, and water bills were seldom collected. When circumstances changed, however, the sharing norm made water unaffordable, yet it proved hard to change even when many people who failed to pay were cut off.

WHAT ARE THE INSTITUTIONS THAT SUPPORT DEVELOPMENT?

Today's successful market economies are characterized by institutions that support impersonal market exchanges, sometimes spanning long distances and extended periods of time. Barter and the bazaar have not been eliminated, and trust and reputation are still important to trade. But these traditional forms of exchange and enforcement exist side-by-side with hands-off transactions between multiple layers of strangers governed by regulators, courts, and police.

Table 2.1   Examples of institutions that foster exchange and constrain state coercion

Foster exchange	Constrain state coercion
Bilateral reputation	Time horizon of dictator
Reputation in business networks supported by family, religious or other social networks	Military norms of non-intervention
	Threat of revolt
	Foreign financing, aid, alliances, threats
Hostages	Democratic elections & norms
Merchants' norms and codes	Separation of powers to assemblies & courts
Commercial codes	Federalism

Sources: Based on Greif (2006) and Shirley (2005a).

Markets require two kinds of institutions to realize the gains from impersonal trade. One set of institutions "foster[s] exchange by lowering transaction costs" (Shirley 2005a, p. 611)[6] (see Table 2.1 for examples). Every transaction has costs: the costs of finding a seller or buyer, getting and providing information, striking a bargain, monitoring the terms, enforcing the bargain, and punishing those who cheat (Coase 1937). Transaction costs are crucial to development; where the costs of transacting are unusually high, opportunities will be forgone. As Ronald Coase famously put it, "If the costs of making an exchange are greater than the gains which that exchange would bring, that exchange would not take place" (1992, p. 197).

Institutions that lower transaction costs cannot do the job alone, however; markets also need institutions that "influence the state and other powerful actors to protect private property and persons rather than expropriate and subjugate them" (Shirley 2005a, p. 611).[7] Effective states monopolize force and use it to secure order and stability, protect property and individuals, and enforce contracts and laws. But a state powerful enough to impose order and monopolize coercion is also powerful enough to expropriate property and subjugate people (North and Weingast 1989; Weingast 1993). Trade requires credible constraints on the state's power to abscond with the gains. Just as institutions that enforce contracts determine the range of transactions that will occur in a market by determining which bargains can be credibly enforced, so institutions that constrain coercion "influence whether individuals will bring their goods to the market in the first place" (Greif 2005, p. 727). Developed countries have evolved institutions that limit the abuse of state power, institutions that are credible to would-be investors (see Table 2.1 for examples).

Thanks to market-supportive institutions, people in developed countries strike countless bargains daily with others whose identity, affiliations, and locations they never know and never need to know. Impersonal exchange in developed economies has evolved to the point where, to take an extreme example, a US investor can go onto the internet; pay a small fee (currently $5 for trades of up to 5000 shares) to a brokerage firm; put in an order to buy a stock at the current market price; and see the order executed within seconds. The investor does not know the identity of the person whose stock is bought, nor the identity of the floor traders and market makers who buy and sell the stock, nor the identity of the brokers who put the order to the traders and post the results. The investor can afford to be ignorant of the personalities involved because a vast and intricate complex of contract-enforcement institutions supports this exchange. Rules, laws, and norms oblige companies listing on the New York Stock Exchange (NYSE) and brokers trading on the NYSE to disclose their prices and performance, to follow instructions, to execute trades promptly and at the best price, and to safeguard investors' money and personal information. In addition, a host of internal rules and norms of operation constrain the behavior of the NYSE and the over-the-counter market, the brokerage firms, the auditors and compliance officers of the firms who register and effect the trade, the Securities and Exchange Commission, the National Association of Securities dealers, and the auditors of the individual firms whose shares are traded. The performance of these individuals and organizations are tracked by newspapers, magazines, credit bureaus, investor newsletters, and blogs, so that individuals and organizations involved in trades comply with the rules or risk costly damage to credit ratings and reputations, fines, or imprisonment.

What stops government actors from confiscating investments through onerous taxes or outright expropriation in our internet trading example? Constitutional rules curb the power of the executive branch and empower the legislature to investigate abuses and pass laws to prevent them. Electoral rules and internal political party protocols reward politicians who oppose expropriation. Norms of civic responsibility and rules protecting the independence of the media check government's arbitrary use of power. Those who benefit from trades – brokerage firms, regulators, industry associations, and others – protest confiscatory laws or regulatory practices that reduce their profits, put them out of business, or just violate their sense of proper commercial conduct. Courts act to redress unconstitutional and arbitrary abuses by the executive. Some of these mechanisms are slow and costly, and they do not always function well in every individual case, but over time and on average they support contractual norms and protections allowing investors to commit their capital in impersonal exchanges with lower transaction costs and a higher degree of confidence that their funds are safe from broker theft or state expropriation.

Internet trading is an extreme case: I can illustrate how institutions function in different societies with a simple real estate transaction. Housing transfers in developed countries are increasingly impersonal thanks to government-enforced rules that protect buyer and seller. In the US more and more transactions rely on escrow agents; the individuals buying and selling the home may not even be present at the transfer. The transaction costs of formal housing transfers are low relative to people's income and the price of houses.

Real estate transactions in poorer countries are more likely to be informal transfers relying on personal reputations because, relative to many people's income, the costs of more formal transactions are high. We can see this in the housing market that developed in the township of Langa, South Africa, in the 1990s after the Cape Town municipal government distributed titles to concrete block houses there (Boudreaux 2007). Although these titles were formal and relatively secure, buyers and sellers used signed affidavits rather than formal sales contracts and did not register their titles in the Registrar's office because they could not afford a formal exchange (ibid.). Incomes were low in Langa. Formal jobs are scarce in Langa because of restrictive labor laws, and many residents work informally, running small shops out of their homes. Informal workers without a steady paycheck were viewed as risky borrowers by banks, which in any case had little tradition of mortgage lending in townships such as Langa. The cost of formal transactions was too high for most Langa homeowners partly because only special conveyancing attorneys could legally transfer title to property in South Africa and these attorneys charged high fees. On top of that, all local taxes and past-due service fees had to be paid in advance, and many poor residents were years behind on their taxes and fees. Informal property markets such as Langa's are a way around these barriers, but they have drawbacks. Sales are confined to buyers and sellers who know one another's reputations and this reduces the size of the market, which in turn reduces the resale value of houses.

How do institutions that support impersonal, sophisticated, and low cost exchanges emerge? Why don't all economies have similar market-supportive institutions? These questions are the subject of the next chapter.

NOTES

1. The extreme poverty definition of approximately $1 per day was calculated to reflect the definition of poverty used in most poor countries (Chen and Ravallion 2004, p. 9). These numbers are converted from local exchange rates using purchasing power parity. PPPs attempt to measure the actual purchasing power of each country's inhabitants, taking account of the fact that prices of the same goods are often lower in poor countries, so a

dollar will purchase more goods in poor countries than in richer countries. The data have problems described in detail in Chen and Ravallion (2004).

2. In 2005 the gross national income per person of high-income countries averaged $32,524 in purchasing power parity terms. The GNI per capita that year of Czech Republic was $20,140, Hungary $16,940, Slovak Republic $15,760, and Slovenia $22,160 (World Bank 2006h).

3. The 2005 GNI per capita in PPP of these countries was Japan $31,410, Hong Kong $34,670, South Korea $21,850, and Singapore $29,780 (World Bank 2006h). The World Bank does not publish data on Taiwan but according to Tiscali Reference Encyclopedia, Taiwan's GNI per capita in PPP was $22,650 in 2002 (Tiscali).

4. "Influence" is measured as the difference perceived by firms and reported in World Bank Investment Climate Surveys between their ability to influence national policy and legislation and the ability of other domestic firms to do so (World Bank 2005f, p. 44).

5. Organizations differ from institutions: "they are groups of individuals bound together by some common purpose to achieve certain objectives," and include legislatures, firms, trade unions, churches, clubs, schools and so on (North 1990, p. 3).

6. These are similar to what Greif calls "contract-enforcing institutions" (Greif 2005, p. 727).

7. These are similar to what Greif terms "coercion-constraining institutions" (Greif 2005, p. 727).

3. Market-supportive institutions

To understand underdevelopment we must first understand development. Even though today's poor countries will follow very different paths from industrializing Europe, European history is our main guide to the forces that shaped modern, open access states. Democracy, unbiased rule of law, largely unfettered access to information and ideas, and competitive market economies only emerged over the last 300 years, but they have roots deep in the past. A voluminous literature analyzes the roots of today's modern, wealthy societies and I cannot do justice to it all. Scholars disagree about what Mokyr has called "the enduring riddle of the European miracle" (Mokyr 2002). I have focused on the explanations favored by institutional economists, especially Douglass North and Avner Greif. These authors give special emphasis to the influence of historically evolved beliefs, knowledge, norms, and rules on economic actors over time, an interpretation that is especially valuable for understanding the effects of ideas and institutions on development today. Even this subset of economic history is large and growing; I can only briefly survey this literature here.

HOW DID MARKET-SUPPORTIVE INSTITUTIONS EMERGE?

For thousands of years people were governed by "tribute-taking empires" such as the Chinese, Ottoman, Persian, or Roman empires (Tilly 1992, p. 21). Tribute-taking empires proved durable, but they never fostered the institutional innovations that led to modern, impersonal markets. The empires' distant central governments provided order and some public goods, but they also engaged in frequent wars with external rivals and suppressed internal rebellions. These perpetual conflicts were financed by often onerous taxes and duties, state monopolies over key commodities such as salt, sale of private monopolies, and similar measures, all with disastrous effects on market development. Some empires were less hostile to commerce than others; the Ottoman Empire at its height did not tax merchants and saw trade as a source of prosperity (Kinross 1977). But even in the Ottoman Empire the emperors' closest allies were large landowners, not merchants. And even in the Ottoman Empire some revenue-raising activities inevitably discouraged commerce. For example, the empire minted money to increase its cash, devaluing the currency. Tribute-taking empires also suppressed commerce by allowing repressive and sometimes corrupt local governments to inhibit competition, place onerous restrictions on trade, and stifle migration, upward mobility, and innovation. The Chinese state, for example, was largely absent from the commercial sphere in the nineteenth century, delegating tax collection and the provision of local public goods to guilds (Greif 2005). The Roman Empire, too, relied heavily on local governments and collaborated with large landowners while usually ignoring merchants, even as sources of credit (Lopez 1966, pp. 12–13).

The collapse of medieval Europe's tribute-taking empire, the Roman Empire, created a vacuum which market-supportive institutions gradually began to fill. Initially the decline of the Roman-imposed order greatly reduced trade. Without Rome, robbers, kidnappers, pirates, vandals, raiders and other mayhem-makers roamed unconstrained. Traders and merchants had to maintain private armies and incur huge costs to protect themselves and their property; costs that could and often did exceed the value of trade. North and Thomas (1973, p. 26) describe Western Europe at the beginning of the tenth century as a "vast wilderness" with little or no economic interaction between thinly-populated villages. Most trade took place within villages where feudal lords enforced order and provided protection from marauding armies. The repulsion of Vikings, Magyar, and Moslem raiders from Western Europe in the tenth century restored enough peace and stability to allow an increase in population. Some villages grew into towns where more traders could be protected and markets could expand. In the thirteenth century some of these expanding towns and cities won increasing degrees of self-government from local lords, bishops, and other powerful authorities. This independence brought greater freedom of movement, fewer burdensome taxes and tariffs, and the right of merchants to come and go without hindrance (Lopez 1966).

New forms of contracting also began to emerge. For millennia people have exchanged goods "hand to hand, eyeball to eyeball; in other words, immediate exchange: goods are sold on the spot, the purchases are taken and paid for then and there" (Braudel 1986, p. 29). Spot markets may seem institution-free, but they are not. Even in eyeball-to-eyeball exchanges, traders needed institutions to reduce their risk of being cheated and to signal to others that they were not cheats. The simplest ones, such as reputation, arose spontaneously as soon as people began to engage in face-to-face barter and found that a reputation for a quality product, true weight, or fair dealing increased business. Gradually people moved beyond face-to-face barter, but they still relied on reputation and still traded mostly with people they knew or people who their friends and relatives knew. Social networks, such as religious, ethnic, or kinship networks, provided information and signaled trustworthiness in less usual trades over longer distances (North 1990, 2005a; North and Thomas 1973). Networks enforced agreements through reputation, loyalty, ostracism, and expulsion, although private coercion, such as the use of armed men to collect overdue debts, continued to be important.

Greif's (1993) description of the Jewish Maghribi during the Middle Ages illustrates the surprising extent to which networks can expand trade. The Maghribi relied on their common religion, social ties, and language to share information about which agents were trustworthy. Armed with this information the Maghribi traded over long distances with Maghribi they did not know, and even hired non-Maghribi as agents. Jews, Armenians, Genoese and other mercantile groups with substantial capital at their disposal also relied on networks to reduce the uncertainty of trade in the Middle Ages, giving group members credit, market information and preferential treatment (Curtin 1984).

Social, religious, and family networks had serious shortcomings. Because they excluded everyone who was not part of the network, they limited trade and specialization, and that restricted growth and development (Keefer and Shirley 2000). But these shortcomings also created an opportunity. As Europe's population grew, there was money to be made trading with people with whom you could not interact "eyeball-to-eyeball," and who were not part of your network. Guilds, business associations, credit rating groups and other new organizations began to enforce more impersonal exchanges, with explicit rules regulating members specifically designed to enhance opportunities for trade (Greif 2005).

Guilds and similar organizations also had drawbacks, however. They enlarged the potential trading group beyond relatives or members of the same religion, but they were still limited to members of the guild. The information costs of adding new members could be high, restricting entry. Information did not flow easily in the Middle Ages and checking on the reputation of a potential new entrant might require a difficult journey or a long wait for an exchange of letters. And concerns about reputation did not eliminate the risk that one party would cheat whenever the value of future relationships was less than the return on cheating (ibid.).

The expanding, semi-autonomous towns and cities in Europe, or communes, developed another institution that allowed impersonal trade without relying on an individual trader's reputation. Foreign merchants at important markets, such as the Champagne fairs, identified themselves as members of a particular commune. The merchant elite and other inhabitants of the town had sworn to defend the rights of the commune (Hyde 1973). So if a foreign commune member was found to have defaulted on a contract by the community court of the town where the fair was held, then that merchant's entire commune was legally liable (Greif 2006). By providing a way to enforce contracts with unknown merchants who were not part of any local social network but who were known in their home communities, commune enforcement was an intermediary between social enforcement and state enforcement, but it fell apart as towns grew and it became easier for cheats to pretend to be members of a commune.

Italian city-states, such as Genoa, introduced other innovations, such as bills of lading and written contracts enforced by laws and courts, and the expansion of literacy spread these innovations, as well as letters of credit and similar documents, throughout Europe (North and Thomas 1973). The Italian city-states also developed institutions to constrain the state. As Greif (2005) describes, Genoa delegated power to an independent ruler (the podestá) who was rewarded at the end of his term for not abusing his coercive power during his tenure. Venice took a different tack and installed a ruler, the Doge, without independent power. The Doge had to mobilize Venetian property holders to back him with their powers, something they would do whenever one of the wealthy families tried to upset the equilibrium among them. Since neither a podestá nor a Doge could pass on power to an heir, Genoa and Venice avoided the deterioration in leadership that plagued hereditary dynasties.

The commercial pre-eminence of the city-states waned in the fifteenth and sixteenth centuries as technological changes in warfare rewarded larger states (Tilly 1992, p. 65). The crossbow, longbow, pike, gunpowder, siege artillery, and similar innovations favored larger, permanent military units manned by specialized, skilled forces. Powerful new weapons such as gunpowder and artillery reduced the protection of the walled city. These new weapons and troops were costly, however, at a time when fiscal revenues were depressed. Throughout the fourteenth and fifteenth centuries plagues and famines decimated the rural labor force, forcing cutbacks in land under cultivation, which reduced earnings from taxes on agriculture (North and Thomas 1973, pp. 79–81). Rulers needed funds to purchase enough weapons to survive invasions, so they tried to consolidate, merge, and conquer, leading to two centuries of wars of conquest in Europe (ibid.). The larger and more prosperous the state, the more resources the ruler could raise to pay for military equipment and mercenaries and the more citizens he could enlist, and the nation-state became the dominant form (Tilly 1992).

Nation-states had commercial advantages too: the rules of trade could be enforced over the entire nation, rather than just within a few communes or among members of a guild or business association. Nation-states could impose rules of disclosure, enforce contracts, and punish violators using the coercive powers of the state – laws, regulations, courts, and police.

Enforcement through public institutions is often time-consuming and expensive and must be paid for by taxes (Williamson 1985), but makes it possible to enforce rules without reliance on personal networks, guilds, or other mechanisms that restrict trade and entry.

Besides the rise of the nation-state, impersonal trade was facilitated by growing wealth. Beginning around 1700 new technologies multiplied agricultural surpluses allowing an expansion in world population (see Figure 2.1; Fogel 2004, p. 22). Family incomes also shot up, as new technologies enhanced productivity and allowed women and indeed children to work outside the home. Commerce also grew. As the scale of war continued to expand during the fifteenth and sixteenth centuries, the European nation-states increasingly encouraged trade as a lucrative source of tax revenue. Rulers began to rely on merchants instead of just large landowners to help finance their wars, gradually expanding the scope for competition and entry and setting the stage for the industrial revolution, a watershed event in human history.

Scholars have different explanations for why the industrial revolution took place in Europe in general and England in particular, which is not surprising since so many forces operated simultaneously and gradually to produce modern markets and polities. According to North (North 1990; North and Thomas 1973) the relative strength of the ruling group vis-à-vis the rising commercial elites was important in determining where secure property rights and third-party enforcement of trade flourished in Europe. In nations where the ruling groups were more powerful than any opposing economic interests, such as France or Spain, the ruler's bargains with merchants and traders did little to open access to political power or to curb state coercion and its threat to property rights. Although the kings of both France and Spain needed money to confront the continual threat of invasion they did not need to make many concessions to get these funds. In France the monarchy relied heavily on the sale of public offices and taxes collected by the nobility and clergy (North and Thomas 1973, pp. 125–7). Hoffman and Rosenthal (1997) argue that while the overall tax burden was relatively low in France and Spain, the marginal tax was high in some sectors, driving investment into activities that were tax exempt, which led the state in turn to try to restrict the mobility of capital. The French state also used monopolies run by nobles and guilds to raise revenues, thereby restricting entry and trade and crippling the development of markets. Rosenthal (1998) has a different interpretation, arguing that the Crown was especially interested in revenue sources that were independent of the nobility, stressing the importance of public borrowing – with occasional defaults – internal tolls, and monetary manipulation. The Spanish Crown had access to the gold, silver, and other riches from its colonies in South

America so it could afford to ignore commercial interests and ride roughshod over private property holders. The Spanish Crown's indifference to private property rights is illustrated by the exclusive rights it gave the sheepherders' guild (the *Mesta*) to drive their sheep across lands owned by others in exchange for taxes, often with disastrous consequences for the landowners' crops (North and Thomas 1973, p. 4).

Institutions evolved differently in Holland and England, however. There the ruling elites were less able to suppress the political ambitions of rising economic groups. Holland's central location and excellent ports facilitated Amsterdam's development as the largest international market in Europe, and that, combined with the establishment of an efficient capital market, enabled the Dutch to build a flourishing economy based on commerce in the seventeenth and eighteenth centuries. Cities grew along Dutch rivers, waterways, and seaports, creating a decentralized and highly urbanized pattern of development (de Vries and van der Woude 1997). Holland's geography also contributed to its political development. To induce farmers to settle and colonize the largely waterlogged areas of the region, with their perennial threat of floods, local lords offered them semi-free tenurial status. Local communities taxed themselves to meet their hydraulic needs, and developed strong traditions of liberty and local autonomy as a result (Schama 1988, pp. 39–40). Reclamation from the sea required increasingly higher-level coordination as well as large capital investments. These large investments would be sunk only if there was a secure way to guarantee that the investor would reap much of the benefits, making private property in land a fundamental institutional arrangement in Holland (North and Thomas 1973, p. 143). After its successful rebellion against Spain in the second half of the sixteenth century, the Dutch republic was ruled by an assembly representing the provincial governments (the States General), which was more powerful than the parliaments in England or France, and a ruler or stadhouder appointed by the provinces who was less powerful than a king. The clergy and the nobles, many of whom remained loyal to the Spanish Crown, lost much of their influence after the revolt against Spain, while the growing merchant elite became increasingly powerful. The urban centers developed a "patrician and oligarchic" political structure, but allowed a great deal of freedom in the economic sphere (de Vries and van der Woude 1997, p. 165). Holland's decentralized government and widely dispersed economic activity favored relatively open trade, religious tolerance, and limited government (Congleton 2006).

Holland adopted and improved on the commercial innovations developed by the Italians and employed them on a larger scale and in a more favorable political climate (North and Thomas 1973, p. 135). Markets using bills of exchange, demand notes, deposit certificates and other credit instruments arose first at fairs, were developed further in Bruges and then Antwerp, and then shifted with commerce to Amsterdam in the seventeenth century (de Vries and van der Woude 1997). Amsterdam also developed a long-term capital market to meet the rising demand for credit from the new nation-states. Facilitating the growth of Amsterdam's capital market was the 1537 Netherlands' law that recognized the assignment of debts as payable to the bearer and a state that enforced the obligation of the debtor to the ultimate holder of the note (North and Thomas 1973, p. 141). Amsterdam's favorable location, strong capital market, and low transaction costs enabled it to emerge in the sixteenth century as the "essential entrepôt," the market where "irregular supplies of goods were stockpiled and held in inventories to accommodate the more regular demand for these goods in their final markets" (de Vries and van der Woude 1997, p. 667).

In the late seventeenth century Holland's economy began to decline as its commercial rivals erected trade barriers, culminating in naval wars with England and the French invasion in 1672. According to De Vries and van der Woude (1997), these external problems were coupled with high internal costs and inefficiencies. For example, guilds made it difficult to reduce Holland's high wages in the face of growing international competition. Longstanding restrictions on internal commerce by cities determined to protect their markets also created costly inefficiencies. Heavy government reliance on bonds resulted in a large public debt and the concentration of wealth in the hands of an ever-narrowing band of bondholders. And finally, efforts to limit competition and hold up sagging prices through protection led to inefficient restrictions on commerce, such as a publishing monopoly over all navigational charts (de Vries and van der Woude 1997). In the eighteenth century Holland was increasingly eclipsed by England, and it was England that became the setting for the industrial revolution.

As in Holland, the balance between rising commercial elites and weaker rulers in England helps explain its adoption of patent laws, joint stock companies, commercial insurance, a central bank and similar institutions. These market-supportive institutions gave the elites greater security of property rights, allowed more room for individual initiative and competition, and encouraged capital mobility (North and Thomas 1973, p. 165). Although the English Crown gave monopolies to selected nobles and guilds, it was not strong enough to enforce its will. Powerful feudal lords forced the king to make concessions to parliament in exchange for their support in raising armies and cash (North and Weingast 1989). Gradually, these concessions evolved into new institutions that further constrained state coercion and made property rights more secure. For example, the common-law courts became an important constraint on the king's sphere of authority as well as a vehicle for contract enforcement. Curbs on arbitrary government action laid the foundation for rule of law, at least for the elites. As wars led to a decline of the nobles in England and the Crown's revenue needs rose further, the state increasingly relied on credit as a way to quickly finance its expanding military needs when war loomed. In the past a new king would simply repudiate the debts of his predecessor, but that changed when the state, as an "impersonal and perpetually lived organization," became the borrower (North et al. forthcoming).

The differentiation between the state as an ongoing, impersonal entity and the king as an individual was facilitated in the seventeenth century in England when civil war and the Glorious Revolution in 1688 created new rules, such as the Bill of Rights, and new organizations, such as the Bank of England, that cemented the constraints on the king's power over the state (North and Weingast 1989). The new king, William III, accepted a permanent parliament that would meet regularly, instead of at the behest of the Crown, and he also agreed to prohibitions against the sovereign's arbitrary use of power and against the creation of a standing army during peacetime. In exchange the king was promised revenue security and support for his war against France. Dutch influence was evident in the English revolution: "All of these substantial constitutional reforms were accepted by a Dutchman who had grown to maturity and held executive power in a republic where policy making and the power to tax were distributed in an even *less favorable* manner for the executive." (Congleton 2006, p. 22; original italics). These reforms did not make England a democracy; the parliament itself violated the property rights and liberties of weaker groups. Nevertheless, the parliament's new powers vis-à-vis the king gave greater security to wealth and contract since the property owners in parliament were now able to mobilize against action by the Crown that would harm their interests. The development of a standing parliament allowed England to make more credible commitments to pay its debts. Loans to the government became laws of parliament, which the king could not simply overturn without the risk of being deposed.[1] More reliable credit gave England an advantage over less credible rival states in raising funds for wars.

Parliamentary law played an increasingly important part in England's development. After the Glorious Revolution, the number of laws passed in a year went from 30 during the seventeenth century to 400 in the late eighteenth century (Bogart and Richardson 2006, p. 1). Much of the growth in laws was in acts that removed restrictions on the use of property and allowed the improvement, sale, and leasing of land (estate acts); acts that shifted property from collective use, such as village pastures, to individual ownership (enclosure acts); and acts that established statutory authorities to build, operate, and maintain infrastructure and to police and collect small debts (statutory acts) (Bogart and Richardson 2006). Such acts allowed individuals more freedom to use and dispose of property and enhance its value through greater security and public infrastructure. In addition, laws were passed that ranked commercial creditors at the same level as Crown creditors (Greif 2006, pp. 343–4). With more secure property rights investors were more willing to sink capital into larger, longer-lived fixed assets, creating greater opportunities to use capital more efficiently. And with rising competition and exchange there was increased division of labor and greater opportunities to use labor more efficiently. As the industrial revolution raised family income, marketing was transformed and goods that had once only been made at home or sold at weekly markets, at occasional fairs, or by roving peddlers could be readily purchased from shopkeepers every day but Sunday (Muller 2002, pp. 58–9). Items that had been luxuries became necessities, such as tea, linens, or crockery, and it became profitable for manufacturers to produce for the expanding consumer market (ibid.). A consumer economy arose and consumerism "permeated down through the social strata" in England (Porter 2000, p. 18).

Through wars, competition, and invasions, favorable institutional innovations in Holland and England spread to other European countries, although at differing rates.[2] The French Revolution and subsequent conquests of Europe by Napoleon from 1799–1815 was instrumental in this spread of institutional changes. Napoleon swept away the nobles, bureaucrats, and clergy who had controlled local politics, while the French Revolution popularized ideas of representation and rule of law, opening the way for new rules and organizations that encouraged markets and development, such as a system of civil law and a centralized and free educational system. Also crucial was the influence of the Enlightenment's new ideas and persuasive intellectuals, such as Adam Smith and John Locke (something I describe in detail in Chapter 7).

Trade gradually became more and more impersonal and new forms of organization emerged, such as corporations and municipalities, that had lives and legal status apart from the lives and status of the individual members. Military force grew more specialized and political control over the military increased. North et al. (forthcoming) portray these developments and the incremental expansion of elite coalitions to include more and more non-elites as a move towards open access economies and polities. This opening of access was sometimes an elite response to the threat of rebellion, but it was often the unintentional result of elite actions aimed at expanding their wealth.[3] Through this process a handful of European societies gradually changed from states where access to political power and economic rents was determined by personal coercive powers, family and kinship ties, and hereditary rights and privileges into open access states.

According to North et al. today's open access states aspire to: (1) free entry into economic, political, religious, and educational activity without restraint, (2) diverse economic, political, religious, and educational organizational forms open to all, and (3) rule of law enforced impartially for all citizens. Open access states have political systems that are not just democratic but highly competitive, combined with highly competitive economic systems. The rules that protect open access have become part of these societies' shared beliefs, fiercely protected by most citizens and organizations, enforced by a largely independent judiciary, and supported by a largely free press.[4] North et al. argue that open access societies are more prosperous because the more open their access, the more credible their commitment to unbiased enforcement of property rights, making them more attractive to investors. Open access societies are also more productive because they create more opportunities for trade, specialization, and entrepreneurial entry, innovation, and exit. So far they have also proved to be enduring. Individuals or groups that try to close access or introduce privileges are opposed by their rivals. This is not to say that modern open access states are free of corruption, political patronage, state secrecy, abuse of power, monopoly power and privilege, unequal access and inequalities, or intolerance of ideas and minorities; they are not. But competition between rival interest groups and organizations acts as an inbuilt corrective mechanism that helps keep abuses in check over the medium term. As I have written elsewhere: "The existence of many organizations in civil society, such as unions, producers' associations, consumer groups, environmental groups, taxpayers associations, and the like, creates competition among organized interests, who act as watchdogs on one another and the bureaucracy. An independent mass media reporting on abuses of power or corruption is another important watchdog" (Shirley 1998). As long as access is open and there is political control over the use of force, whenever one group begins to dominate its rivals, the others will organize to protect the open access system and hold the dominant group in check.

I have tried in this highly condensed history to give an overview of how institutionalists explain the emergence of modern, impersonal market exchange and open, democratic polities in Europe and elsewhere. Although there are still controversies and gaps in our understanding of how European economies developed market-supportive institutions, considerable progress has been made. Far less progress has been made in explaining why most other countries in the world have not developed these favorable institutions, which is the subject I turn to next.

WHY DO COUNTRIES FAIL TO DEVELOP MARKET-SUPPORTIVE INSTITUTIONS?

Most of the world has not been able to replicate the beliefs and institutions that characterize developed, open access societies. Many underdeveloped countries do not even pretend to open access rules. Others in Latin America (for example, Argentina or Chile), the Middle East (for example, Turkey), and Asia (for example, the Philippines) have installed the same rules as open access societies; they have competitive elections, market economies, diverse civil societies, religious tolerance, active universities, a free press, and the like. Yet these rules do not function in the same way as they do in richer open access economies. Although access is nominally open to all, as we saw in Chapter 2, non-elites face large transaction costs and informal barriers to starting a new business, getting credit, or finding a job in the formal economy. They also face high costs and barriers to creating a political or civil organization, getting a response from their political representatives, or negotiating with the bureaucracy.

A large and growing literature purports to explain why most countries failed to develop the market-supportive institutions and beliefs that were so important to European development. Elsewhere I have grouped these explanations into four broad categories (Shirley 2005a):[5]

1. Colonial heritage
2. Factor endowments plus colonial heritage
3. Conflicts
4. Beliefs and norms

The forthcoming book by North et al. steps back from these explanations and provides a set of deeper reasons that I will term:

5. The natural state

I briefly summarize each of these explanations below.

Colonial Heritage

Most of today's underdeveloped countries were once colonies, but not all former colonies are underdeveloped. This observation has led some institutional economists to propose that the rules, norms, and organizations installed by the colonial powers explain their colonies' subsequent institutional evolution, and determined their long-run rates and patterns of economic growth.

North (1990) has pointed out that England transplanted its rules and organizations constraining state powers and enforcing contracts to the United States and Canada. In contrast, Spain transplanted its powerful, centralized, and bureaucratic state apparatus and its system of property rights favoring a narrow group of elites to much of Central and South America. When the former Spanish colonies became independent they evolved very differently from the former British colonies in North America. "Without the heritage of colonial self-government and well-specified property rights, independence disintegrated into a violent struggle among competing groups for control of the policy and economy. Capturing the polity and using it as a vehicle of personal exchange in all markets was the result" (North 2005b, p. 112). Latin America's shared beliefs about the importance of personal relationships and the region's lack of shared beliefs about the legitimate role and limits of government are another inheritance from its colonial past (ibid.).

This explanation leaves one important question unanswered. Why did countries such as the US, Canada, or New Zealand inherit favorable beliefs and institutions from England, while other British colonies, such as Ghana, Jamaica, or India did not? It may be that the institutions of the indigenous inhabitants interacted with colonial institutions in harmful ways, although this would not explain outcomes in countries such as Jamaica where native inhabitants died of disease soon after their first encounter with Europeans. In those cases slavery may have strongly influenced future development. Or it may be that colonies with abundant natural riches or large populations were governed differently under colonialism in ways that left a harmful institutional heritage, as argued by the literature on factor endowments that I review later.

A prolific set of authors argues that one colonial institution in particular – the legal system – had a profound effect on the subsequent development of financial and political institutions (La Porta et al. 1997, 1998, 1999, 2000). Although these studies do not set out to explain economic development, one conclusion from their cross-country regressions is that countries whose early legal origins are grounded in English common law have an advantage over countries with other legal origins, and especially over those grounded in French civil law. Common law combines laws passed by the legislature with customary rules and norms and with the precedents set when judges adhere to prior judicial rulings in making their decisions. Civil code or statute law has its roots in Roman law and requires judges to uphold the laws as written by the legislature, with less room for judicial interpretation or discretion and less adherence to custom or precedents. Laws originate in a more decentralized, bottom up fashion under common law than under civil law. Common law and civil code law arose from very different traditions. Common law evolved in England partly as a way to protect private property against the king's encroachment. As I described earlier, the nobles' demand that the Crown not make common law subservient to royal prerogative was part of the struggles that led to the dethronements of the king in 1614 and again in 1688 (North and Weingast 1989). The French civil code was a product of the French Revolution's backlash against the corrupt French legal system that was subservient to the king and the nobility (Arruñada and Andonova 2005).[6] Civil law was implemented as an attempt to protect property and individuals from judicial abuse by binding judges to laws protecting rights.

La Porta et al. assert that English common law facilitated the development of more effective institutions to enforce contracts and constrain state coercion than French civil code law. They argue that legal systems based on the French civil code tradition provide much weaker protection of property rights and fewer checks on state coercion than those that are part of the English common law family. They also assert that civil code origins lead to a legal system that is more formalistic and less adaptable to changing circumstances (Beck and Levine 2005; La Porta et al. 1997, 1998, 1999). French civil law (and socialist law) origins are statistically correlated with more government interventionism, greater bureaucratic inefficiency, and less democracy than common law or German or Scandinavian civil law origins (La Porta et al. 1999). Countries with legal systems in the French civil code "family" also afford less legal protection to minority shareholders and to creditors than systems from the common law "family" (La Porta et al. 1998). Although legal origin is not significantly correlated with economic growth, common law origin has a strongly positive association with the development of banks and stock markets and with other measures of financial development, and these financial development measures have been shown to be correlated with growth (see studies cited in Beck and Levine 2005). French civil code origins also have a strong negative association with the Heritage Foundation's index of how well a country protects its citizens' property rights (Beck et al. 2003), and as we have seen protection of property rights is also strongly associated with growth.

The argument that differences in legal origins explain differences in contemporary institutions or property rights has been challenged (see, for example, Arruñada and Andonova 2005; Hadfield 2005; Shirley 2005a). Few dispute the importance of an effective legal system to economic and political development or the key role of the development of common law in the early industrialization of England or in the subsequent development of the United States. What is questionable is whether a country's legal family, imposed or adopted decades or centuries ago, determines how well it protects property rights and constrains state coercion today.

A number of critics question whether it is appropriate to categorize countries as part of the French civil law family or the English common law family based on laws on the books. Siems suggests that the "origins" classifications are arbitrary and insufficiently precise for econometric analyses (Siems 2006). There are large differences between the legal systems in France and those of the former French colonies or former Dutch, Portuguese, or Spanish colonies, yet all are classified in the French civil law family. Large differences also exist between the English legal system and that of the United States or between states within the US (see papers cited in Levine 2005, p. 66).[7] Some countries that initially adopted one legal tradition were subsequently strongly influenced by other legal traditions. For example, Japan's laws were modeled on German civil law, but were also strongly influenced by the US occupation (Siems 2006). Dam (2006) points out that Latin American law is categorized as of French civil code origin, but most Latin American countries have constitutions modeled on the US and many allow judicial review of administrative acts. There are also big differences in how countries with similar legal traditions enforce laws today. Not surprisingly, laws in practice turn out to be much more important for financial development than laws on the books (Pistor et al. 2000).

Another objection is the emphasis on a single set of institutions, the legal system. The essence of North's argument above is that a colonizer, such as Spain, imported not just a legal system but an array of rules, organizations, and belief systems to its colonies and it is this institutional complex, not just the judicial system, that influenced the subsequent development of the country's institutional environment.[8]

Much has changed in the years since France adopted the civil code in 1801, and these changes cast further doubt on the premise that legal family determines current protection of property rights. As we have seen, La Porta et al. find that civil law countries provide less shareholder and creditor protection than common law countries, and for that reason they are less financially developed. But financial development in European civil law countries has not consistently lagged behind common law countries; this seems to be a post-World War II phenomenon (Rajan and Zingales 2003). By many measures France and other civil law countries in continental Europe were more financially developed than the United States in the early 1900s (ibid.). Furthermore, legal systems in civil law and common law countries have been converging (Arruñada and Andonova 2005; Hadfield 2005; Rubin 2005). For example, the US created the Securities and Exchange Commission (SEC) and a number of other regulatory structures precisely because common law was seen as providing weaker protection for investors than regulation based on statute (Roe 2002). In both common and civil law countries current corporate and bankruptcy laws largely rely on recent statutes rather than judge-made common law or nineteenth-century civil law codes (Dam 2006, pp. 8–9).

The legal origins literature sheds little light on the question of why some countries are underdeveloped while others are not. Nor can the very different development paths of, for example, modern Chile and Argentina be explained by differences in legal origins, since both are in the French civil law family. Anglophone and francophone Africa have similar development problems despite their different legal origins. And it seems inappropriate to classify China's rapidly changing, highly idiosyncratic set of property rights into a single legal family (Ohnesorge 2003). Moreover, there is some evidence that it is the very weakness of the Chinese legal system that enables the private sector to divert funds from the inefficient state sector and make the investments responsible for Chinese growth (Lu and Yao 2003).

Factor Endowments plus Colonial Heritage

The endowment literature agrees that colonial heritage is indeed important to development, but argues that former colonies differ not because of where the European colonizers came from, but because of what they found when they arrived. Acemoglu et al. (2001, 2002) argue that Europeans settled in larger numbers in countries, such as Canada or the northern US, with lands and climates ill-suited for large plantations and with native populations too sparse or too hostile for plantation work. To govern themselves in their new circumstances, these settlers created or adapted institutions that protected property rights, enforced contracts, and limited state intervention. In places with mineral riches, such as Peru, lands and climates suited to plantation agriculture, such as Jamaica, or large populations that could be enslaved, such as Mexico, European colonizers immigrated in much smaller numbers and set up very different "extractive" institutions to exploit these endowments. These extractive institutions were designed to "concentrate political power in the hands of a few who used their power to extract resources from the rest of the population." (Acemoglu et al. 2002, p. 14). Extractive institutions endured after independence as postcolonial elites used them to enrich themselves. Regions where extractive institutions were prevalent had weaker property rights and fewer opportunities for innovation, and as a result were slower to industrialize. Economic development in these regions lagged behind more equitable regions, and that explains why they have a lower per capita income today.

These authors find that the differences in colonial inheritance that North (1990) describes have no effect on subsequent institutional development. Acemoglu et al. (2002) argue that, regardless of where colonizers came from, they created institutions to protect property rights and enforce contracts wherever they settled in large numbers, and created extractive institutions to exploit human and natural resources wherever they did not have large settlements. They attribute the low levels of institutional and economic development in Africa, with its variable factor endowments and low population density, to high mortality rates that kept settlers away.[9] Beck et al. find that the Acemoglu et al. measures of mortality rates for soldiers and bishops during the colonial period have a strong negative association with the Heritage Foundation index of contemporary property rights (Beck et al. 2003).

This argument is controversial. Easterly (2006) points out that there was large European migration to some high mortality areas, such as the southern US and the Caribbean, while from 1630 to 1780 net British migration to low mortality New England was zero. Glaeser et al. (2004) argue that settler mortality is not a valid instrument for institutions that protect property rights, because settlers brought not just institutions but educated people and schools. They argue that human capital determines institutions, not the other way around, although this assertion falls prey to dueling specifications.[10] Another issue is that Acemoglu and co-authors do not directly test the causal relationship between endowments and modern institutions, and are vague about the details of the damaging extractive institutions.

Sokoloff and Engerman (2000; Engerman and Sokoloff 2002) agree that factor endowments help explain large differences in contemporary institutions in the New World; they also provide more details about how this happened. In locations where endowments favored large plantation agriculture with imported slaves, such as the southern US or the Caribbean, and in places with large indigenous populations that could be enslaved, such as Mexico or Peru, elites limited access to property, suffrage, education, and credit, and designed legal, political, and social institutions to preserve their power. The inequality that resulted created a persistent disparity in political power, wealth, and human capital. In places less favorable to plantations and with indigenous populations too small or too hostile for a ready supply of slave labor, such as Canada and the northern US, colonial settlers came in larger numbers and promulgated rules favoring equality and homogeneity, expanding the franchise, investing in schooling, encouraging immigration, promoting secure land rights, and protecting intellectual property. They did so to benefit themselves and also to attract migrants to areas where labor was scarce. Engerman and Sokoloff (2005a) find evidence that the distribution of the indigenous population during colonization influenced the design of political and suffrage rules. As a result North America differed from much of South America (including the southern US) in many specific and lasting ways. For instance, Sokoloff and Zolt (2005) show that early in their histories, Canada and the US had far more progressive tax structures than Latin America; they also raised more revenues for local governments, and their local governments directed the funds to more socially progressive spending on projects such as schools, roads, or health care.

Engerman and Sokoloff do not ignore the influence of metropolitan institutions on the colonies, but argue that these institutions had to be adapted to the settlers' new circumstances. That explains why, even though former British colonies are all governed by British laws, they differ from one another depending on their location in temperate or tropical areas and their initial resource endowments (Engerman and Sokoloff 2005b). In the case of slave labor, for example, "climate and resources were the most powerful determinants of the geographic incidence of slave labor, irrespective of the metropolitan institutional structure" (ibid., p. 650). Engerman and Sokoloff advise caution in making claims about the effects of institutions on growth. If institutions are endogenous to endowments and other factors, then the focus should be on the factors influencing the rate and direction of institutional change, rather than a "set of institutional structures that would be universally effective at promoting growth" (ibid. 2005b, p. 662).

Conflicts

The central role of conflicts over borders in the evolution of European institutions has led some scholars to argue that the absence of border wars accounts for underdeveloped institutions in poorer countries. As we saw earlier, the need to raise revenues for conquests and defense led English monarchs to make concessions to nobles and merchants. These concessions strengthened institutions such as parliament, common law, and courts; institutions that later evolved into market-supportive rules and organizations. Tilly (1992) argues that colonies suffered because they did not go through the conflicts that built European nation-states. Instead their governance institutions were built under the control or influence of a dominant foreign power. Boundaries of countries that became independent in the twentieth century were made permanent by great powers. Although the big powers did not permit border conflicts, they did provide military aid and training to their client states, and these weapons and armies were used, not for external conflicts, but for internal control.

Bates argues that military aid and foreign aid more broadly reduced the incentives for poorer states to "forge liberal political institutions." Support from the international community freed them from having "to seek ways to get their citizens to pay for defense and other costs of government" (Bates 2001, p. 83). Herbst (2000) suggests that colonizers in Africa drew state boundaries in ways that concentrated opposing ethnic groups in urban areas with vast stretches of largely empty territory between them. This empty land provided shelter for rebel armies, setting the stage for continual civil wars. After independence, the great powers prevented these former colonial boundaries from being redrawn through border wars, since local wars did not suit their Cold War interests. They also propped up weak and venal governments with aid. Robinson (2002) argues that this view pays too little attention to the pernicious effect that slavery had on Africa's development. He suggests that pre-colonial African states organized themselves for slave raiding and predation rather than for providing public goods. During colonization, he asserts, dangerous diseases kept Europeans from migrating in large numbers, leading colonizers to build on the existing exploitive institutions that supported slavery, rather than building new, more participatory institutions such as democracy or universal schooling.

The emphasis on war in this literature seems misplaced. Although war played a nation-building role in medieval Europe, it was not the only cause or even the predominant one. As we have seen, new belief systems, increasing trade and competition, the growing power of the commercial classes, a historically weaker king in England, and the pressures to raise revenues to fight increasingly expensive wars facilitated the institutional innovations that prompted market development. Institutional innovations did not emerge in those warring nations, such as France or Spain, where some of the necessary elements were missing.

One intriguing feature of these studies is their view of the role played by foreign military and economic aid. To Bates and Herbst, outside funds have largely relieved African rulers from the need to encourage commerce and make concessions to merchants and investors in order to raise revenues. In this view aid seems to have played a similar role in Africa as that played by New World riches in Spain, where wealth from its colonies exempted the Spanish Crown from pressures to compromise or reform. I return to the role of foreign aid later in Chapter 4.

Beliefs and Norms

Some institutionalists, notably Greif and North, stress the importance of beliefs and norms in motivating people to adhere to laws and rules or to change them. People hold a set of beliefs about the world and expectations of what others believe and how others will behave that directly influence their own behavioral choices (Greif 2006). Consider my earlier driving example. Drivers in Cairo or Washington are powerfully influenced by their belief that straddling lanes is appropriate or inappropriate behavior, their expectations that other drivers will or will not do the same, and their presumptions that other drivers will expect them to straddle or not to straddle lanes. A change in the formal rules that govern driving will not change behavior unless it changes such internalized expectations and beliefs. Since beliefs influence how people learn by determining how they interpret new experiences, beliefs determine the sorts of institutional changes that will be accepted (North 2005b).

Greif (1994, 2006) emphasizes the importance of individualism in supporting Europe's move to impersonal exchange. Individualism had roots in early Greek and Roman beliefs and in Christianity's focus on the individual; it was reinforced by feudalism with its emphasis on the obligation of the individual to his or her lord. He contrasts how the collectivist beliefs of the Jewish Maghribi traders led to different institutions from those developed in individualistic Christian Genoa. As we have seen the Maghribi collectivist system relied on community ties and enforced bargains through fears of losing reputation and ostracism. As a result the Maghribi did not develop formal contracts or courts to support the expansion of trade. In contrast, Genoa relied more on written documents, contracts, and courts, and less on shared information and collective punishment. Another element in Europe's transformation according to Greif (2006) was religious doctrine. Unlike much of the world, medieval Europe moved from social structures built around family, clan, or tribe to social structures based on mutual interests, such as corporations. The Roman Catholic Church encouraged this shift by weakening kin-based social structures through its prohibitions against marrying relatives and its bans on practices that enlarged the family such as polygamy or divorce and remarriage. By encouraging consensual marriages instead of controlled marriages within extended families and by urging that inheritances be donated to the Church instead of to heirs, the Church also weakened the hold of kin-based networks (ibid., p. 252).

Beliefs and institutions are intimately interrelated. Indeed for Greif (2006), beliefs are part of institutions; beliefs motivate the behavior that makes an institution self-enforcing. To North, beliefs are separate from institutions but are intimately related to them since, "the institutional structure reflects the accumulated beliefs of the society over time" (North 2005a, p. 49). Beliefs explain why attempts to change institutions so often fail. Beliefs and norms tend to be durable, changing gradually through learning and new ideas. When intellectual ferment is stifled through repression, muted by brain drain, or discouraged by an uninformed, apathetic, or illiterate public, there are fewer opportunities for learning and change and beliefs stagnate (for more on this issue see Chapter 7).

The Natural State

North et al. (forthcoming) argue that most countries have underdeveloped institutions not because of any single determinant, but because they are natural states. In their view natural states emerged 10,000 years ago in an effort to reduce the endemic violence common to primitive societies, and have been the dominant social order ever since. In their concept, groups or coalitions naturally formed around specialists in violence who had the potential to protect non-military elites, such as traders, educators, clergy, or politicians. The elites had an incentive to form coalitions and to strike deals with other elites to enforce their property rights to land, labor, and capital, because rents are higher when there is social order rather than civil war. The ruling elites use economic rents to bind the coalition together, and use the state to generate these rents by providing elite groups with economic privileges and by limiting access to markets or power to members of the elite (ibid.). Thus, property rights and legal systems have their origin in the definition of elite rights.

What keeps this system from beggaring itself, which would happen if elites took the entire surplus and prevented markets from expanding? Sometimes nothing, as we see in many African countries today. Greif (2005) suggests that ruling elites could be constrained if they believe that an abuse of power would lead to a decline in trade and future financial losses that would out-weigh any gains from present abuse. He argues that this incentive is self-enforcing if the elites expect to be around long enough to reap future gains from trade. Dominant elites may still be bandits, but if they are "stationary bandits," they care about safeguarding property rights in order to foster eco-nomic growth and reap bigger rewards over time (Olson 1993). Ruling elites without an absolute monopoly over coercion can also be constrained by a fear of retaliation from other powerful actors, but that fear protects only the rights of those with the power to retaliate (Greif 2005).

According to North et al. (forthcoming), members of an elite group have an incentive to increase its size, since that will make their coalition more powerful. But they also have a countervailing incentive to limit access so that their rents are not dissipated. This results in a limited access order where the state controls trade and only enforces property rights for elites. Elites hold power by virtue of their personal position in the dominant coalition, and non-elites seek their patronage and protection. Although the individuals may change, elite incentives remain the same, so that the insti-tutions that perpetuate elite power persist (Acemoglu and Robinson 2006). Market organizations, such as corporations or unions, and social organ-izations, such as clubs, arise in the natural state, but the state only enforces the rules and rights of organizations created or dominated by elites (North et al. forthcoming). Natural states are stable only as long as powerful elites believe they are better off remaining in the coalition than using their mili-tary power to overturn and replace it; this explains why many natural states succumb frequently to violence and military coups.

As natural states mature they introduce some of the same formal rules and organizational forms as open access states, including competitive elections, political parties, a complex body of public law enforced by police and courts, division of powers between government branches and jurisdictions, taxation, market pricing, limited liability corporations, contracts and private laws, unions, banks, and stock markets. But these institutions and organizations function very differently in the North et al. natural state from the way they function in an open access society. Laws, contracts, and rights are only enforced for elites, and organizations are only effective when they serve elite purposes. Markets are not fully competitive because of elite monopoly powers and privileges. Non-elites pay high transaction costs when they try to set up businesses or create other new organizations, borrow money, pay their taxes, comply with government regulations, and the like. Transaction costs are high for everyone, but elites have ways around them. For example, banks will accept and indeed prefer personal guarantees rather than collateral for loans; bureaucrats will expedite administrative procedures for bribes or in response to potential or perceived pressure from politicians on behalf of influential persons.[11]

Although the work of North and co-authors is still preliminary, there is evidence supporting their model of the natural state in today's underdeveloped countries. Kathy Fogel (2006) finds evidence that personal power and relationships are relatively more important in poorer countries. In these countries wealthy families control ownership of the largest domestic, nongovernmental businesses, and more family control is associated with more government red tape, more intervention through regulation, more state ownership, more bureaucratic delays, more frequent price controls, and less protection of shareholder rights.[12] Large costs imposed by the state protect these powerful family firms from competition. It is not well established whether the inefficiencies and intervention of the state lead to family ownership, or, as North and co-authors argue, the economic importance of certain families and high transaction costs imposed by government developed simultaneously as two mutually dependent components of the natural state.

Faccio (2006b) provides insights into why elite-owned businesses prosper in high transaction cost economies, which are reminiscent of the World Bank's findings on influential firms. She finds that large firms in many countries have strong political connections thanks to relatives and friends of the owners or major shareholders of the firm who are cabinet ministers or members of parliament.[13] Political connections are more likely in countries with high ratings of corruption, greater restrictions on foreign investment, and fewer regulations restricting the business activities of public officials (ibid.). Even though politically connected firms underperform non-connected firms, connected firms enjoy higher leverage, lower tax rates, and larger market shares (Faccio 2006a). Connected firms are also more likely to be bailed out by governments than similar non-connected firms, yet exhibit significantly worse financial performance when they are bailed out and over the following two years (Faccio et al. 2005). More research is needed to establish whether political connections and family-dominated firms are the product of poor institutions that permit corruption, related lending, and government bailouts, or whether politically connected business and the corresponding institutional failures form part of the equilibrium of the natural state as North et al. assert.

THE CHALLENGE AHEAD

Although we have made considerable progress in understanding the institutions that led to development, our understanding of what led to under-developed institutions is less advanced, and we still have very partial knowledge of how institutions change. Institutions are persistent, but they are also endogenous. The challenge ahead is to move our understanding of institutions beyond the present abstractions and provide findings that are more useful for decision-makers and citizens of poor countries. In the next chapter, I analyze how our poor understanding of institutions has had important implications for foreign aid. Chapter 5 discusses the problems of measuring institutions given our current state of knowledge.

NOTES

1. The result was that England had what North et al. (forthcoming) call the doorstep conditions for transition to an open access state: rule of law for elites, perpetual forms of organizations for elites (including the state and corporate forms), and political control of the military.
2. Spain and Portugal were late in adopting modern market-supportive institutions. Revenues from their overseas empires allowed their kings to wage wars without making the same concessions to asset holders and merchants (North and Thomas 1973).
3. Acemoglu and Robinson (2005) model how this might occur in response to rebellion where to avoid civil war and offer a credible bargain to the rebels, the dominant group allows democratic institutions.
4. North et al. (forthcoming) term these rules, "constitution," which in this context refers not to a written document, although that could be part of the constitution, but to the set of ideas, norms, and rules that are accepted as part of a societal consensus. (For more on how constitutions become self-enforcing see Weingast 2005).
5. This section draws heavily on Shirley (2005a).
6. Arruñada and Andonova (2005) show how both systems developed as an attempt to install market-oriented legal systems. English judges were former barristers who understood the fundamentals of a market economy and were allied with the merchants

and landed gentry in parliament against the encroachments of the king. In contrast, *Ancien Régime* judges in France were the product of a doctrinaire course of study, had little previous practice, and in some cases had purchased their positions from the king. They provided no check on state power.

7. Large parts of the United States have a civil law heritage that still affects state laws, such as community property laws in California, Texas, and other former parts of Mexico.

8. Siems asserts the importance of taking into account more than just the explanatory force of legal families in regressions in assessing the role of legal systems, citing a paper by Mark West showing that French legal origin is positively correlated with success in the football World Cup (West 2002, cited in Siems 2006, p. 8).

9. The Acemoglu et al. (2002) mortality rates are not in fact those of settlers, but are based on the non-combat deaths of European soldiers in European colonies in the nineteenth century and of bishops in Latin America from the seventeenth to the nineteenth century. Whether these rates are themselves accurate and accurately reflect settler motivation is open to question. Government policy in restricting immigration and awarding monopoly rights was probably as or more important in discouraging settlement in some colonies, such as Spanish America or Dutch Indonesia. This may support Acemoglu et al.'s argument that the mortality rates instrument captures exogenous sources of variation in institutional quality.

10. Acemoglu et al. (2005) argue that including time dummy variables in the Glaeser et al. (2004) regressions eliminates the effects of education on institutions (specifically on democracy).

11. There is a large literature on the importance of elite economic power in economic development; see the cites in Morck et al. (2005).

12. Among the countries where more than 90 percent of the top largest conglomerates are family controlled are Belgium, Brazil, Chile, Greece, India, Malaysia, Mexico, Pakistan, Peru, Philippines, Portugal, Thailand, Turkey, and Venezuela (Kathy Fogel 2006, table I).

13. Countries where more than 10 percent of all firms are politically connected include Indonesia, Italy, Malaysia, Mexico, Russia, and Thailand (Faccio 2006b).

4. Can foreign aid promote development?

The preceding chapters described how institutions emerged to support increasingly open access to economic and political activity and allowed the specialization and innovation that were critical to the evolution of today's wealthy, developed countries. These crucial institutions are weak or missing in today's underdeveloped countries. Instead, poor societies are characterized by high transaction costs, corrupt and inefficient bureaucracies, weak enforcement of laws, lax protection of property rights, and the absence of mechanisms to hold bureaucrats and politicians accountable for their actions. Access to economic opportunities, rule of law, and protection of property and persons are privileges available only to elites. Can foreign aid change these damaging circumstances and help nurture the institutions that promote development?

Is it fair to ask whether foreign aid can promote development? Much aid is dedicated to reducing the immediate misery of people in poverty, not to development. But improving the lot of direct beneficiaries by distributing food, shelter, health care, or money is not the only mission of aid-giving agencies. Aid organizations are also dedicated to the proposition that underdevelopment can be eliminated and poverty eradicated. The World Bank mission statement is emblematic: "Our dream is a world free of poverty." Increasingly aid agencies also recognize that development requires improved institutions, as these quotes show:

- "Addressing the challenge of building effective institutions is critical to the Bank's mission of fighting poverty." (World Bank 2002, p. iii)
- "Sustainable and equitable development requires a democratic, modern and efficient state that promotes economic growth, establishes a regulatory framework conducive to the efficient functioning of markets, that guarantees a stable macroeconomic environment, that is capable of adopting social and economic policies appropriate for poverty reduction and environmental preservation, and that implements such policies in an efficient, transparent and accountable manner. In the development debate a consensus has formed that the quality of public institutions is an essential, and perhaps the most

47

important ingredient for sustainable economic growth." (Inter-American Development Bank 2003, p. 9)

- "Development interventions are more likely to succeed if they promote improvements in wider institutional competencies as well as in technical competencies." (United Kingdom, Department for International Development 2003, p. 5)

Thus it seems not just fair but imperative to ask whether aid agencies can promote the institutions that underpin growth and development. This chapter addresses this question, focusing on aid targeting development, not on humanitarian aid.

THE FOREIGN AID COMMUNITY IS BURGEONING

It is easy to lose sight of how large aid has grown when donors are being widely condemned by celebrities and politicians as doing too little, too late. Over the past five decades official development aid has totaled more than $2.3 trillion in nominal dollars, and the foreign aid community has burgeoned. From an almost non-existent base, the aid community has grown to 21 multilateral and 36 bilateral agencies and numerous private organizations (Table 4.1). In 2003 there were another 59,003 international, non-governmental agencies or NGOs (Anheier et al. 2004, p. 320), and innumerable local NGOs. These aid-givers were responsible for $186 billion in gross, or $120 billion net, disbursements in 2005. Aid is projected to accelerate in the near term. If major donor governments deliver on the public pledges of their officials, net official development assistance in constant dollars will climb almost 65 percent, from almost $79 billion in 2004 to close to $130 billion by 2010 (OECD, DAC 2006).[1] As we shall see in this chapter, this boom in aid-giving comes even though there is no robust evidence that aid contributes to growth – or to good institutions.

Despite the dreams, money, and good intentions of aid-givers, most people in aid-recipient countries still live in appalling poverty. Jeffrey Sachs and the team at the United Nations Millennium project argued that this was mostly because foreign aid has been too small (Sachs 2005; UN Millennium Project 2005b). They pointed out that, despite the volume of aid shown in Table 4.1, few donor countries reached the target ratio of 0.7 percent of their gross national income (GNI). The approximately $79 billion of net official development assistance in 2004 was on average 0.25 percent of the GNI of donor countries. Achieving the 0.7 percent target would therefore require a drastic increase in aid. But the 0.7 percent target has a dubious history. It is an arbitrary target that began life as a "lobbying tool" (Clemens and Moss

Table 4.1   Size of the aid community, 2005

Type of aid agency	Number	Gross assistance[a] 2005	Net assistance[a] 2005
International financial institutions	10		
African Development Bank		1,839	685
Asian Development Bank		4,791	866
European Development Bank		1,597	85
Inter-American Development Bank		3,013	595
International Monetary Fund		596	(714)
World Bank (IBRD, IDA, IFC)		22,030	4,139
Other (Caribbean Development Bank, Council of Europe, Int'l Fund for Agric. Dev., Nordic Development Fund)		174	109
Total IFIs		34,040	5,765
United Nations agencies (UNDP, UNFPA, UNHCR, UNICEF, UNRWA, UNTA, WFP, other UN)	7		
Total UN		3,777	3,659
Other multinational aid agencies	4		
European Community		11,640	10,282
Rest (Global Environmental Fund, Montreal Protocol Fund, Arab Funds, GFATM)		1,684	1,514
Total		13,324	11,795
Bilateral aid[b]			
Development aid, OECD members of DAC[c]	22	117,428	82,133
Development aid, non-DAC members[d]		2,399[e]	2,399
Total	14	119,827	84,532
Grants by private voluntary organizations		14,721	14,712
Total assistance		185,680	120,464

Notes:
a.   US dollars millions. Concessional and non-concessional disbursements to underdeveloped countries (as defined by the OECD) with promotion of economic development as the goal at current prices converted to US dollars at current exchange rates.
b.   Includes grant and grant-like contributions (including technical cooperation, development food aid, emergency and distress relief, contributions to NGOs, and administrative costs), debt reorganization, and new development lending.
c.   Australia, Austria, Belgium, Canada, Denmark, Finland, France, Germany, Greece, Ireland, Italy, Japan, Luxembourg, Netherlands, New Zealand, Norway, Portugal, Spain, Sweden, Switzerland, UK, US.
d.   Czech Republic, Estonia, Hungary, Iceland, Israel, South Korea, Kuwait, Latvia, Lithuania, Poland, Saudi Arabia, Slovak Republic, Turkey, and United Arab Emirates.
e.   Net.

Source: Author's calculations (based on OECD, DAC 2007, tables 13, 17, and 33).

2005, p. 2).[2] Clemens and Moss show that "the 0.7 percent target was calculated using a series of assumptions that are no longer true, and justified
by a model that is no longer considered credible" (ibid.). Applying the
same methodology to today's conditions would produce a target of only
0.01 percent of wealthy countries' GDP for aid to the poorest countries and
negative aid flows to the rest. As Clemens and Moss point out it would be
more meaningful to set aid targets on the basis of recipient need combined
with a model of how aid affects development.

The UN Millennium Project nonetheless called for massive increases in
aid to achieve the Millennium Development Goals. These are a set of laud-
able and ambitious goals that grew out of a UN meeting in Monterrey on
21–22 March 2002 (the goals are shown in Table 4.2). The report of the UN
Millennium Project did not ignore the presence of weak and damaging
institutions in poor countries. Instead it argued that increasing aid would
improve institutions, because institutions are partly endogenous to income:
"good governance helps achieve higher income, and higher income supports better governance" (UN Millennium Project 2005b, p. 110). The
assumption that money could buy better institutions is crucial to the UN
Millennium Development Project, as the report asserted:

> The upshot is that while good governance can contribute to economic growth
> and bad economic governance can certainly impede growth, governance itself
> can be improved by investing in other factors (such as education and health) that
> support overall economic growth and human capital accumulation. This two-
> way causation is hugely important from the vantage point of the Millennium
> Development Goals. It underscores the importance of a broad-based strategy to
> meet the Goals, directly through good governance practices and indirectly
> through investments in human capital, public sector management, and infra-
> structure. (ibid., p. 112)

According to the report of the UN Millennium Project there are two
kinds of poor countries, the few with "truly rapacious government leadership" that lack the "volition" for improving governance and the many with
"well intentioned" governments that lack the resources for improving governance (p. 113). The report called for rich nations to provide more money
to the "well intentioned" countries in order to support public administration, strengthen the rule of law, increase transparency and accountability,
promote political and social rights, promote sound economic policies, and
support civil society (p. 114). The report also urged donors to support
investments in the other Millennium Goals to lift the recipient country out
of its "poverty trap" (p. 32). The project laid out detailed programs to
achieve its set of goals and called for poor countries to develop extensive
plans on how they will implement these programs.

Table 4.2   Millennium Development Goals

Goals	Targets
1. Eradicate extreme poverty & hunger	• Halve % people whose $Y = <\$1$/day between 1990–2015 • Halve people hungry, 1990–2015
2. Achieve universal primary education	• By 2015
3. Promote gender equality & empower women	• Eliminate gender disparity in primary & secondary ed. by 2005 & in all education by 2015
4. Reduce child mortality	• Reduce 1990 under-5 mortality rate by 2/3 by 2015
5. Improve maternal health	• Reduce 1990 maternal mortality rate by 3/4 by 2015
6. Combat HIV/AIDS, malaria, & other diseases	• Halt & begin to reverse spread of HIV/AIDS by 2015 • Halt & begin to reverse incidence of malaria & other major diseases by 2015
7. Ensure environmental sustainability	• Integrate principles of sustainable development into country policies & programs & reverse loss of environmental resources • Halve % people w/o sustainable access to safe drinking water & basic sanitation by 2015 • Significantly improve lives of at least 100 million slum dwellers by 2020
8. Develop global partnerships for development	• Develop open, rule-based, predictable, nondiscriminatory trading & financial system • Address special needs of least developed countries • Address special needs of landlocked & small island underdeveloped countries • Deal comprehensively with debt problems of underdeveloped countries through national & internt'l measures to make debt sustainable in long term • Develop & implement strategies for decent & productive work for youth in cooperation w/ underdeveloped countries • Provide access to affordable essential drugs in underdeveloped countries in cooperation w/ pharmaceutical companies • Make available benefits of new technologies, esp info & communication, in cooperation w/ private sector

Source: Adapted from UN Millennium Development Goals at: www.un.org/millenniumgoals.

Developed countries have responded by pledging to increase aid dramatically, especially to Africa, and to write-off large amounts of official debt. The IMF predicts that if the levels of financial assistance envisioned by the UN Millennium Report are achieved, aid will finance an average of about 60 percent of government expenditures in low-income African countries (International Monetary Fund 2005, p. 147). Yet, as the next section shows, the track record of aid provides no reason to assume that aid can promote sustainable development or improve institutions, and many reasons to believe that large amounts of aid are damaging to weak institutional environments.

AID HAS A POOR TRACK RECORD IN PROMOTING GROWTH OR IMPROVING INSTITUTIONS

Aid and Growth

A controversy has raged about the effect of aid on growth; a debate that has been traced by one survey back to 1970 (Clemens et al. 2004). A profusion of recent papers presents conflicting statistical evidence on the effects of aid on growth. Two frequently cited papers by Burnside and Dollar (2000, 2004) find a positive association between aid and growth, but only in better policy and institutional environments. There are a host of challenges to this finding, however (for a survey see Harms and Lutz 2004). For example, Easterly et al. (2003) reproduce Burnside and Dollar's methodology, but when they add additional countries and years the positive growth effect of aid in good policy environments loses its statistical significance. Burnside and Dollar's results were also found to be fragile to changes in the specification of the policy and institutional variables (Brumm 2003; Easterly et al. 2003; Harms and Lutz 2003). And Roodman (2004) finds the Burnside and Dollar result is weak in empirical tests.

Some argue that aid has a positive but non-linear effect, perhaps because of decreasing returns to aid (see studies cited in Harms and Lutz 2004). But others find no evidence of decreasing returns (Gomanee et al. 2003). Clemens and his co-authors find a positive short-term impact of aid on growth by separating that part of aid that seems likely to have a growth impact in four years from humanitarian aid and aid likely to be effective only in the long term (Clemens et al. 2004). Yet another paper slices and dices aid differently and finds a beneficial association between very long-term growth and what they classify as "development aid," defined as aid from multilateral agencies and the Nordic countries plus other so-called "better" donors (Reddy and Minoiu 2006). This positive impact only occurs after several decades.

Rajan and Subramanian (2005) tried to put all these dueling regressions to rest. They did an extensive analysis of the effects of aid on growth over different time horizons, looking at different kinds of aid from different sources. Specifically, they divided aid into 10, 20, 30, and 40-year time periods, separated out aid designed to stimulate growth from humanitarian assistance or food aid, and distinguished between bilateral and multilateral aid. They looked at the effects of aid on countries that have adopted better policies or have better institutions, and on countries in different geographical settings. Their bottom line: there is *no* robust evidence of either a positive or a negative impact of aid on growth.

Evidence from specific countries supports the null impact of aid on growth. There is little evidence that foreign aid was important for economic outcomes in China, for example. For one thing, in the 1980s and 1990s when China was growing rapidly foreign aid was trivial, only 0.4 percent of China's gross domestic product (Easterly 2002a). For another, one of the main engines of Chinese growth, the township and village enterprise, was neither created nor supported by foreign aid, as I discuss below. Other fast-growing countries tell a similar story. In the 1980s when Chile introduced the reforms that led to its subsequent rapid growth, it was not receiving foreign aid, instead it was repaying in full its debts to official and private lenders. South Korea's growth accelerated only after the decline in US aid and only after South Korea followed many policies contrary to US aid officials' advice (Fox 2000). An important reason why Taiwan introduced more market- and export-oriented policies that stimulated its subsequent growth in the 1960s was to reduce its dependency on US aid (Haggard and Pang 1994). In contrast, the countries where aid has been the most important have been among the slowest growing. For decades, those African countries where aid represents the highest percentage of gross domestic product have had the slowest rates of per capita growth.

Aid and Institutions

Perhaps even more disturbing than the failure of aid to spur growth is the absence of any beneficial effect of aid on institutions. Burnside and Dollar (2004, p. 4) cite a number of studies that support this finding, concluding that "there is broad agreement that giving a large amount of financial aid to a country with poor economic institutions and policies is not likely to stimulate reform, and may in fact retard it". Other studies find that aid has a *negative* effect on institutions. These studies argue that aid fostered so much rent-seeking and corruption and tied up so many valuable resources in unproductive administration, that its negative effects counteracted any good outcomes from aid projects (Bauer 1991; Kanbur 2000; cited in Harms and Lutz 2004). Easterly argues that the large and cumbersome bureaucracies required to implement aid projects and meet aid reporting requirements have contributed to excessively centralized administrations and higher transaction costs and divert government time and effort from governing (Easterly 2002a). For example, Tanzania has to produce more than 2400 reports a year for donors and to host 1000 annual visits from aid agencies (Easterly 2002a). Bates (2001) suggests that foreign aid helps non-reforming governments survive by making the cost of non-reform cheaper, and also makes governments less dependent on their citizens for revenues and therefore less accountable. Whatever the reason, higher aid levels have been significantly correlated with lower indexes of bureaucratic quality, corruption, and rule of law in one study (Knack 2000), although a subsequent study finds no effect on these or other economic institutions (Coviello and Islam 2006). Higher aid levels have been associated with slower adoption of market-oriented economic policy reforms from 1980 to 2000, although aid's negative correlation with reform was more pronounced during the 1980s than in the 1990s (Heckelman and Knack 2005). Foreign aid has also been shown to have a negative association with democracy (Djankov et al. 2006). An IMF study of a sample of 105 countries from 1970 to 2004 identified 36 instances where institutions were transformed for the better according to various measures of institutional quality (these measures are discussed in detail in the next chapter). Using a probit model, the report estimated how much foreign aid, trade, freedom of the press, and other variables affect the probability of a positive institutional transition, and find that aid has a negative association with the probability of transition to more economic freedom (International Monetary Fund 2005, p. 139). This finding, however, could reflect reverse causality: the possibility that aid flows are greater to countries with conditions that impede institutional transition (ibid., p. 141).[3]

Most of these studies use cross-country regressions, which have well-documented flaws (see, for example, Durlauf et al. 2005; Levine and Renelt 1992; Rodrik 2005). Nonetheless, it is revealing that so many different specifications and authors should find that aid has nil or negative effects on growth and institutions. Even if cross-country regressions cannot establish causal relationships, they do allow us to weed out hypotheses that are consistently rejected in most specifications. The premise that aid promotes development is just such a rejected hypothesis. Attempts to find a positive association between aid and growth have become increasingly strained. Take, for example, the implausible finding that the effects of aid only appear decades after the money has been disbursed. Anyone who has visited aid-funded roads or schools some time after the assistance has ended, as I have, will be struck by the absence of sustainable effects rather than their persistence. I remember my taxi inching its way into and out of the series of craters that was all that was left of an aid-funded road in Tanzania or being ushered through ante-rooms to the palatial office of the Nicaraguan Minister of Education in what was originally intended to be an aid-funded school building.

Cross-country regressions are not the only evidence of aid's ineffectiveness in improving institutions. The World Bank is one of the few donors that does serious evaluation of the outcomes of its projects, and its judgment of the results of institutional support is damning. The World Bank's projects to improve public administration, strengthen rule of law, or otherwise develop institutions were judged "largely ineffective" by its Operations Evaluation Department (Girishankar 2001). Ratings of World Bank efforts to improve institutional performance in Africa record a train of failures (reports cited in World Bank 2005b, Annex A, pp. 47–9):

- 1990: "The main goal of freestanding TA [technical assistance] is to enhance the capacities of borrower institutions and government agencies to perform their work on a sustainable basis. The record of the Bank is poor: only 3 out of the 19 Bank projects reviewed were rated as having satisfactory outcomes."
- 1994: "The use of TA as a means to develop institutional capacity has had very limited success in Africa. Instead of transferring expertise, this approach has created dependency on foreign experts that has not diminished over the years."
- 1999: "Bank-supported civil service reforms were largely ineffective in achieving sustainable results in capacity building or institutional reform."
- 2004: " 'Big bang' approaches have failed because they overstrained limited implementation capacity. What is needed is 'strategic incrementalism' – highly focused and pragmatic interventions that are better grounded in the political realities and consistent with the capacity constraints of the country concerned."

The World Bank projects supporting institutional reform are arguably the most comprehensive and serious of any aid-givers. We can only speculate how much worse the judgment would be if applied to projects of other, less self-reflective givers.

My Own Experience with Aid and Reform of State-owned Enterprises

The finding that aid fails to spur growth or improve institutions is consistent with my experience during 35 years working on development, 21 of them doing research at the World Bank. I worked on reform and privatization of state-owned enterprises long before it became fashionable in the aid community. In 1981 I led the first joint World Bank/IFC mission advising the Peruvian government on selling state enterprises.[4] I visited countless state-owned firms that had received aid from the World Bank and many other donors, and analyzed a number of different "solutions" designed to improve management of state-owned enterprises (SOEs), such as special ministries dedicated to oversight of SOEs, special units within ministries dedicated to improving SOEs, holding companies managing a portfolio of SOEs modeled after Italy's IRI, performance contracts between SOEs and governments modeled after France's *contrats de plan*, and better rules for SOE boards of directors (Shirley and Nellis 1991). All of these "solutions" attempted to engineer a organizational remedy to what were essentially political problems. State-owned enterprises performed badly for all the reasons identified in agency theory: they had multiple and conflicting objectives; they answered to multiple principals; they reported to supervisory ministries that interfered in day-to-day operations for political or corrupt reasons; they were not permitted to raise prices, lay off workers, close uneconomic lines of businesses, or go bankrupt; they were forced to hire surplus workers and provide extensive social benefits and training to staff; they were run by managers and board members who were political appointees, often unqualified, who changed whenever the political leadership changed; they were monopolies or protected from competition; they received directed credit from state-owned banks and government-guaranteed loans and were allowed to roll over their bad debts or foist them onto the treasury (Shirley 1999). There are multiple examples of the political roots of SOE problems. To mention a few: Thailand's government appointed generals to the boards of SOEs in order to secure support from the powerful military; India's government propped up state-owned textile and coal companies that had lost money since their inception to secure patronage jobs; China's government used the banking system to keep its large and unprofitable SOEs alive in order to avoid politically dangerous unemployment. Aid-funded projects that relied on organizational engineering could not address these root causes of poor performance. When aid agencies subsequently embraced privatization of SOEs in the mid-1980s, aid to SOEs continued, but now to rehabilitate state-owned firms prior to sale, to finance advice from investment bankers, and to reward governments who sold their SOEs with structural adjustment loans.

The SOE example illustrates a fundamental paradox of aid: many of the changes that are most needed do not require money or technical assistance. No money, training, or advice is necessary for governments to stop interfering in SOE operations, to appoint competent managers, to allow competition, or to decide to privatize, for example. Quite the contrary, these reforms often generate additional revenues by removing a fiscal drain or putting SOEs in the private sector where they can be taxed. Aid money may have been useful in paying for retrenchment and retraining, but only where the decision to reform was serious. What reforming countries most need is not aid but a much scarcer commodity, what the donor community calls "political will," that is, the readiness to take politically difficult decisions. As we know from the previous discussions, political will is endogenous to the beliefs and institutions that shape politicians' incentives. It is not surprising that privatization was disappointing wherever institutions supported the dominance of powerful elites and governments privatized in order to transfer rents to powerful individuals.

In the 1980s the World Bank introduced a new tool, the structural adjustment loan. The genius of the structural adjustment loan was that it dodged the problem of what to fund in the absence of political will. Structural adjustment loans disbursed funds for government promises to implement reforms, called conditionality. In some cases reforming governments used this money to pay off those who would lose from reforms. Argentina, for example, used foreign aid to pay severance pay to civil servants and SOE employees who were laid off in the process of downsizing government and selling SOEs.[5] Others simply took the money and failed to keep their promises. Zaire was one of the most egregious cases; massive inflows of foreign assistance continued despite poor performance and corruption. According to the World Bank (1998), "While the former Zaire's Mobuto Sese Seko was reportedly amassing one of the world's largest personal fortunes (invested, naturally, outside his country), decades of large-scale foreign assistance left not a trace of progress".

WHY AID AGENCIES ARE POOR TOOLS TO PROMOTE INSTITUTIONAL REFORMS

Why has aid been so unsuccessful in promoting growth and market-supportive institutions? Some argue that aid performs poorly because of principal–agent problems. Principal–agent problems arise when a principal, such as the manager of a firm, is monitoring and motivating an agent, such as an employee, and the agent has more information about her performance than the principal (Laffont and Tirole 1993). The agent may use her information advantage to shirk, or the principal may pay the agent more than is needed to motivate her to perform. Agency problems are worse when performance has to be judged against many, conflicting, and hard to measure objectives, and when there are multiple principals with different objectives, conditions that are endemic in aid agencies (Martens et al. 2002).[6]

Aid agencies have multiple objectives. Besides eliminating or alleviating poverty, and completing specific projects, such as building health clinics, they are increasingly expected to improve the environment, help women and minorities, protect human rights, strengthen democracy or civil society, and much more. (For a sense of these goals, see the list of criteria used to rate country eligibility for the World Bank's soft credits (IDA) in Table 5.2.) Objectives of aid organizations are frequently amorphous, far harder to measure than profits, and place conflicting demands on staff and management. Sometimes the objectives conflict, for instance, when aid-assisted civil organizations oppress women or pollute the environment, or when aid-encouraged elections lead to governments whose decisions harm the economy and the poor (see my discussion of democracy in Chapter 5). Even if objectives could be properly measured and weighted, it would be hard for a principal to hold aid-givers accountable since they operate in sovereign countries; moreover, aid may be relatively small compared to other capital sources such as remittances or private investment.

Besides multiple objectives, aid organizations also have multiple principals: donor governments, donor citizens, and governments, beneficiaries, and interest groups in recipient countries. The board of directors of the World Bank alone has 24 directors representing 184 donor and recipient governments. The board's role is not trivial; it meets twice a week to vote on all loans, guarantees, and country assistance strategies, as well as administrative budgets and new policies. The European Union's administrative body, the European Commission or EC, answers to 26 different national governments through its Council, "which is composed of serving politicians whose main focus is on their domestic interests" (Seabright 2002, p. 37). Bilateral aid agencies respond to their governments' different ministries and legislatures, as well as numerous interest groups. Ostrom et al. posit an aid octangle in which (1) an aid agency interacts with (2) other donors including private foundations and NGOs, (3) parliament, ministries, and different line agencies in the donor country, (4) the recipient government, (5) ministries and government agencies in the recipient government, (6) implementing organizations such as consulting firms and NGOs, (7) organized interest groups and civil society organizations in both the donor and recipient countries, and (8) the target beneficiaries (Ostrom et al. 2002, p. 61). These multiple principals have more than the usual collective action problems and more than the usual information asymmetries vis-à-vis the agency's staff.

Agency problems are common to all public bureaucracies and may not necessarily be worse in aid agencies. What complicates aid is the moral hazard problem between the aid-giver and the aid recipient. As Ostrom et al. note (2002, p. xviii), "The availability of aid creates a moral hazard, since the aid helps to ensure [sic] incompetent governments from the results of their actions, thus weakening their incentive to find alternative revenue sources or better policies". The recipient government may balk at policies that alleviate poverty or increase its revenues if they would reduce aid funds. This situation was described by Buchanan (1977) as the "Samaritan's Dilemma". The payoff is highest to the Samaritan if the Samaritan provides aid and the beneficiaries respond by exerting high effort. But the payoff is highest to the beneficiaries if they receive aid without increasing effort. In countries with stronger political institutions such a game is harder to play. Media report on politicians' actions; political competitors hold their opponents accountable; interest groups provide oversight; and citizens vote out incompetent governments. The weaker the institutions, the greater is the risk of the Samaritan's Dilemma.

If institutions in underdeveloped countries could be strengthened, it would be at least plausible that foreign aid could promote development. Yet foreign aid does not promote, and may even undermine, the very rules and norms necessary for effective aid. There is a fundamental mismatch between the characteristics of institutions and the characteristics of aid, a mismatch that will not be corrected merely by solving agency problems. The literature I summarized in Chapter 3 suggests three characteristics of institutions that are particularly relevant to foreign aid. To recap:

1. A society's fundamental beliefs, norms, and rules tend to be durable, often lasting for centuries. Changes occur on the margin in less fundamental laws or organizations, but these are seldom sustained if the broader institutional framework remains unchanged.
2. Institutional frameworks endure because they are congruent with underlying power structures. Powerful groups who benefit from the institutional status quo will actively oppose changes that threaten their power and wealth. Even without active opposition, humans' habits and beliefs tend to resist revolutionary change. Without drastic changes in power structures and shared beliefs, institutional reforms in most poor countries will lead to large disparities between laws on the books and laws in practice, and between how laws are applied to the powerful and to the powerless.
3. Sometimes changes in beliefs, power structures, and institutional frameworks do occur and move countries incrementally toward more open access to economic and political power. Sustainable progress results from heterodox experiments that evolve gradually in response to competition and through adaptation to local conditions.

Table 4.3   Comparison of the characteristics of institutional frameworks and foreign aid

Institutional frameworks	Foreign aid
Deeply rooted and usually durable	• Focus on policy, organization, sector rules • Three-year projects • Staff rotates every 3–5 years • Rewards for approval, not sustainability • No long-run accountability
Supported by power elite and beliefs	• Requires support or permission of incumbent government • Staff incentives to cooperate to win more project approvals • Revolutionaries would be asked to leave

Changes are often idiosyncratic and experimental	• Focus on Western best practices
	• Prefer that changes are
	  ○ Rapid
	  ○ Measurable against benchmarks

By contrasting these characteristics of institutions with the characteristics of aid and aid organizations we can see why foreign aid has been a poor tool for reforming institutions. In the next few pages I consider these contrasts in detail; Table 4.3 summarizes this discussion.

1. Institutional frameworks tend to be durable, but sustainable reform depends on changing them

The information, knowledge, and incentives of aid agencies are not focused on changing underlying institutional frameworks. Aid is aimed at changing policies, sector regulations, or organizations, not constitutions, norms of behavior, or shared beliefs. This short-term focus is inherent in the nature of aid (see point 2 below), and has persisted even as donor rhetoric has changed.[7]

Even if aid were redirected toward changing deeply-rooted institutional frameworks, its tools and incentives are poorly suited for such long-term efforts. Aid projects tend to be relatively brief, less than three years, and project staff is rotated frequently, typically every five years.[8] Because of rotation, those supervising the execution of the project are seldom those who designed it. (Staff members sometimes support rotation for the wrong reasons. As one World Bank colleague put it to me, you should "move before your mistakes catch up with you.") Rotation gives staff little time to understand the local norms and networks that determine power structures in a recipient country, which may be hard for an outsider to know in any case.

Even without rotation, staff members have little incentive to challenge fundamental beliefs, rules, and norms. Despite much rhetoric to the contrary, aid staff are rewarded for project approval, not for long-term project sustainability. Studies document the aid focus on "moving the money."[9] In any case it would be difficult or impossible for aid agencies to reward or penalize their staff because client countries hit or missed their long-run development goals. Development is multifaceted and hard to measure and governments are ultimately sovereign, making it impossible to assign responsibility for economic outcomes to the actions or advice of individual aid staff. Those aspects that are most easily monitored, namely project approval and disbursement of funds, are the ones most likely to influence careers (Martens et al. 2002, p. 20).

2. Institutional frameworks endure because they are supported by powerful elite groups who benefit from the status quo

Aid-givers are not in the business of fomenting revolution and would soon be required to leave if they were. Donors work with the acceptance of governments in the recipient country and any project they finance requires a supportive or at least a permissive government. Even when the aid agency works with a non-governmental agency or a private enterprise, the government in the recipient country must at least tacitly permit the project to go forward. Rulers who allow aid projects that foment revolutionary changes do not last very long. Local political, business, religious, social, and other leaders would oppose aid payments designed to alter institutional frameworks in ways that might undermine their rents, authority, and power. This is the case regardless of whether the leadership is what the UN Millennium Project (2005b) report calls "larcenous" or what the report deems "well intentioned". Government and leaders of powerful interest groups could conceivably be won over through persuasion, reassured through additions to their power in other spheres, bought off with side payments, or neutralized through publicity campaigns. But until recently most aid agencies have resisted playing such a direct role in financing change and co-opting its opponents. This was seen as outside their mandate or as dangerous meddling in internal politics.[10] Some bilateral aid agencies and international NGOs fund organizations opposing the incumbent government or lobbying for radical policy changes, although the amounts and specifics are hard to document and little is known about the outcomes. Such support could have unintended consequences. It could make it more politically acceptable for the incumbent government to suppress opposition groups and it could provoke a backlash against foreign "meddling" in domestic politics.

Sometimes the most effective option is to refuse further support, especially since foreign aid can reinforce the existing power structures, causing unintended consequences that aid officials cannot anticipate. Donors lose leverage once a project is over, so it makes sense to hold new projects hostage to government's performance on its earlier commitments. Staff members in aid agencies, however, have strong incentives to cooperate with incumbent governments.[11] Bad relations with the ruling government disrupt the project pipeline, and an inactive aid recipient can adversely affect an aid staff member's budget, prestige, power, and prospects for promotion. Staff members rewarded on the basis of project approvals have little incentive to delay new projects in order to improve the outcomes of ongoing projects – projects that were probably designed by their predecessor.[12] Even aid staff members who are not especially focused on their careers will try to work with incumbent governments rather than recommend suspending assistance. Aid agencies hire highly motivated, skilled, and altruistic individuals with a bias towards optimism and activism, the sorts of individuals who would be reluctant to classify any government or problem as intractable.

3.   Effective institutional changes arise locally and incrementally from heterodox experiments

Aid agencies are bureaucracies accountable to donor governments, and that has consequences for the design of aid projects. Aid bureaucracies prefer to support changes that can be instituted rapidly and generate measurable benchmarks for dispersing funds and assessing outcomes. This emphasis on swift and measurable results creates a bias among aid staff towards pro forma rather than de facto change. De facto change is often slow and sustainability can only be measured after the project is ended. I illustrate this problem in the case of SOE performance contracts below.

Aid agencies also prefer to support Western best practice, which can be more easily defended to their sponsoring governments than homegrown reforms. Yet heterodox reforms are often characteristic of meaningful institutional change. China's experience illustrates this challenge to aid. China's federal system allowed provinces and local governments to compete by experimenting with different economic rules as long as the dominance of the Communist Party went unchallenged (Weingast 1995). China's institutional experiments had to be adapted to Communist ideology, totalitarian rule, tenuous property rights, and weak rule of law. The TVE or township and village enterprises were an example of a successful experiment. Townships and villages permitted private investors to run government-owned enterprises in exchange for regular payments to the local government that "owned" the firm. TVEs allowed capitalistic incentives to flourish within an officially socialist system, contributing to China's surge in growth (Keefer and Shirley 2000). But aid-givers neither sanctioned nor supported TVEs, despite their resounding success. This is not surprising since aid agencies have no mandate to promote heterodox experiments such as TVEs. TVEs secured investor's property rights through informal ties to the locality and payoffs that could be considered a form of corruption. It would have been hard to defend TVEs to the representatives of Western governments who sit on the boards of aid agencies. Nor did the TVEs need outside assistance; quite the contrary, aid would have undermined their profit motive, distorted their market, and muddied their accountability to investors.

Given this disconnect between the characteristics of foreign aid and the nature of institutional change, it is unsurprising that economists find no robust, positive association between aid and institutions. The disconnect is recognized by some in the aid community, but it is usually viewed as surmountable. Some argue, with Sachs (2005), that more aid would promote institutional improvements by increasing income. Others argue that aid's disabilities can be cured to make it an effective tool for institutional change. Both these arguments ignore the history of foreign aid and the deeply-rooted nature of institutions. They also ignore the contradictions inherent in foreign aid, such as the need to win the approval of governments that are themselves major obstacles to development or the incentives to move the money while simultaneously threatening to withhold support for noncompliance.

AID IN INHOSPITABLE INSTITUTIONAL ENVIRONMENTS LEADS TO PRO FORMA REFORMS

Since aid-givers want to assist even in inhospitable institutional environments, they sometimes accept pro forma reforms. Pro forma reforms include laws without meaningful enforcement; government bureaus without adequate staffing, budgets, or mandates; or state enterprises without competition or competent corporate governance. Because of the pressure to lend, past failures may not affect donors' future willingness to give. For example, "during a 15-year period, the Government of Kenya sold the same agricultural reform to the World Bank *four times*, each time reversing it after receipt of the aid" (Collier 1997; original italics). Ironically, aid directed at institutional reforms may make these problems worse, because institutional projects lack tangible outputs, making impact "more diffuse and hard to verify" (Martens et al. 2002, p. 17).

I can illustrate how pro forma reforms work in practice with the "performance contract": contracts signed between a government and the managers of its state enterprises. Performance contracts were championed as a way to improve SOE performance by giving managers incentives to achieve specified targets; they enjoyed a vogue among aid agencies in the 1980s (Shirley and Xu 1998). One survey found performance contracts in 33 countries in the mid-1990s (Shirley and Xu 1998, Table One). Yet in five of the six cases studied, governments signed performance contracts but failed to negotiate tough targets, demand the information needed to judge performance, pay promised bonuses for good performance, impose promised punishments for bad performance, or provide promised autonomy to lay off workers or close plants (Shirley and Xu 1998). Targets were weak and distorted. For example, targets in Senegal were set below prior years' performance and in India negotiations over targets dragged on so long that some targets were set equal to actual performance (ibid.). Philippines Electricity achieved its expenditure targets by cutting investments that were badly needed to upgrade its infrastructure; India Oil achieved its target number of wells drilled by drilling more unproductive wells (ibid.).

All the sample firms achieved their targets, but showed no statistically significant improvement over pre-contract trends in total factor productivity, labor productivity, or return on assets (Shirley and Xu 1998; World Bank 1995). Shirley and Xu (2001) found similar outcomes in over 500 performance contracts in China: after controlling for selection bias and unrelated reforms, there was no statistically significant positive correlation between contracts and improvements in total factor productivity. In simulations, a hypothetical, ideal performance contract did improve performance in China, but these contracts were not the norm. On the contrary, on average China's performance contracts had a negative effect. The dismal performance of large Chinese state-owned enterprises since this study was done offers little comfort to those who argue that performance contracts can improve SOEs' performance in adverse institutional circumstances.

Why were performance contracts so widely supported by aid-givers? One reason is that recipient governments liked performance contracts because they could sign contracts and achieve their targets without politically costly actions. State enterprise managers could be forced to sign the contracts, and contract targets could be achieved without layoffs, plant closures, firing of incompetent managers, or other politically risky changes. Aid officials also liked performance contracts. Funds could be disbursed against a tangible action – signing the contract – and results gauged by a tangible outcome – achieving the targets. Performance contracts allowed projects to go ahead where privatization was politically unacceptable and where poor SOE performance made it difficult to justify further assistance without some "evidence" of effort. Aid staffers had few incentives to scrutinize the ex post effects of contracts, since staff were rewarded for project approval and disbursement, not subsequent performance. High rates of staff rotation and constraints on staff time also made scrutiny of such apparently successful projects unlikely.

After we published our finding that performance contracts did not improve performance (Shirley and Xu 1998, 2001), we were strongly criticized by some colleagues for robbing them of an important lending instrument. This "robbery" was not long lived, however, since performance contracts are still advocated by some staff (see, for example, Kingdom et al. 2006). Recent reports are optimistic that contracts will be more effective because of "recent comprehensive reforms" in recipient countries (World Bank 2006b, p. 16) and make vague references to "promising" results (Baietti et al. 2006, p. 32). These reports assert that contracts will at least improve information on state enterprises, despite our finding that timeliness and accuracy of information did not improve, while distortions increased. This optimism suggests that the perverse incentives that produce pro forma reforms are still at work.[13]

A BIAS TOWARDS OPTIMISM

World Bank reports on performance contracts illustrate a more general bias towards optimism common to aid documents. Many aid reports are written in a style my World Bank colleagues and I jokingly called the "future presumptive," upbeat and forward-looking. Easterly (2006, p. 139) gives some examples of this style in quotes about Africa from World Bank reports:

> From 1983: "many African governments are more clearly aware of the need to . . . improve the efficiency . . . of their economies."
> From 1986: "Progress is clearly under way. Especially in the past two years, more countries have started to act, and the changes they are making go deeper than before."
> From 1994: "African countries have made great strides in improving policies and restoring growth."
> From 2000: "Since the mid-1990s, there have been signs that better economic management has started to pay off."
> From 2002: "Africa's leaders . . . have recognized the need to improve their policies . . ."
> From 2004: there has been "remarkable progress in several African countries over the past year."

Aid staff have strong incentives to be optimistic, incentives that also make them reluctant to confront chronic problems, such as corruption. For example, a 2007 report on corruption in World Bank lending commented:

> There is a tendency . . . to shrink from confrontation with borrowing countries who are members of the World Bank Group and sovereign countries in their own

right. That tendency is reinforced by a culture of the Bank that favors seeking out lending opportunities rather than simply responding to borrowing countries' initiatives and felt needs . . . There is a natural discomfort among some line staff, who are generally encouraged by the pay and performance evaluation system to make loans for promising projects, to have those projects investigated *ex post*, possibly exposed as rife with corruption, creating an awkward problem in relations with borrowing clients. (Volcker et al. 2007, p. 8)

Another illustration of uncritical optimism is the ready supply of "successful" projects promoted as models well before outcomes can be measured. A prime example is Pakistan's Hub River Power project that during the 1990s was hailed by some as an innovative model for private participation in large-scale infrastructure.[14] By the late 1990s there were widespread accusations that the project was rife with corruption and unfair dealing, and had produced overcapacity in energy generation combined with insufficient transmission and distribution capacity to keep pace with the planned expansion (Fraser 2005). In 1998 the government cancelled contracts amounting to two-thirds of the contracted private power capacity. In a subsequent report, the World Bank Group did an about face and congratulated itself for "facilitating an orderly resolution of the IPP [independent power producers] disputes and helping to avert a wider Government default on IPP contracts which could have had macroeconomic implications for Pakistan" (ibid., p. 1).

The Chad–Cameroon Pipeline also exemplifies the rush to optimistic judgment. This project financed a pipeline to transport oil from Chad, which is landlocked, to the coast of Cameroon for export. Since Chad had a long history of civil war, instability, widespread corruption, and abysmally weak institutions, the project included innovative revenue arrangements meant to ensure that the oil windfall would reduce rather than exacerbate poverty and instability in Chad. Part of the oil revenue was earmarked for investment in five priority sectors: education, health and social services, rural development, infrastructure, and environmental and water resources, and an independent oversight monitoring and control committee was appointed to oversee the management of the funds. The project was touted as a prototype in the World Bank and was nominated for the President's Award for Excellence in 2000. In 2002 the Central Africa representative of the International Finance Corporation asserted, "This is going to be the model for every single project of this type worldwide" (Mohammadou Diop in an interview on 25 September 2005 cited in Gary and Reisch 2005, p. 4). By 2005, however, the Catholic Relief Services described the pipeline as "a 'model project' hanging by a thread" (ibid., p. 88). As they put it, ". . . the elaborately constructed technocratic 'quick fix' for Chad's governance problems could go up in smoke" (ibid.). And,

"Everything in the Chad 'model' rests on the enforcement of the law and sanctions for violators in a country with a history of neither. This is a tenuous basis for hope" (ibid., p. 89). In January 2006 the World Bank suspended disbursements on all its projects in Chad to protest the government's amendments to the revenue law. The government and the World Bank reached a new agreement in July 2006, but it would still be wildly inappropriate to label the Chad pipeline project a "success" or a "model." I was one of only two members of the World Bank committee allocating the President's Awards for Excellence who initially protested giving an excellence award to the Chad–Cameroon Pipeline, but our skepticism won over the rest of the committee.

We might expect that a bias towards optimism would eventually be countered by poor outcomes. But most aid agencies do little serious evaluation of their projects, and any such evaluation comes late in the process. For example, staff in SIDA complained that evaluations were often written to justify decisions already made and "to represent the vested concerns of various interested parties . . ." (Ostrom et al. 2002, p. 152). Although the World Bank does much more serious evaluation than most aid agencies, it typically measures success without reference to costs versus benefits or to what would have happened without the aid project, that is, the counterfactual. A recent report on 14 evaluations by the World Bank Impact Evaluation Group found simple counterfactuals in 12 of the cases, but only 5 did any sort of cost/benefit analysis (World Bank 2006d). Cost/benefit and counterfactual analyses have shortcomings: they are heavily dependent on assumptions and available data. But without them it is impossible to judge whether the intervention was worthwhile and worth the money. Aid agencies seldom collect even the data necessary to do a proper factual, much less a proper counterfactual or cost/benefit analysis.

Proper evaluation can change the conclusions about project outcomes. We can see this in the World Bank education projects in Ghana that financed the construction of schools closer to students and other improvements in infrastructure. Evaluators found that enrollment increased by 4 percent from 1988 to 2003, but that the project was responsible for only one-third of this increase (World Bank 2004a). Exogenous causes – improvements in household income and parents' education – were responsible for most of the gain in enrollments. Test scores also improved, which could be partly attributed to the project's support for textbooks, but better teaching was also responsible. Again, causes exogenous to the project were responsible for better teaching, including an increase in teachers' salaries prior to the 1992 election.

Besides ex post evaluation we could measure performance through experiments. Not providing assistance to everyone intentionally sets up a counterfactual. Experiments get a lot of lip service but are rare in foreign aid. Some projects, such as the Chad–Cameroon pipeline, are one-of-a-kind projects that do not lend themselves to experiments. But even in instances where experiments are feasible, they are seldom tried. My colleagues in the World Bank's research department designed experiments on occasion, but operational staff generally objected to the delay, cost, and uncertainty. Experiments take time and the atmosphere in the aid bureaucracy gives staff a constant sense of urgency. Development problems are large and the stakes are huge; the "window of opportunity" when the "local champions" will support reforms seems narrow; at the same time the project approval process is slow, cumbersome, and opaque, requiring consensus from many parts of the aid bureaucracy, including other donors, as well as recipient agencies, interest groups, and NGOs. In my experience, aid agency staff members worked very hard, under constant pressure to persuade doubters in the aid community and cajole reluctant reformers in the recipient country. There was no room for a pilot project or experimental phase in this hothouse atmosphere.

Experiments also have a major drawback from the perspective of aid staff: they require the aid-giver and the recipient government to admit ignorance about the outcome of the project. Recipient governments object to this as politically suicidal; some also view experiments as morally reprehensible since they deny the project's benefits to the control group. As for aid staffers, as we have seen they rush to portray even highly risky projects as models of success. The staff members who are devoting their lives to these projects have become their champions; they are seldom willing to admit that the outcome of their projects is unknown. I recall a blistering battle with the project officer for the aforementioned Pakistan Hub River project over my refusal to portray the project as a model in a report to the board on private sector development. Experiments run against this bias towards optimism. Since aid projects are designed under the fiction that the outcomes are known to be beneficial, neither staff nor governments wanted to lift the veil and reveal that many aid interventions are in fact unscientific experiments.

CAN AID AVOID THE ILL EFFECTS OF DAMAGING INSTITUTIONS?

I do not mean to give the impression that aid-givers ignore damaging institutions; they have tried to protect their projects from damaging institutional environments in three ways: (1) creating project implementation units insulated from the problems of the recipient country's government; (2) bypassing recipient governments to work directly with NGOs; and

(3) working directly with groups of beneficiaries. Each of these approaches has drawbacks, however, and none of them addresses the root institutional causes of underdevelopment.

1. Project Implementation Units

Dedicated project implementation units or PIUs are supposed to avoid the poor incentives, corruption, and incompetence of the recipient's bureaucracy. Although nominally part of the recipient government, PIUs are the creature of the donor agency. They operate as islands within the host government, staffed by the country's most highly skilled civil servants or consultants whose salaries are topped up by aid funds to many multiples of official salaries. For example, a World Bank agricultural project in Kenya paid eight local staff between $3000 and $6000 a month compared to the $250 monthly salary of a senior economist in the civil service (World Bank 2005f, p. 206). Project implementation units illustrate how donor expediency can hamper institutional improvement. Because aid-givers cannot effectively change the institutions found in the field, they create their own virtual office, an insulated island of competence in the host government. The high salaries of PIU employees creates resentment, while the low pay and status of the regular civil service leave the PIU staff with no competent counterparts in the rest of the government.

There is no evidence that PIUs improve project success and considerable evidence that they harm sustainability and public management. Yet a 2000 survey of 17 bilateral and 9 multilateral donors in Bolivia, Ghana, Romania, Uganda, and Vietnam found that PIUs are pervasive (World Bank 2003a). From 55 to 87 percent of donors in the five sample countries used PIUs and on average half planned to continue using them. This despite the finding by a multi-donor assessment that PIUs "have undermined mainline public sector capacity and demoralized low-paid civil servants" (World Bank 2003a). Field visits to six African countries (Benin, Ethiopia, Ghana, Malawi, Mali, and Mozambique) found that "stakeholders in all six case study countries heavily criticized the [World] Bank's use of PIUs . . . They consider that PIUs have promoted rapid and efficient project implementation at the expense of long term capacity building" (World Bank 2005b, p. 31). Studies of the World Bank's experience in hundreds of projects in South America and Eastern Europe and Central Asia showed that project implementation units ". . . have no significant positive impact on project outcomes, while the likely sustainability of results clearly suffered" (World Bank 2004b, pp. 205–6).

It's not surprising that when the projects ended and the PIUs disappeared sustainability "suffered." The rest of the government has neither the incentives nor the capacity to monitor and maintain the project. The failings of PIUs have been known for years, yet they persist because donors are often unable to function without them. Indeed, one reason why structural adjustment projects and budget or program support were enthusiastically embraced by donors was because these types of projects can be implemented without creating a virtual office.

The alternative to PIUs is to enhance the effectiveness of government bureaucracies and that has proved to be beyond the capacity of foreign aid. Civil service reforms in underdeveloped countries face supply-side and demand-side problems. Supply of talented bureaucrats is low because civil service pay is low, below subsistence in many of the poorest countries. You might wonder why anyone would agree to employment at less than a living wage. Probably because the job offers opportunities for bribes or special privileges, or because it is so undemanding that the wage is virtually a gift. It is not unusual in my experience to visit ministries in some of the poorest countries and find one unoccupied desk after another and the few staff members present talking on the phone about their other, outside jobs. In Cambodia, to take an extreme example, government public health staff received $10 to $12 a month, compared with a minimum of $100 needed to achieve a basic standard of living (Disease Control Priorities Project 2006). Absenteeism was high, staff sometimes worked only one to two hours a day, and drug theft and dual practice were common (ibid.). Even where the civil service pays a living wage, it can take months or years to hire new staff because of cumbersome administrative procedures, norms of patronage and control, and bureaucratic turf battles and inertia. Under such circumstances it is not surprising that projects aimed at improving the civil service have a generally poor track record.

Aid has sometimes undermined the capacity of the public service. Donors finance training that has improved skills, but has also kept public servants away from their desks and helped better government workers qualify for jobs outside the public sector, often with NGOs or aid agencies themselves (World Bank 2004b, pp. 206 and 207). Donor top-ups of the salaries of civil servants have contributed to corruption and patronage without producing meaningful reforms in the management and functioning of the bureaucracy.

Pay increases and training also failed because they did not address the second problem, demand for reform. As Barbara Geddes (1994) points out, civil service reform is a collective action problem. Even though most citizens would benefit from a more competent state bureaucracy, many well-organized groups, including bureaucrats who are currently employed, oppose reform. The dominant party in the legislature has little incentive to give up the spoils of office. Presidents use patronage jobs in the civil service to keep their party or coalition together, to prevail in future elections, to stay in office when coups threaten, or to be influential when out of office. In democracies, civil service reforms occur only in those rare instances when electoral and political party rules motivate politicians differently, insulating them from threats of the loss of power, prestige, and wealth if they reform the bureaucracy. In authoritarian regimes, civil service reform may seem easier because decision-makers are "insulated from many of the political clientele networks that pervade society, as well as from most organized interest groups" (ibid., p. 191). But dictators are also insulated from democratic norms of public disclosure and accountability and there are fewer checks on them if they choose instead to plunder the treasury, divert aid funds, and employ incompetent relatives and cronies (ibid., pp. 192–3). Reforms under dictatorships also lack legitimacy and often collapse when previously excluded party politicians once again compete for power with promises of patronage.

Geddes (1994) describes how reform-minded presidents in Latin America tried to create a few competent bureaucratic agencies in key policy areas and insulate them from political pressures, agencies that seem very similar to aid-sponsored PIUs. Just as most PIUs leave no traces of competency in the civil service after the aid project ends, the autonomy of home grown "islands of excellence" seldom survives when the president supporting them leaves office or withdraws support. For example, President Kubitschek of Brazil (1956–61) created "grupos executives" through executive decrees (see Geddes 1994, pp. 64–5). The "grupos" had financial autonomy and operational flexibility and were empowered to implement the administration's economic goals in specific sectors, insulated from politics and the bureaucracy. "They were separate from the federal bureaucracy. In fact they were officially charged with circumventing the bureaucracy" (ibid., p. 64). The "grupos executives" were very effective at getting things done, but they depended on the personal support of Kubitschek and could not survive his departure. The insulation and professionalization of agencies such as the "grupos executives" or PIUs is not contagious. Such agencies are indeed islands in a sea of bureaucratic incompetence and paralysis, and their status and survival depends on the intervention of a president or aid donor.

PIUs may assume other guises, but they are unlikely to disappear. Donors will not tolerate the delays, corruption, and incompetence that are endemic in countries with poor public management. And public management is unlikely to improve because of aid, since the institutional reforms required for effective civil service reform are not motivated by foreign aid.

2. Non-governmental Organizations

Aid to non-governmental organizations or NGOs constitutes another attempt to reduce the problems caused by corrupt, incompetent, uninterested, or repressive governments (Martens et al. 2002). NGOs are non-profit organizations that come in many guises. The ones of interest to the aid community focus on improving general social welfare and reducing poverty, protecting the environment, promoting democracy, safeguarding human rights, expanding access to education or health services, eradicating specific diseases such as malaria or AIDS, supporting women, providing humanitarian aid after disasters or wars, and the like. Some are religious. Some are affiliated with corporations, trade unions, political parties, or other social organizations in the donor or the host country. Because many NGOs are staffed by volunteers and visionaries dedicated to their mission, their proponents argue that NGOs will be less bureaucratic and less subject to the moral hazard problems of official aid-givers. Visionaries are presumably less interested in money than private consultants are, hence they are also expected to require less monitoring by the donor agency and to be less ready to collude with recipients than profit-oriented consultants. Martens, for instance, argues that "NGOs may push harder to achieve their goals, even at the cost of forgoing some or all of the profits on a contract" (Martens 2002, p. 183). "Furthermore, to the extent that NGOs are able to find and collaborate with like-minded recipient groups in beneficiary countries, preferences of donors and recipients will be aligned and conflicts of interest can be avoided" (ibid., p. 185).

The number of NGOs operating internationally now exceeds 60,000. Aid channeled through these NGOs has also grown rapidly in recent years, doubling between 2001 and 2005. Grants by international NGOs were about $15 billion in 2005 (OECD, DAC 2007, Table 2). These larger international NGOs often work through local NGOs, and these too are growing fast. Data on local NGOs is poor, but one source reported that in 2003 there were 22,000 registered NGOs in Bangladesh alone (OECD 2003, p. 75) although another study found only 7643 (Gauri and Furuttero 2003, p. 5).

International NGOs have been famously effective in delivering humanitarian assistance and are often the only provider in remote and war-torn locations. They also work effectively at lower costs and smaller scales than official aid agencies and can be more flexible and more sensitive to the needs of beneficiaries. In Zambia, for example, health-care NGOs count many more poor people among their clientele than government or private providers (World Bank 2004b, p. 103). Local NGOs often have a better understanding of local conditions than aid staff or outside consultants, and can be effective at winning popular and government support for aid projects. In some places NGOs are the main or even only source of outside aid for such vulnerable groups as women, children, and minorities. In Brazil, for example, NGOs combating AIDS reached prostitutes and other high-risk groups that usually avoid public programs and distributed 2.6 million contraceptives (World Bank 2004b, p. 104).

Reliance on NGOs has drawbacks, however. Unelected NGOs controlling large caches of aid can become powerful alternative power structures, undermining societies' efforts to build representative and responsible political institutions. Many NGOs are single-issue groups focused only on, for instance, the environment, women and minorities, or individual diseases such as AIDS or malaria. In developed countries with strong institutional rules and norms, there are checks and balances that keep any single interest group from dominating resource allocation over the long term. But in weak institutional frameworks, the influence that NGOs gain over donor policy and the funds they command can distort country priorities and derail projects that fail to meet their single-minded criteria.[15]

Pressures from NGOs for aid agencies to address their issues have led to mission-creep, or more accurately, mission-leap. For example, the World Bank's Country Policy and Institutional Assessment (CPIA) has 52 criteria that it uses to determine the allocation of the World Bank's concessional funds. Many of these were included in response to pressures from NGOs (see Table 5.2 below; the CPIA is discussed in Chapter 5). Another drawback is that donors and international NGOs have little information about local NGOs in places where transparency, accountability, and oversight are weak. As the World Bank points out, "Donor enthusiasm has led to a massive proliferation of NGOs, many of them not at all motivated by altruism. Indeed, many appear to be run by former civil servants who have lost their jobs as a result of the downsizing of public sectors but who know how to approach donors and government contracting agencies" (World Bank 2004b, p. 104).

It is questionable whether NGOs are better conduits for assistance because they are altruistic and mission-focused. Although they may not be profit-oriented, NGOs need resources and cannot afford to be unresponsive to donors. A study of Bangladesh, for example, found that the location of new NGO programs is not significantly correlated with measures of poverty, landlessness, or illiteracy (Gauri and Furuttero 2003). Instead NGOs preferentially locate new programs where they have no established programs. This is not out of a concern for duplication: the study finds that NGOs put programs in new locations that do not duplicate their established programs; it also finds no evidence that NGOs are concerned with duplicating the efforts of other NGOs. Rather, the authors assert, NGOs try to locate their programs as widely around the country as possible in response to donor preferences to channel funds to NGOs with broader geographical coverage.

3.   Participation of Beneficiaries and Community Groups

Participation, like NGOs, has been touted as a means of improving aid-targeting, delivering benefits more cost effectively, and reducing corruption and rent-seeking; it is also purported to "empower" local communities. Proponents argue that greater participation of beneficiaries in the design and implementation of projects allows donors to bypass the central governments' poorly performing delivery mechanisms, introduce more intergovernmental competition, and create checks against government abuse of power. By involving the intended beneficiaries in the design, construction, and maintenance of aid projects, aid agencies can also tap into local knowledge of needs and conditions, and generate contributions towards the project's cost, such as labor. Prichett and Woolcock (2004) suggest that participation and community involvement is especially useful in providing needed flexibility and local commitment to delivery of "transaction intensive services," such as allocation of irrigation water or classroom teaching, which necessarily give considerable discretion to the provider. But they also point out that there is considerable disagreement about whether solutions such as participation will work under all or even most conditions and for all or even most projects (ibid.).

The World Bank is consulting much more with "civil society," a term that seems to encompass any local non-governmental group. Civil society could be an "administratively defined locale such as a village . . . or a common interest group, such as a community of weavers or potters" (Mansuri and Rao 2003, p. 10). Some of these civil society organizations are pre-existing groups, but many are formed as part of the project. The World Bank reported that in 2006 it consulted with civil society in preparing 72 percent of 217 projects compared to 32 percent of 50 projects in 1990 (World Bank 2006e, p. 23). There has been even faster growth in projects involving local community groups in implementation or giving them control over resources and decisions, from just 2 percent of all World Bank projects in 1989 to 25 percent in 2003 (World Bank 2005d, p. ix).

As with NGOs, participation of local groups can have undesirable consequences. Local beneficiary groups and leaders who are empowered do not always represent all beneficiaries. As Platteau suggests, "It is in fact plausible to argue that, at least in situations of high inequality, the poor and the minorities are more easily oppressed by local power groups that can easily collude beyond the control of higher-level institutions and the attention of the media" (Platteau 2003, p. 6). Bardhan (2002, p. 202) points out that "structures of local accountability are not in place in many underdeveloped countries, and local governments are often at the mercy of local power elites who may frustrate the goal of achieving public delivery to the general populace". Selecting or creating groups that are not part of the local power hierarchy is not a good alternative. Such groups often have little local support and tend to disappear when donors leave (World Bank 2005d, p. 40). Another risk is that participants are pressured to donate costly amounts of labor. Governments sometimes exploit this unpaid labor to shift the cost of service delivery to poorer communities (Mansuri and Rao 2003). Finally, technology is sometimes scaled back to make community implementation possible, driving costs up and reliability down.

Evidence about the effects of participation is limited and ambiguous. Under the right circumstances, participation has improved the success of individual aid projects and the lives of their direct beneficiaries (see cites in Mansuri and Rao 2003; Prichett and Woolcock 2004). But empirical evaluations of decentralized service delivery are few and largely descriptive, with insufficient data to compare centralized and decentralized programs (Bardhan 2002). Case studies of projects involving local communities in their design and implementation have contradictory findings and lack adequate counterfactuals (Mansuri and Rao 2003, pp. 40–43). Mansuri and Rao found some evidence that participatory projects were better targeted to poor communities than more centralized projects, but no evidence that participatory projects were better targeted to the poor within the community and some evidence that local inequality worsened.

The World Bank's evaluation of its participatory projects is even more sobering. These projects have not performed better; there was no statistically significant difference in the percentage of projects with and without community involvement that were rated satisfactory (World Bank 2005d, p. 78). Projects with and without community involvement had similarly low ratings of institutional impact (ibid., p. 79). Participatory projects were different in one way, however; they received a statistically significant lower rating on sustainability (ibid., p. 78).

Participation also turned out to be an ineffective tool for avoiding unfavorable institutions. Quite the contrary, the success of participatory projects depends on a favorable institutional environment. Mansuri and Rao find that sustainability of participatory projects "depends critically on an enabling institutional environment," that is, on line ministries that are responsive to the needs of communities and national governments and that are committed to "transparent, accountable, and democratic governance" (2003, p. 42). They also find that success is more likely when the leaders of the local communities are "downwardly accountable" to the beneficiaries and that success is crucially conditioned by the "local cultural and social

systems" (p. 43). Bardhan points out that "the logic behind decentralization is not just about weakening the central authority, nor is it about pre-
ferring local elites to central authority, but it is fundamentally about
making governance at the local level more responsive to the felt needs of
the large majority of the population" (2002, p. 202). Far from bypassing a
dysfunctional central government, decentralization in Bardhan's view
demands an activist state that mobilizes people to participate in local development, neutralizes the power of local oligarchs, provides support to
pump-prime local finances, and provides services to build local capacity
(ibid., pp. 202–3).

Ultimately neither NGOs nor beneficiary participation avoid or solve the
problems caused by damaging institutions. There are some noteworthy
exceptions, but generalizing from these exceptions is risky. As Prichett and
Woolcock (2004) point out, successes grow out of local conditions that may
not exist in other institutional or political circumstances. Because understanding of local institutions is limited, most sober assessments call for
learning-by-doing and an experimental approach with more careful studies
of outcomes. Such sobriety has not constrained the sudden explosion of
NGOs and community-driven projects, however. And as I argued earlier,
experiments in aid projects are the exception, not the rule.

NEW INSTITUTIONAL ECONOMICS IS NOT GOOD NEWS FOR FOREIGN AID

Most aid-givers embraced the idea that institutions matter, but did not consider the implications for their business. A fundamental premise of foreign
aid is that people and societies will choose best practice policies and
improved institutions if they can be shown that they will be better off and
if there are funds to help defray the costs of change. The UN Millennium
Project is an example of this reasoning. Unfortunately human history does
not support this premise. North (2004) shows how damaging institutions
have endured throughout history because change was opposed by powerful people who believed they benefited from the status quo, and resisted by
less powerful people unwilling to risk chaos or to change their beliefs. But
without fundamental changes in institutional frameworks, foreign aid ends
up financing fleeting or pro forma reforms.

The point of this chapter is not that foreign aid is useless. Foreign aid has
provided important, often life-saving benefits to many poor people. Aid
agencies provide vital humanitarian assistance and are an invaluable source
of knowledge. But in the final analysis, foreign aid has not improved –
indeed I have argued that it cannot improve – the fundamental institutions

necessary for a market economy. As a result aid has not promoted development in countries with damaging institutional frameworks. Sometimes aid has even harmed institutional progress by providing funds and credibility that prolonged the life of corrupt and incompetent governments and reduced the pressures for reforms.

Opportunities for changing fundamental institutions do arise in underdeveloped economies, but not because of aid. And aid-givers exceed their mandate and their welcome if they try to engineer opportunities for change in deeply-rooted rules and norms. Nor can they control the direction of change and assure that the outcome is for the better. Beneficial change is often heterodox, contrary to donors' best practice and received wisdom. Aid could perhaps be effective if it was directed only to countries that are already creating the institutional prerequisites and political circumstances to use aid effectively. But targeting demands wholly different incentives and organizational structures from the present aid model. A new aid paradigm is theoretically possible but faces formidable practical challenges. The first and foremost challenge seems deceptively simple: to identify and measure institutional change. Yet, as I show in the next chapter, current institutional measures are woefully inadequate.

NOTES

1. Official development assistance includes bilateral concessional grants and loans by OECD member countries and their contributions to multilateral agencies. These numbers differ from the totals in Table 4.1 because the table includes bilateral grants and loans by OECD member and non-member countries and concessional and nonconcessional disbursements by multilateral agencies and NGOs.
2. Clemens and Moss also show that, contrary to assertions in UN documents, no country in a UN forum ever agreed to actually reach 0.7 percent although many pledged to move towards it (Clemens and Moss 2005, p. 2).
3. Since cross-sectional and panel data show no robust relationship between aid and the quality of institutions in the IMF study, it seems more likely that reverse causality is at work.
4. An event occurred during this visit that is curious in light of the World Bank Group's later enthusiastic support for privatization. Our team suggested that the IFC advise the Peruvian government on its privatization program. The Belaunde government was positive, but when the IFC staff members called headquarters their managers at the IFC rejected the idea because privatization was "too controversial." Subsequently, the IFC sought to be the investment adviser in many state-owned enterprise privatizations, pursuing the opportunity so aggressively that private investment banks complained to me that IFC was unfairly using its association with the World Bank to "cream-skim" the best opportunities.
5. The General Council of the Bank initially objected to this because the World Bank at that time still adhered to the fiction that loans should be investments that generate sufficient funds in the future to permit countries to repay the debt. This principle was also the reason why the World Bank at one time calculated the rate of return on every project.

6.   As Martens et al. (2002) point out, there are also principal–agent problems between the aid-giver and the consultants or NGOs it hires to implement its projects.

7.   Donor rhetoric may not have changed as much as it appears at first reading. Although aid documents propose institution-building, they often define institutions broadly to include rules or organizations that are more tractable to outside influence than embedded rules and norms. For example, World Bank *World Development Reports* defined institutions to include policies such as interest rates and organizations such as banks (World Bank 2002, 2003b).

8.   World Bank and IMF staff members are encouraged to move every three to five years and promotions often require experience in different regions or sectors. SIDA's average staff time in one assignment is four years (Ostrom et al. 2002, p. 143). Consulting firms working with international financial agencies have claimed that "high staff rotation" causes a lack of institutional memory which leads to "very inefficient and ineffective work" (BIMILACI 2001, p. 2).

9.   See Ostrom et al. (2002). (See also Easterly 2002a; Martens et al. 2002.)

10. The bylaws of the World Bank require it to be apolitical. The European Bank for Reconstruction and Development and some bilateral agencies are required to support democracy in recipient countries, but they too avoid involvement in politics and require *de jure* evidence of elections rather than de facto proof of representation and accountability.

11. This has an effect on reporting. World Bank reports that criticize an incumbent government are held in limbo or censored by project staff if they could adversely affect the project pipeline or influence an election. For example, a research report critical of the Fujimori government's mismanagement of Lima's water system reform was held up by staff working in the World Bank operations department responsible for Peru. The paper analyzed the government's political motivations, and attributed the failure to privatize to the president's desire to win votes. The operations staff deemed the paper a "liability" to the World Bank since it would be seen as attacking the president before the next election when he was running as a candidate. They asked the researchers to meet with one of Fujimori's advisers to discuss changes which would make the report acceptable to the government. Even after the agreed changes were made, the report was only released for publication after Fujimori was ousted in a scandal in 2000.

12. This incentive problem can be tempered if a staff member has several client countries or if the recalcitrant government is not particularly important to a donor's portfolio of projects. It can be heightened if responsibility for, or influence over, project approval is in field offices, since the careers of many individuals who are dedicated to that country's aid program would be harmed if the project pipeline slows or dries up. I know a prominent economist who was not allowed to work on World Bank analyses in several countries because field officers there decided his analysis was too critical of the government or of the World Bank's project and would harm the "country dialogue."

13. The evidence goes beyond performance contracts. For example, one World Bank report brings up the long discredited idea of a centralized body to exercise government's "ownership function" for SOEs, separate from regulation or sector policymaking (World Bank 2006b). Such bodies were deemed to be mostly useless and sometimes harmful in the early 1990s (Shirley 1989; Shirley and Nellis 1991).

14. For example, the World Bank's 1994 *World Development Report*, while criticizing the project as too large and complex, still described it as "an early and innovative effort using project finance for power generation . . ." (World Bank 1994).

15. In his biography of James Wolfensohn, Sebastian Mallaby asserts that this happened in several cases in the World Bank (see Mallaby 2004).

5. Can we measure institutions and institutional change?

Measuring institutions turns out to be far more difficult than it sounds. Economists have put considerable effort into defining and testing institutional variables for cross-country growth regressions, but far less effort has gone into measuring institutions in specific countries. Specificity is crucial because, as North et al. (forthcoming) argue, the same institutions work very differently in limited access and open access societies. I describe this problem for democracies later in this chapter. Because they lack specificity, few current institutional measures are what Steve Knack calls "actionable," that is, able to help researchers analyze the causal effects of specific institutions, help citizens demand better institutions and hold leaders accountable, help reformers design successful and sustainable improvements in institutions, and help aid-givers judge when countries are able to use aid more effectively (Knack 2006).

In this chapter I first consider the evidence that institutions are correlated with growth and how this literature measures institutions. I next discuss specific problems of measuring democracy. If institutions matter for growth then democracy should matter, since democracy represents a prime subset of institutions. Yet it has proved impossible to find a clear relationship between democracy and long-run growth, probably because we cannot measure institutions adequately. Despite such weaknesses, institutional indicators are widely used by aid agencies. The previous chapter concluded that aid can neither improve nor avoid harmful institutions, but at least in theory aid could usefully assist countries that are already improving their institutions. The last two sections of this chapter review two efforts to do just that, one from the US and the other from the World Bank, and the serious practical obstacles hampering efforts to measure institutional change.

HOW TO BE PRECISE THOUGH VAGUE

M.J. Moroney (1951) in his classic book on statistics, *Facts from Figures*, titled his chapter on estimation and confidence limits, "how to be precise though vague." This title aptly applies to the institutional variables in cross-country growth regressions. Cross-country regressions persistently demonstrate large and statistically significant correlations between institutional variables and growth in GDP per person. Specifically, growth in GDP per capita is significantly and positively correlated with (i) protection of property rights and enforcement of contracts; (ii) measures of economic freedom such as voluntary exchange, free competition, and protection of property rights; (iii) civil liberties; (iv) political rights and democracy; and (v) institutions supporting cooperation, such as trust, religion, and social clubs and associations (see Table 5.1). Growth is negatively correlated with (vi) political instability, defined as coups, revolutions, riots, and deaths from political violence. Political instability is treated as a proxy for weak institutions to mitigate conflict and promote civic order, such as the absence of laws and norms prompting people to express their grievances peacefully. These institutional measures have large and significant correlations with growth even when different measures from different sources are used, including voice and accountability, regulatory burden, rule of law, graft, constraints on executive power, or property rights (International Monetary Fund 2003, Figure 3.3). Furthermore, in horse races between variables an index of institutional quality "trumps" measures of geography or trade as an explanation for levels of development, although geography and trade also have effects on institutional quality (Rodrik et al. 2002).

The econometric evidence correlating institutions with growth is precise, but vague. The studies in Table 5.1 are painfully precise, testing a multitude of different specifications with a host of control variables and numerous tests for robustness. The institutional variables are also precisely measured, using painstakingly-selected experts or large surveys with carefully defined terms. Yet these variables, so painstakingly measured and regressed, are nevertheless vague. Some are abstractions, such as democracy, that encompass a plethora of individual norms, rules and enforcement characteristics (see the next section). Many are outcomes, the product of institutions rather than institutions themselves.

The use of outcomes has led some to declare these exercises tautological. These critics argue that high scores on civil liberties, rule of law, democratic politics, secure property rights, enforcement of contracts, political stability, cooperative social norms, and trust are the definition of development. In contrast, proponents view these variables not as institutional outcomes, but as measures of institutional quality (Rodrik et al. 2002) or "clusters" of institutions (Acemoglu 2005). Some propose "unbundling" institutions, by separating the effects of, for example, "property rights institutions" and "contracting institutions" (Acemoglu and Johnson 2005), but even these unbundled institutions are still broad abstractions.

Table 5.1   Studies showing significant correlations between institutional variables and growth and levels of per capita GDP

Institutional variables	Number of studies

Protection of property rights and enforcement of contracts
    As measured by: ICRG, BERI, Business International
    risk indicators, Rule of law (World Bank Institute
    Governance Indicators)
	17

Economic freedom (voluntary exchange, free competition,
    protection of people and property)
    As measured by: Fraser Institute (Gwartney and Lawson)
	19

Civil liberties As measured by: Freedom House	13
Political rights and democracy As measured by: Freedom House	13
Political instability As measured by: Barro; Taylor and others; Banks	15

Institutions supporting cooperation (trust, religion, social
    clubs, etc.)
    As measured by: World Values Surveys; Putnam social
    capital; Banks
	6

Sources: Author's calculation based on studies surveyed in Aron (2000) and Berggren (2003), combined with: Acemoglu et al. (2001, 2002, 2005), Dollar and Kraay (2003), (Rigobón and Rodrik (2005), Rodrik et al. (2002); Roll and Talbott (2001). Indicators are: ICRG (International Country Risk Guide) at www.ICRGonline.com; BERI (Business Environmental Risk Intelligence) at www.BERI.com; Business International (now part of the Economist Intelligence Unit) risk indicators at www.eiu.com; World Bank Institute Governance Indicators available at: www.worldbank.org/wbi/governance; Fraser Institute/ Gwartney and Lawson economic freedom index available at www.freetheworld.com; Freedom House civil liberties and political rights index available at www.freedomhouse.org; Barro are data from various publications of Robert J. Barro; Taylor is Charles Taylor and others, *World Handbook of Political and Social Indicators* (various); Banks is Arthur Banks, editor of the *Political Handbook of the World* (various); World Values Survey available at www.worldvaluessurvey.org; Putnam's social capital measure is in Putnam (1993). Some studies are counted twice; there are 59 individual studies.

In Table 5.2 I list some widely used measures of "institutions."[1] The first five are rankings by experts. The sixth, the World Bank governance index, is an aggregation of rankings and public opinion polls. The seventh, the World Bank Doing Business indicators, uses surveys of lawyers and other local experts about the cost of government regulations for a hypothetical firm to undertake common business activities, such as starting a business, hiring a worker, getting credit, paying taxes, and the like. (I discuss the World Bank governance index and Doing Business indicators in more detail below.) The Polity Project (number 8 in the table) rates countries on

Table 5.2   Commonly used measures of institutions

Variables	Type	Measures
1. Country risk: ICRG[a], www.icrgonline.com	Expert ratings	Corruption in government Rule of law Expropriation risk Repudiation of contracts by government Quality of the bureaucracy
2. Civil liberties index: Freedom House, www.freedomhouse.org	Expert ratings	Freedom of expression & belief Associational & organization rights Rule of law Personal autonomy & individual rights
3. Political liberties index: Freedom House, www.freedomhouse.org	Expert ratings	Electoral process "free & fair" Political pluralism & participation Functioning of government (Accountable? Corrupt? Open?)
4. Corruption: Transparency International, www.transparency.org	Aggregation of expert ratings and opinion surveys	Perceptions of corruption of businesses & experts
5. Economic freedom: Fraser Institute, www.freetheworld.com	Expert ratings	Size of government expenditures, taxes & enterprises Legal structure & security of property rights Access to sound money Trade barriers, taxes, & size, black market premium, & capital market controls Regulation of credit, labor & business
6. Governance indicators: World Bank, www.worldbank.org/wbi/governance	Aggregation of expert ratings & surveys	Voice and accountability Political stability and absence of violence Government effectiveness Regulatory quality Rule of law Control of corruption
7. Doing Business: World Bank, www.doingbusiness.org	Surveys of lawyers & others	Formal business regulation & protection of property rights based on a similar hypothetical company and circumstance

Table 5.2   (continued)

Variables	Type	Measures
8. Polity Project: Center for Global Policy, U. Maryland, www.cidcm.umd.edu/ polity	Scholars' judgment	Competitiveness of executive recruitment Openness of executive recruitment Constraints on chief executive Regulation of participation Competitiveness of participation
9. Database of political institutions: World Bank, econ.worldbank.org search for wps 2283	Data on political variables	Chief executive background, election Political parties of executive, legislature Legislative elections, special interests Electoral rules Checks & balances Federalism

Note: a. BERI (Business Environmental Risk International) provides similar information for a smaller number of countries.

Sources: Author's calculations based on sources of indicators described.

the basis of political criteria: do changes in the executive occur through forceful seizures of power, by designation within the political elite, or by competitive elections? The World Bank Database on Political Institutions (9) provides specific data on political systems: does the chief executive have a finite term in office, how long is that term, what party does the executive belong to, does that party control all relevant houses of the legislature, and so on?

These indicators are an advance considering our prior ignorance about institutions. Economists used to assume away institutions; using these indicators they find institutions have large and consistent effects on growth and development. Unfortunately there are also serious problems with the current indicators and with the way they are being used. I can illustrate this best with some specific examples and these are the subject of the rest of this chapter.

THE DEMOCRACY DEBATE

Cross-country growth regressions find no consistent, statistically significant association between democracy and long-run economic growth (see, for example, Przeworski et al. 2000; Przeworski and Limongi 1993). Several authors have found that the transition to democracy has a positive and significant relationship to short-term growth (Papaioannou and Siourounis 2004; Persson and Tabellini 2006; Rodrik and Wacziarg 2005, and, using a new different dataset described in Beck et al. 2001, Keefer 2004).[2] Since democracy embodies many important institutional features, the failure to find a robust relationship with long-run growth has led some to argue that institutions have only a second order effect on economic performance. "The first order effect comes from human and social capital, which shape both institutional and productive capacities of a society" (Glaeser et al. 2004, p. 26). These critics point out that measures of institutional outcomes bear little relationship to the specific rules that are presumed to produce these outcomes. For example, the ICRG measures of expropriation risks (number 1 in Table 5.2) , the World Bank's measure of government effectiveness (a subcategory of 6), or the Polity Project measures of constraints on the executive (8) have little correlation with constitutional constraints such as electoral rules or courts (Glaeser et al. 2004, p. 8). Furthermore, dictators, who presumably can "freely choose" good policies, score as high on the ICRG or World Bank measures as do democratic governments constrained by elections and other rules (ibid.). Glaeser et al. conclude that institutional research must "focus on actual rules, rather than conceptually ambiguous assessment of institutional outcomes" (ibid.).

Why should we expect democracy to cause growth? Recall from Chapter 3 that market-supportive institutions reduce transaction costs and protect persons and property from expropriation. Is democracy such an institution? Theories about democracy fall into two camps. One camp argues that democracies will grow faster because governments accountable to voters are motivated to protect individuals and property rather than expropriate them. The other camp counters that democracy slows growth because voters demand redistribution, threatening the security of property rights and lowering the returns to investment. Neither point of view is supported by cross-country growth regressions because democracy shows no consistent effect on growth, negative or positive.

It seems plausible that the way democracy is measured accounts for much of this ambiguity. The cross-country growth literature relies heavily on the Polity data and the Freedom House data. Polity experts rank the competitiveness and openness of recruitment of chief executives, the extent to which chief executives can act on their own discretion, and the regulation and competitiveness of political participation. Freedom House experts rank political participation and civil liberties, determining whether there are free and fair elections for the executive and legislature, whether political parties compete, whether opposition parties are allowed to take power, whether political participation is open to all citizens, and so forth.[3]

These measures are abstract, subjective, and hard to decipher. They aggregate heterogeneous laws and norms, some electoral, some non-electoral. For example, Polity mixes legal and legislative rules, asking, for example, is there is an independent judiciary and can the legislature initiate legislation? Freedom House mixes audit rules and legislative rules, asking, for example, is there an independent auditing agency and can the legislature review the budgetary process? This mingling makes it impossible to determine which kinds of institutions are driving the relationship between democracy and growth: is it the judiciary, checks and balances, auditing rules? Not all the measures in Table 5.2 suffer from these problems. The Database of political institutions (9) uses more objective criteria to judge competitiveness of elections. For example, instead of asking experts if they believe elections were competitive, it measures whether multiple parties competed and no single party or candidate got more than 75 percent of the vote (Beck et al. 2001). It excludes outcomes, for example, did the opposition party take power? And it does not confound measures of electoral institutions with measures of other institutions, such as judicial independence or auditing rules.

Even the best current measures of democracy exclude political institutions that are hard to quantify or require country-specific knowledge. Yet these excluded variables are crucial to how democracy functions, such as franchise rules (for example, who can vote?), electoral regulations (for example, how are ballots designed?), political party rules (for example, how are candidates determined?) Also excluded are laws affecting voter access to information such as rules governing the media (for example, is there censorship of the opposition?) or candidate disclosure (for example, must candidates reveal their funding sources?) Nor do they cover constitutional divisions of power that affect which issues are salient in national or local elections or legislative or executive elections (for example, do candidates talk about national budget deficits or federal funding for local roads?), norms that govern how people view voting (for example, I always vote for my father's party) or corruption (for example, all politicians are crooked so what difference does it make?), and many more.

Furthermore, even the institutions that are measured have aspects that are not measured, but that determine how the institutions function in practice. Consider the problem of measuring whether elections are competitive. We do not know if incumbents can freely use the resources and power of government to crush their opponents. Cross-country growth regressions do not specify such underlying causal institutions, and for good reason. It would be a daunting task to discover comparable data on how effectively incumbents are restricted from abusing the power of their office to defeat their electoral opponents. Measuring legal restrictions on the incumbent is not enough; we must also know if the laws are enforced and how easily restrictions can be overturned.

The problem of measuring democracy goes even deeper. If North et al. are correct, then similar institutions perform very differently in open access and limited access societies because they serve very different political and economic ends (see North et al. forthcoming, pp. 182–93). Elections in open access societies work to align, at least partially, the interests of those in power with the interests of voters, because citizens can freely form political organizations, lobby the electorate, and vote to dismiss leaders who fail to serve their interests. In limited access societies, however, not all citizens can express their interests in the same way. Restrictions make it costly and difficult for non-elites to organize politically or to mobilize against illegal state actions such as calling off elections. Limited access societies also lack civilian control over the military and as a result the outcomes of elections are often threatened by coups or by incumbents who refuse to give up power. Democracy variables record coups, but they do not capture the chilling effects of the perennial threat that the military will intervene, that losers in elections will be imprisoned or exiled, or that opposition supporters will lose their assets and rights. In limited access societies elections allow peaceful power sharing within the dominant elite coalition and give the state legitimacy in international circles; they are not meant to make the state more responsive to powerless non-elites. Should non-elites gain power through elections (and not be overthrown by a coup) they seldom change these rules, instead they use their new powers to suppress their opponents.

These differences between "democracies" in limited and open access societies may explain why Keefer (2007) finds much larger policy differences between rich democracies and poor democracies than between poor democracies and poor autocracies. Poor democracies perform about the same or somewhat worse than poor autocracies, and considerably worse than richer democracies, on inflation, corruption, bureaucratic quality, rule of law, contract enforcement, and customs delays (ibid.). Governments in poor democracies spend much less than governments in rich democracies, which is not surprising. But they also spend less than poor autocracies, contradicting the theory that democracy is bad for growth because poor democracies will redistribute more.

Keefer also documents how political institutions that are nominally the same function differently in different settings (Keefer 2005). In richer democracies political parties are identified with well-established programs dealing with issues of broad public concern. Countries with these "programmatic" parties have less corrupt governments that are more likely to provide public goods and less likely to target goods to narrow groups of voters. Keefer argues that programmatic parties allow politicians to make credible promises because voters can assess how well their promises fit with the party's program. Credibility allows politicians to appeal to a large constituency so they are less likely to pursue distortionary policies that benefit narrow social interests. If politicians cannot make credible promises, they tend to appeal to a small group of influential patrons who can deliver the votes of their clients in exchange for favors. In these circumstances politicians earmark revenues for jobs and investments to pay off their patrons, not to serve a broad constituency of voters. As a consequence, poor democracies provide far inferior services and infrastructure than richer democracies, even though they spend almost the same share of GDP on public sector wages and more on public investment. For example, poor democracies spend almost the same median share of their GDP on public education as rich democracies – 2.6 percent compared to 2.9 percent – but their secondary school enrollment is over 50 percentage points lower (ibid., p. 8).

Democracies where politicians court patrons and clients rather than appealing to broad groups of constituents are vulnerable to replacement by autocracies because they are not very different from their non-democratic alternatives. Indeed, one reason why some poor autocracies grow faster than poor democracies is that poor autocracies are less prone to change. Investors are likely to believe they face less risk of expropriation from autocrats with a long political horizon and few challengers than from politicians in volatile democracies.

In summary, institutionalists confront a serious empirical challenge to measure democracy. If North et al. (forthcoming) are correct then electoral rules can appear similar in open access and limited access countries, but operate in very different ways. To understand democracy we need to delve deeper into the rules and norms that support elections and into the broader voting environment. The same is true for other rules and norms, such as rule of law or protection of property rights. Although enormous progress has been made in understanding institutions, most institutional measures fall far short of this challenge. This is not an esoteric issue. Large amounts of money ride on institutional measures, and that is the subject of the next two sections.

MONEY FOR "GOOD" INSTITUTIONS: THE MILLENNIUM CHALLENGE ACCOUNT

Allocating aid based on the abstract measures of institutions in Table 5.2 is ill-advised, as we can see in the US government's Millennium Challenge Account (MCA). The MCA was created in 2002 to disburse funds only to those very poor countries that are performing well on its criteria.[4] In 2006 some 99 countries were potentially eligible: 69 had per capita incomes of $1675 or less, while another 30 were low to middle-income countries with per capita incomes between $1675 and $3465. To qualify for assistance a potentially eligible country must score at or above the median of its income group on control of corruption. The country must also score at or above the median of its income group on at least half of the criteria under each of the three performance dimensions shown in Table 5.3 (Millennium Challenge Corporation 2006). Only 22 countries met these conditions, and by the fall of 2006 only nine of them had signed agreements. The MCA's selectivity also slowed disbursements. The MCA was allocated $4.2 billion, but by mid-2006 had disbursed only $25.1 million (Center for Global Development 2006).[5]

According to MCA documents the criteria in Table 5.3 "are intended to assess the degree to which the political and economic conditions in a

Table 5.3   US Millennium Challenge Account performance criteria, 2006 (institutional variables in italics)

Performance dimension	Performance criteria	Type of measure
Ruling justly	*1. Civil liberties*	Ratings of experts
	2. Political rights	Ratings of experts
	3. Voice and accountability	Index of ratings & surveys
	4. Government effectiveness	Index of ratings & surveys
	5. Rule of law	Index of ratings & surveys
	6. Control of corruption	Index of ratings & surveys
Investing in people	1. Public expenditures on health	Expenditure/GDP
	2. Immunization rates DPT3 & measles	Average rates of immunization
	3. Public expenditures on primary education	Expenditure/GDP
	4. Girls' primary completion rate	Female graduates/population in cohort
Encouraging economic freedom	*1. Cost of starting a business*	Estimate of lawyers
	2. Inflation	Change CPI
	3. Fiscal policy	Budget deficit/GDP
	4. Days to start a business	Estimate of lawyers
	5. Trade policy	Average tariffs + trade barriers
	6. Regulatory quality	Index of ratings & surveys

Source: MCC, Report on the Criteria and Methodology for Determining the Eligibility of Candidate Countries for Millennium Challenge Account Assistance in FY 2006, September 8, 2006. Available at: www.mca.gov/about_us/congressional_reports/FY07_Criteria_Methodology.pdf.

country serve to promote broad-based sustainable economic growth and reduction of poverty; and thus provide a sound environment for the use of MCA funds" (Millennium Challenge Corporation 2006, Annex A, p.11). Selecting aid recipients on the basis of objective, scholarly criteria seems like a good idea in principle, but in practice MCA holds countries accountable for improving indicators that are neither transparent nor amenable to change (see Knack 2006, on this point). Since the MCA policy measures are endogenous to institutions, my discussion focuses on the institutional indicators, the six MCA criteria under "ruling justly," the cost required to start a new business, the time required to start a new business, and regulatory quality. We have seen these institutional measures before as measures of institutions in econometric studies. MCA uses two kinds of institutional measures: indices based on expert rankings and opinion surveys and the Doing Business measures, and I will consider each in turn.

Experts and surveys have well-known problems. Experts can be biased because they know how others regard the country; they have a favorable view of the country for irrelevant reasons; they are swayed by recent news coverage; or, since you cannot be an expert on everything, they extrapolate from their knowledge of only one aspect of the several criteria they are judging. Opinion surveys are also flawed. People's answers to surveys can be biased by the latest information they receive, by the way the questions are asked, by the order in which they are asked, by poor or inaccurate memory, or by the respondent's tacit metric that may be different from what another observer may use. Tacit metrics are important. For example, responses to questions about corruption will differ if respondents typically measure their country against Switzerland or Nigeria.

The MCA indicators for "ruling justly" and "regulatory quality" have serious measurement problems, some of which are described by Kaufmann and Kraay (2002), Kaufmann et al. (2005) and Arndt and Oman (2006). As a result they also have large margins of error or confidence intervals. We cannot draw any conclusions by comparing two points that fall in overlapping confidence intervals, since there is no statistical difference between them. Kaufmann et al. give confidence intervals or margins of error with a 90 percent probability that the "true" point estimate falls within the interval. The confidence intervals are large, so large for the estimated corruption measure that it is impossible to say with 90 percent certainty whether 30 of the 70 target countries are eligible for aid or not, that is, whether they rank in the top half or the bottom half of the sample (Kaufmann et al. 2005, p. 10). Ninety percent certainty sounds deceptively high, but it means that in one out of ten cases the estimate is outside the confidence interval. Arndt and Oman (2006) argue that the margins of error could be even larger if the errors of the sources used to construct these measures are correlated with each other. They regard this as likely because some of the sources rely on each other when doing their ratings (see section on CPIA below). Since the differences in ratings between the MCA countries are generally small, these large margins of error make the allocation exercise suspect.

Errors and biases do less injury to cross-country regressions because they are not focused on individual rankings. Bias does not matter in cross-country regressions as long as it causes a consistent over- or under-measurement over time. And errors in a large sample do not matter as long as they are not correlated with each other, so they cancel each other out. Biases and error do matter, however, for exercises such as the MCA, in which individual countries must qualify for aid based on their ranking in a group.

Some of the specific criteria also raise concerns. The criteria under "ruling justly" in Table 5.3 are not just abstract and general, they are aggregates of measures that are themselves abstract and general. Rule of law, for example, is "an index of surveys that rates countries on: the extent to which the public has confidence in and abides by rules of society; incidence of violent and non-violent crime; effectiveness and predictability of the judiciary; and the enforceability of contracts" (Millennium Challenge Corporation 2006, Annex A, p. 1). A large number of specific rules and norms underpin each of these concepts, just as we saw with democracy. Take "enforceability of contracts." It is affected by commercial norms in different types of businesses; laws governing different mortgages, leases, purchase agreements, marriages, and other types of contracts; laws governing contracts between private persons, local manufacturers, banks, foreign conglomerates, governments, or other categories of individuals and organizations; rules governing availability and costs of arbitration and courts; codes of ethics of reputation-based business groups; accounting rules and their enforcement; and much more. There is no way of knowing how any specific law or norm affects the rank of any individual country on enforcement of contracts, or how enforcement of contracts affects the country's rank on rule of law. Again, this is less important for cross-country studies but it matters greatly for the MCA. The MCA needs to know more than whether a country qualifies for aid, it needs to know specifically what the country is doing right or wrong and how to measure the success of specific reforms. Such abstract and general measures make this task impossible.

There is also a dynamic problem. Since progress is the goal, logically the MCA should judge countries on changes in their rankings rather than on their static ranks, but broad measures such as rule of law change very slowly or not at all for most countries. When these measures do change it may not mean that the country's performance changed. According to the authors of the World Bank governance indices, smaller changes are probably caused by changes in the sources for the data, not by changes in the real world (Kaufmann et al. 2005, p. 13): "At a most basic level, it should be clear that the presence of measurement error in the underlying data implies that we should be cautious about reading too much into observed changes in individual and composite measures of governance, both subjective and objective" (ibid., p. 16). Should these measures be used to determine aid allocation, especially for countries that are very similar on a world scale, ranking in the bottom tier on most indicators?

The other set of MCA measures, the costs of doing business, may seem more precise than broad aggregates of opinions, but they are not necessarily more accurate. Nor are objective measures necessarily free of subjectivity, since analysts must select which "facts" to report, and how to define and measure them. The two quantitative measures of institutions in the MCA criteria – days to start a business and cost to start a business – come from the World Bank "Doing Business" reports, which survey lawyers, accountants, and other professionals about legal formalities in their countries. These measures only reflect reality if laws on the books bear some resemblance to performance in practice, which is probably rare in the poor countries targeted by the MCA.

How different are the Doing Business measures from reality? Doing Business instructs its respondents to list each step required by law for starting a new firm and allot at least a day to each procedure, except for procedures that take place simultaneously. It assumes that all steps are completed without facilitators, such as lawyers, and without bribes. Yet surveys of Brazilian and Peruvian garment firms found that the majority used facilitators, and many reported that bribes could accelerate the process. Doing Business also fails to measure the opportunity cost of time for the entrepreneur, arguably the most important measure of the cost of entry. In the Lima and Sao Paulo surveys the opportunity cost of entrepreneurs (the time they reported multiplied by their salaries) and the fees of facilitators were the single biggest costs of registration, yet neither cost is included in the Doing Business measure. Doing Business differs from other surveys even when they measure the same thing, such as the time to register a new firm. The World Bank's investment climate surveys, which cover hundreds to thousands of firms in each country, show large discrepancies between firm responses and the Doing Business data. For example, new firms in Honduras report close to 40 days *more* to register than the Doing Business data, while firms in Nicaragua report more than 40 days *less* than the Doing Business data. There is no statistically significant correlation between the days to start a business measure and firms' perceptions about the ease of starting a business in surveys in 56 underdeveloped countries (Kaufmann et al. 2005, p. 60, Table 8).[6]

Which should we believe, Doing Business or firm surveys? Lawyers or entrepreneurs? The Doing Business measures are judgments about a hypothetical firm that is probably not representative of most firms in the smaller and poorer countries eligible for the MCA. The hypothetical firm is a limited liability firm operating in the most populous city and employing up to 50 employees. It has five owners, a start up capital of 10 times per capita income and a turnover at least 100 times per capita income (World Bank 2006a). In contrast, the survey of garment firms in Lima, Peru found that most are not limited liability companies and have far less start up capital and fewer partners than the Doing Business hypothetical (Jaramillo Baanante 2004). Even in a large market such as Sao Paulo, Brazil, only 64 percent of garment manufacturers are limited liability companies, and only 10 percent of them have more than two partners (Zylbersztajn et al. 2004).

Given our current state of knowledge, there is no way to know if the MCA criteria correctly gauge whether a country is creating the institutional framework necessary for development. Even if the criteria were correct and appropriately measured, there is no way to know what threshold a country must attain to create an aid-supportive environment. The MCA assumes that a country that does better than half of the eligible poor countries on half of its criteria will use aid well, but there is no empirical basis for this assumption. It seems more plausible that aid will only make an effective contribution to development above some unknown but potentially measurable threshold level of institutional quality.

Aid targeting confronts a root dilemma: cross-country institutional measures are inadequate to judge whether countries are improving their institutions enough to use aid well. The governance indices are too abstract, aggregate, and error-prone for this purpose. The Doing Business measures are more concrete and specific, but measure a hypothetical situation that bears little relationship to the actual situation. Since Doing Business measures legal inputs rather than performance outputs, a country can improve its rating just by changing its rules on the books, without reducing the burden on firms. Might specific country ratings from aid agencies do a better job at directing aid to where it will be most effective? To answer this question I turn to another set of indicators, the World Bank's CPIA.

THE PROBLEMS WITH AID AGENCY RATINGS: THE WORLD BANK'S CPIA

Given the problems with aggregate ratings, it might make sense to rate countries using an aid agency's in-house expertise. The World Bank's Country Policy and Institutional Assessment (CPIA) does just that. The goal of the

CPIA is to direct more aid to countries which implement "policies that promote economic growth and poverty reduction" (World Bank 2006c). It is used to allocate funds to the poorest countries from the Bank's soft window, IDA (International Development Agency).[7] Ratings by World Bank country experts make up 80 percent of a country's score on the CPIA; the remaining 20 percent is based on the proportion of the country's World Bank projects that are judged to be "at risk" in the annual review of project performance.

Indicators representing real country conditions have the unavoidable disadvantage of being complicated, and the CPIA is complicated, with 16 components grouped into four clusters. Each component is broken into two to six sub-components, or dimensions as the Bank calls them, for a total of 52 separate criteria. Many of the criteria, shown in Table 5.4, are institutional. Initially the clusters are equally weighted in calculating the average score for the CPIA, but in a later calculation the public sector management and institution cluster is given a greater weight.[8]

New procedures were introduced in 2004 to make the rankings more consistent and to base them on specific policies and institutions rather than outcomes. Country experts now get details about what each subcomponent means and how it should be rated (World Bank 2005c, p. 32). They also get data on benchmark countries in a given region and "guideposts" on their country, such as the World Bank's governance indicators. Staff rate country performance on each subcomponent from one to six; the subcomponent scores are usually equally weighted to get a total component score.

How well do the CPIA ratings reflect reality? Even knowledgeable staff will be hard pressed to judge how countries rank on all but the extreme ends of these measures. Consider the six possible ratings for the "legal basis for secure property and contract rights" (World Bank 2005c, p. 33):

1. Formal property rights are hardly recognized, and informal rights are seldom enforced. Formal contractual arrangements are little used. Manipulation of property and contract rights is endemic.
2. Enforcement of contracts and recognition of property rights depend largely on informal mechanisms. Property and contract rights are subject to manipulation by government officials or other elites.
3. The law protects property rights in theory, but in fact registries and other institutions required to make this protection effective function poorly, making the protection of private property uncertain.
4. Property rights are protected in practice as well as theory. Contracts are enforced, but the process may be lengthy and expensive.
5. All property rights are transparent and well protected. Property registries are current and non-corrupt. Contracts are routinely enforced.
6. Criteria for "5" on all four sub-ratings are fully met. There are no warning signs of possible deterioration, and there is widespread expectation of continued strong or improving performance.

Table 5.4   World Bank performance-based allocation system for IDA funds

Country Policy and Institutional Assessments (80 Percent)	
Cluster	Components
Economic management	1. Macroeconomic management
	Monetary & exchange rate policy aimed at stability
	Aggregate demand policy for external balance
	Crowding out private investment
	2. Fiscal policy
	Primary balance sustainability
	Public expenditures/revenues flexibility to shocks
	Provision of public goods
	3. Debt policy
	Debt burden sustainability
	Coordination debt & macroeconomic policies
	Adequacy & timeliness information
	Debt management unit
Structural policy	4. Trade
	Trade regime restrictiveness, transparency, & predictability 75%
	Custom & trade regime corruption, transparency, timeliness 25%
	5. Financial sector
	Financial stability
	Financial sector efficiency, depth, & resource mobilization strength
	Degree of access to financial services
	6. Business regulatory environment. Burden, cost, rigidity, restrictiveness of:
	Regulations of entry, exit, and competition
	Regulations of ongoing business operations
	Regulations of factor markets (labor and land)
Policies for social inclusion/equity	7. Gender equality
	Equality of access to human capital development
	Equality of access to productive and economic resources
	Equality of status and protection under the law
	8. Equity of public resource use
	Consistency of government spending with poverty reduction
	Progressiveness of taxes & alignment with poverty reduction

Table 5.4 (continued)

Country Policy and Institutional Assessments (80 Percent)	
Cluster	Components

	9. Building human resources. Access to and quality of:
	  Health and nutrition services
	  Education, early childhood development, training and
	    literacy
	  Prevention and treatment of HIV/AIDS, tuberculosis,
	    malaria

	10. Social protection & labor
	  Social safety net programs adequate & enforced
	  Protection of basic labor standards (e.g. child labor
	    prohibited)
	  Labor market regulations protect labor, don't
	    discourage hiring
	  Community driven initiatives
	  Pension and old age savings programs adequate &
	    enforced

	11. Policies & institutions for environmental sustainability
	  Adequacy & enforcement of regulations & policies
	  Availability of public information
	  Capacity & application environmental assessment
	    system
	  Environmental priorities set & adhered to
	  Sector policies incorporate environmental concerns
	  Inter-ministerial coordination

Public sector
management &
institutions
	12. Property rights & rule-based governance
	  Legal basis for secure property and contract rights
	  Predictability, transparency, and impartiality of laws &
	    regulations affecting economic activity, & their
	    enforcement
	  Crime and violence as impediment to economic activity.

	13. Quality of budgetary & financial management
	  Comprehensiveness & credibility budget, link to policy
	    priorities
	  Effectiveness of financial management systems that
	    ensure budget is implemented as intended in controlled
	    & predictable way
	  Timeliness & accuracy of accounting and fiscal
	    reporting

	14. Efficiency of revenue mobilization
	  Quality of design & degree distortion of tax system
	  Quality, complexity, costliness, corruption,
	    transparency of tax administration

Table 5.4   (continued)

Country Policy and Institutional Assessments (80 Percent)

Cluster	Components
	15. Quality of public administration
	Mechanisms for policy coordination
	Design of administrative systems, business processes
	Merit based hiring & promotion, extent of corruption
	Public employment, pay & wage bill adequacy
	16. Transparency, accountability, & corruption in the public sector
	Accountability of executive & public employees
	Access of civil society to information on public affairs
	State capture by narrow vested interests.

Annual Review of Project Performance (20 Percent) Score based on percent of World Bank projects judged at risk.

Source: Author's calculations based on World Bank (2005c).

Most poor countries have a mix of the conditions in ratings 2–5, model laws combined with spotty enforcement, manipulation, and informality. Would outsiders know whether contract enforcement is lengthy and expensive (rating 4) or uncertain (rating 3) on average and across most kinds of contracts in most parts of a country? How would they weight routine enforcement (rating 5) of corporate contracts or sales contracts against uncertain enforcement (rating 3) of leases and mortgages? How will they assess differences in enforcement across different groups? In the natural state described by North et al. (forthcoming), property rights and contract enforcement are effective and low cost for elites, and ineffective and costly for non-elites.

Differences such as these are hard for outsiders to evaluate without studying the issues at length. Yet World Bank staff visit client countries for a few weeks at a time perhaps three or four times a year and have many tasks to accomplish. It would not surprise me if busy staff relied heavily on other expert ratings, the "goalposts," to make or at least reaffirm their judgments. In that case the information added by this exercise is very little. It is also worrying because the CPIA is a component in the aggregate governance indicators, and the aggregate governance indicators are part of the goalposts. Even assuming the country teams compile the CPIA ratings in a serious and informed fashion, we cannot ignore their incentives to lend or the more generalized bias towards optimism that I described in Chapter 4. Optimistic staff may prefer to give the benefit of the doubt to a country that is embarking on a reform project, since this would increase its chances of getting more aid.

Many of the components in the CPIA are based on Western ideas of best practice or political correctness, rather than empirical evidence that these institutions spur growth or reduce poverty. China, for example, probably scores quite low on the CPIA's ratings of formal property rights, budgeting, financial sector, equity of public resource use, the business regulatory environment, environmental policies and regulation, social protection and labor, and transparency, accountability, and corruption in the public sector. There is strong theoretical and empirical evidence that low inflation has a causal effect on growth and poverty reduction (for a review of this literature see Lopez 2004). But social protection, if it enters into growth equations at all, enters as the product of increased income, not as a cause.

If the CPIA trumps other indicators it is because of its country specificity. But the CPIA reduces the impact of country differences by assigning common weights to the subcategories and the ratings (a point also made by Kanbur 2005). Development is not only multifaceted, it is driven by interactions between different causal variables, interactions that are likely to vary from country to country.

Some critical variables that are salient for aid effectiveness are not measured at all. Wane (2004) shows that the most important determinant of the quality of World Bank projects was the quality of project design.[9] In Wane's regressions the usual governance indicators used by Burnside and Dollar or the MCA did not predict project performance once quality of design was taken into account. Rather, quality of project design was endogenous to the borrower's capacity to select better projects and reject worse ones. In other words, the quality of aid depends on selectivity on the demand side more than on the supply side. In countries where the government has the "capacity to screen and select projects conducive to development," and where they are "held accountable enough to their citizens to be deterred from accepting bad aid projects," design quality and, hence, impact of aid will be higher (ibid., p. 1). Wane's findings are supported by the experience of successful developers such as Chile and China (see Chapter 7). The institutions that determine the quality of aid are therefore likely to include variables not included in the CPIA, such as political rules or norms that reward selection of better projects, by, for example, giving leaders longer time horizons and holding them accountable for growth. As we saw in the discussion of democracy above, such institutions are hard to measure comparatively.

HOW CAN WE IMPROVE INSTITUTIONS IF WE CAN'T MEASURE THEM?

The measurement of institutions is still in its infancy. Although important regularities have been discovered, the current measures are not actionable. They are too crude to help aid agencies, policymakers, and concerned citizens design reforms and gauge their outcomes. The devil is truly in the detail, and the current set of measures may be seriously misleading about the micro developments. Part of the fault for the weakness of the measures lies with researchers who have focused their attention and efforts on variables that can be used for cross-country growth regressions. Actionable variables are not likely to be useful for papers worthy of peer-reviewed journals, but they are essential for a useful understanding of institutions.

I have gone to some lengths to critique the measures used by the MCC and the World Bank yet they are among the few aid-givers who have made any serious effort to assign aid where it is likely to be used effectively. Most donors allocate assistance on the basis of their national foreign policy aims, past practice, or some broad criterion such as countries below some per capita income level. The better ones piggyback on the World Bank CPIA or similar efforts.

If aid can be effective in promoting development it must begin with better measures. There has been progress in developing more sophisticated, usable measures, such as the World Bank's database of political institutions, and aid-givers could systematically collect specific country data on other institutional variables. I am not hopeful this will happen, however. The World Bank has the funds and expertise to collect comparative data, but is capricious towards standardized measures. There are exceptions, such as the Living Standards Measurement Surveys, the Database on Political Institutions, or some firm-level surveys, but generally the Bank aggregates data from other sources or collects simpler measures, such as Doing Business.

Developing more useful measures of institutions will not be simple. Ultimately, consistent, comparative case studies will be crucial if we are to understand the complex nature of institutions and institutional change and develop more specific and accurate measures. It would also be helpful to analyze the MCA and CPIA rankings retrospectively to see how accurately they predicted relative performance. As we will see in the next chapter, there are a large number of institutions that determine outcomes in only one sector, water. But even though measuring institutions is hard, it is not impossible and it is too important a task to neglect.

NOTES

1. These are not the only measures available. For a more comprehensive list and description see link to indicators at www.worldbank.org/publicsectorandgovernance (see also Arndt and Oman 2006, Box 4.1).
2. Keefer found that competitive elections at the beginning of the period explained growth in a 1975–2000 cross-section, but only after controlling for endogeneity (Keefer 2004).
3. Some scholars use both Polity and Freedom House rankings and add their own assessments as well. For example, Papaioannou and Siourounis (2004) combine the Polity data with the Freedom House measures, and also rate countries based on their own readings of historical information on whether and when the country introduced elections deemed "free and fair" by international observers or adopted a new democratic constitution (Papaioannou and Siourounis 2004, p. 8).
4. The US government set up a government-owned corporation, the Millennium Challenge Corporation or MCC, to administer the MCA separately from its bilateral aid agency, the US Agency for International Development.
5. The MCC also provides assistance to "threshold" countries, which are countries that do not meet all the criteria, with the objective of helping those countries meet its criteria. In the fall of 2006 there were 14 countries eligible for its Threshold Program.
6. The days to start a business measure has a significant negative correlation with the ease of starting a business in underdeveloped countries only when measures of perceptions of administrative regulations and control of corruption are included in the specification (Kaufmann et al. 2005, p. 60, Table 8). Interestingly, the Doing Business measures seem to be more accurate in wealthier economies; the days to start a business measure is significantly correlated with firm perceptions in 25 developed and newly industrialized countries. This suggests, logically enough, that *de jure* measures are accurate reflections of real-world conditions where there is a higher probability that laws are enforced.
7. Only countries with a per capita income below a cut off threshold ($1025 in 2005) are eligible for IDA. A similar rating system is used for countries receiving IBRD money, which are loans under the World Bank's usual terms, but the criteria have not been made public.
8. In this calculation the combined scores on the CPIA and project performance are multiplied by a governance factor, which is the unweighted average of the CPIA ratings under public sector management and institutions and the procurement practices component of the project performance evaluation. The allocation process does not end here. This so-called governance rating is then divided by 3.5, which is the midpoint of the 1 to 6 range used for the ratings, and then raised by an exponent of 1.5 to create a so-called "Governance Factor;" that is, Governance Factor = (average governance rating / 3.5) $^{1.5}$. The country's overall rating is then multiplied by the Governance Factor to give the Country Performance Rating, or CPR. The actual IDA allocation is a function of the CPR, population, and per capita income, with greatest weight given to the CPR as follows: IDA Country Allocation = f(CPR$^{2.0}$, Pop$^{1.0}$, GNI/Cap.$^{-0.125}$) (World Bank 2005e).
9. Based on internal evaluations of project and design quality.

6. Institutions and the reform of urban water systems

Reform of urban water and sanitation systems provides a good illustration of what we see when we unpack the black box of institutions. Water and sanitation are interesting because they are critical goods, yet appallingly mismanaged. Even though clean water and adequate sanitation are essential to prevent disease and premature death, as many as 1 billion people lack access to safe drinking water and 1.2 billion people lack access to adequate sanitation. As a result millions of poor people, mostly children, become ill and die from diseases such as cholera or diarrhea. The UN's Millennium Development Goal aims to halve the percentage of people without access to safe drinking water and basic sanitation by 2015 at an estimated cost of $101 billion (UN Millennium Project 2005a).

Money alone will not achieve the UN Millennium Development Goal, which is evident from the history of water and sanitation reform. Despite large volumes of aid, urban water systems in many poor countries are the epitome of government waste, inefficiency, and underinvestment. Huge volumes of water are lost because of leaks and wasted because of low prices. Paradoxically, those cities depleting their raw water the fastest have some of the lowest prices and largest losses from leaks and waste. For example, in 1992 half of the water produced in Mexico City was unaccounted for, 30 percent was lost to leaks (Haggarty et al. 2002, Table 5.4). Mexico City has pumped so much water from its aquifer that the city has been sinking (Haggarty et al. 2002). To avoid depleting its aquifer further the city pumps about a third of its water from distant rivers up over the mountains, and to avoid contaminating the aquifer, pumps the waste back over the mountains, polluting the rivers for downstream users. But prices for water in Mexico City do not reflect these costs; they have been well below those of cities such as Buenos Aires or Santiago that have cheaper, more abundant sources of water (Shirley and Ménard 2002, p. 34, Table 1.11).[1]

Multitudes of urban poor are not connected to the water and sewerage system at all. Instead they pay exorbitant prices to water vendors or wait for hours in lines at public standpipes. Their sanitation is largely unaddressed and so is sewage treatment: most poor and many middle-income cities dump their untreated sewage into rivers and oceans. Yet in many of these cities, governments charge even wealthy consumers low prices. Some customers receive water for free because billing and collection are lax. In Guinea, one of the poorest countries in the world, the government itself failed to pay its water bills. The utility covered the revenue shortfall by raising prices for its other customers, so in essence, Guinea's government was free-riding on its bill-paying citizens (Ménard and Clarke 2002b).

Water utilities are poorly managed in most poor countries. Many are overstaffed, with far more employees per connection than in developed countries, yet service is abysmal. These excess wage bills, along with failure to bill and collect and underpricing starve water and sanitation utilities of the funds they need for basic maintenance. As a consequence few utilities in poor cities have the funds to extend the system to all residents.

A number of cities, mostly in middle-income underdeveloped countries, reformed their water systems in the 1990s with support from large volumes of aid. World Bank lending for water and sanitation alone averaged \$2 billion a year in the early 1990s (World Bank 2006f). The overall outcome of these reforms is hard to assess, as I describe below, but some studies report considerable improvements in performance. Many water systems were not reformed, however, and some reforms led to backlash and reversals.

In the next section I summarize what economists generally agree about water and sanitation. I then review what little we know about the outcomes of the reform efforts in water and sanitation and consider the difficulties of analyzing outcomes econometrically. Next I discuss how institutions have affected outcomes in ways that confound economic theories, and compare the Buenos Aires water concession and Santiago's reform as examples of the effects of beliefs, norms, and local political institutions on reforms.

WHAT ECONOMISTS GENERALLY AGREE ABOUT WITH RESPECT TO WATER AND SANITATION

Private Good/Public Benefit

Water falls from the sky and is abundant in rivers and oceans, but when it is supplied by a utility it meets the economic definition of a private good. According to Samuelson a pure public good is non-rival and non-excludable. Water is a rival good – one person's consumption of clean water reduces the amount available to another. And piped water is excludable – a utility can cut off service to customers who do not pay their bills and can exclude users from boring wells into shared aquifers or diverting water from rivers or reservoirs.

Piped water has some public good characteristics that call for government involvement, however. Since water is essential to life, the state may need to ensure that all its citizens have access to some minimal amount of water. Very little drinking water is required to sustain human life, however, about two liters a day in temperate climates and four liters a day in hot climates. But water is also essential for hygiene, and hygiene has positive externalities; the benefits from reducing communicable diseases because of adequate hygiene have a greater value to society than the benefit to any one individual. Again the amounts are small: Rijsberman estimates that poor people without washing machines or gardens need only 20 to 50 liters of water per day for all domestic purposes (2004, p. 499). Sanitation also has positive externalities, and access to safe water without adequate sanitation will not by itself prevent diseases. Epidemiological studies suggest that young children only show reductions in incidents of diarrhea when clean water is provided on the premises combined with improved sanitation (Esrey 1996).[2]

Pricing

Despite water's public good characteristics, most economists agree that water prices should be set to cover the marginal cost of efficient operation, including a return on investment (Noll et al. 2000). Such a price gives consumers an incentive not to waste water, gives utilities the funds they need to maintain and expand the system and compensate users for unabated pollution, and gives regulators the information they need to judge the economic value of competing uses for water. Although economists may disagree about how best to measure the costs of water supply or how best to set tariffs that increase information and minimize costs, they agree that in principle consumers who can afford to pay should pay a tariff that covers the costs of an efficient operator (see the discussions in Munasinghe 1992; Noll 2002).[3]

Subsidies

Economists differ about whether it is necessary to subsidize water to make it affordable to the poor. Surveys suggest that people are willing to pay relatively high prices for drinking water; many poor consumers without connections are already paying very high prices to water vendors. Since the amount of drinking water needed to survive is small, it is less clear whether people are willing to pay high prices for piped water connections (see the discussion below on the saliency of water to consumers). Economists do agree that if subsidies are used, they should be strictly targeted to low-income consumers and be only as large as necessary to make water affordable. Subsidized rates for all consumers encourage waste and deprive the utility of the resources needed to maintain and expand the system. Across-the-board subsidies are also regressive. The poorest consumers are often not connected to the system at all, and are harmed by subsidies that deprive the utility of the funds it needs to bring them piped water. Many economists are critical of increasing bloc tariffs, a widely used form of subsidy where lower volumes of consumption are charged at a price below operating cost and the price goes up as the consumption volume increases. They argue that increasing bloc tariffs subsidize wealthier customers, yet may not provide sufficient subsidy to poorer users, an issue I explore in the next section. Increasing bloc tariffs also lead to inefficient use of water since conservation within a bloc does not reduce consumers' bills.

Metering

Some economists recommend metering water only when the savings from conserving water are larger than the costs of metering. Metering and meter reading are expensive, and these economists argue that metering has net benefits only where the supply of raw water is scarce and likely to be depleted at projected rates of consumption (Munasinghe 1992) or where there are problems disposing of waste water.

Operation

Water systems were long viewed by economists as classic natural monopolies. It would be inefficient to build competing networks of pipes, plus there are economies of scale in pipes.[4] Government ownership was once widely viewed as a remedy for natural monopoly, under the false assumption that governments are composed of perfectly informed agents aiming to maximize social welfare. Economists today no longer assume that government agents are well-informed servants of the public good, or that simply creating a government department will assure an adequate and efficient supply of clean water and sanitation. Instead most economists agree that water systems should be operated by companies, whether public or private, that are regulated in a way that motivates them to operate efficiently and to connect the entire population in their service area. Economists also generally agree that the government needs to monitor water quality, regulate monopoly providers, and require companies to reduce negative externalities from the diminution and pollution of water sources that others use. Optimal regulatory design envisions a politically independent regulator setting rates and monitoring performance based on objective and verifiable information, with right of appeal to neutral and independent arbitrators or courts (for a good sense of this literature see Armstrong et al. 1994; Joskow 2000).

Many, but not all, economists argue that private operation motivates water utilities to operate efficiently and to expand. A profit-maximizing operator has an incentive to extend service and keep costs down as long as the tariff structure rewards that behavior. The experience with state ownership shows that it is difficult, although not impossible, to replicate this sort of profit-maximizing behavior in state-owned enterprises (Shirley 1999, 2002; World Bank 1995).

Although most economists view urban water systems as a natural monopoly, some see opportunities for competition (Noll 2002). Water vendors already operate alongside piped water systems in many poor cities, but water vendors typically do not compete with piped systems; they operate only in neighborhoods without access to piped water. Nevertheless, competition is theoretically possible in a water system with multiple reservoirs. Each reservoir could compete to supply the system much as electricity generators compete to supply the grid, and a competitive wholesale water market could direct water to the piped network much as wholesale electricity markets do for electricity (Noll 2002, pp. 46–7).[5] Water systems with multiple wells could have competing well owners and a centralized body could manage depletion of the aquifer similarly to the centralized management of competitive wells in petroleum and natural gas fields (ibid., p. 47). To my knowledge this has not been tried in developing countries.

HOW WATER AND SANITATION SYSTEMS USUALLY OPERATE IN THE REAL WORLD

Private Good/Public Benefit

Despite twenty years of reform, most urban water systems operate very differently from conventional economic wisdom. The idea that water is a private good is highly controversial, something I describe in detail in the later section on beliefs. Much of what economists recommend is ignored in practice. Below I consider each topic in turn.

Pricing

Prices are seldom set to allow cost recovery. A survey of 132 major cities worldwide found that prices in most cases did not allow a return on investment (Global Water Intelligence, 2004 cited in Komives et al. 2006, p. 4). To the contrary, average tariffs were below operating and maintenance costs in all water utilities surveyed in South Asia, Eastern Europe, and Central Asia and in more than half of all water utilities surveyed in East

Asia, the Middle East, and North Africa (ibid.). Utilities had cost-recovery prices only in Latin America, and even there, only half of those surveyed had high enough average prices to fund operation, maintenance, and a portion of capital costs (ibid.). Prices are zero for many consumers in poor cities because utilities are lax in billing, collecting, and detecting and punishing thieves. Moreover, governments often require water to be supplied free to hospitals, schools, religious orders, government offices, powerful politicians, and other consumers.

Subsidies

Few underdeveloped countries target subsidies to the neediest. Targeted subsidies are complex; they require the government to monitor the income of the recipient and even reform-minded politicians will be reluctant to entrust this task to incompetent or corrupt bureaucracies. Less high-minded politicians may prefer indiscriminate subsidies to large numbers of consumers if that has a bigger political payoff than assisting only the poor. This may explain why so many poor countries continue to use increasing bloc tariffs under the pretext that poorer consumers will benefit. As some economists predicted, however, increasing bloc tariffs have not helped most poor consumers and have benefited many rich and middle-class ones. An analysis of subsidy programs of 13 water utilities in poor cities around the world found that increasing bloc tariffs were highly regressive, benefiting the rich disproportionately more than the poor (Komives et al. 2006). Most of the bloc prices were set below average costs, so virtually all consumers received some subsidy. In La Paz, Bolivia, in the late 1990s, for example, only 1 percent of households consumed enough water in a month to pay tariffs above average cost (ibid., p. 13). Poor consumers receive less subsidy than richer consumers under increasing bloc tariffs because they are often higher volume users; they share connections, have larger households, and sell water to unconnected neighbors (Munasinghe 1992). Moreover, bloc tariffs require meters, and poor households are less likely to be metered in cities where utilities charge customers for meters; instead they pay a higher flat rate. This is a drawback to not metering that economists failed to recognize and it is not the only one, as I discuss below.

Subsidies based on need target the poor more effectively than increasing bloc tariffs, but they are not the sure-fire solution that economists predicted either. Such means-tested subsidies provide no benefit to unconnected households. For example, Paraguay's means-tested subsidy excluded 93 percent of the urban poor (Komives et al. 2006, p. 16). Poor consumers who are connected to piped water are also sometimes excluded from the subsidy by overzealous administrators trying to avoid subsidizing the non-poor (ibid.).

Most subsidies never reach the poorest residents because they live in slums where there is no water or sewerage network. Newer slums are often outside the utility's service area, while utilities are typically prohibited from providing service to illegal squatter settlements even if they are inside the network. Those poor who do have legal and physical access to the network often cannot afford the cost of a connection or the household fixtures required (ibid., p. 12). Providing free water from public standpipes in slums is a simple way to target subsidies and include poor households without connections. In Bangalore, India, for example, the poor were four times more likely to use public taps than the non-poor (ibid., p. 17). But stand-pipes can only assist those consumers who are near enough to benefit – only 44 percent of the poor in Bangalore. The poor in peripheral slums and illegal settlements where the utility has no network are too far from public standpipes to use them. Public standpipes also have high opportunity costs for the poor because waiting times can be very long, robbing them of time for working, child-rearing, or schooling. For example, consumers in Lima wait an average of one hour and must make as many as seven trips a day during the dry season when cut-offs are common (Webb and Associates 1992). Standpipe water has another drawback; it is associated with higher incidence of diseases than piped water. Standpipe water can be contam-inated during transport or storage, and families are less willing to use such costly water for hygiene, a problem with water from water vendors as well. As a consequence, the availability of water from public standpipes does not reduce the prevalence of diarrhea among young children (Esrey 1996).

Metering

In purely economic terms, it does not make sense to meter systems with enough low-cost raw water to meet foreseeable future demand, as long as disposal of waste water is not a problem. London provides a prime example of a large, modern city with ample water that functions with almost no res-idential water meters. Economists' advice, however, ignored important, non-economic consequences. Without meters the poor cannot benefit from subsidies for low volume consumption and cannot reduce their water bills by curbing consumption. Economists could argue that they were justified in ignoring the consequences of metering for the poor, since they also rec-ommended direct, targeted subsidies, not subsidies based on consumption volumes. But was it realistic to assume that poor countries with little bureaucratic capacity would be able to introduce means-tested subsidies?

Economists' advice against metering also overlooked the political conse-quences. After reform many consumers confronted private, often foreign, management of their water company, and were rightly suspicious of their government's ability and incentive to control the water utility's monopoly powers. They also confronted higher water bills where reforms led to more comprehensive billing, better collection of bills, cut-offs of customers who failed to pay, and price increases. Without meters consumers had no information to challenge their bill and no way to reduce their bill by using less water. It seems plausible that metering could have helped increase consumer acceptance of water reform; the comparison between Chile and Argentina below is suggestive, but more work is needed.[6] Finally, economists' advice against metering may have also underestimated the environmental benefits from encouraging conservation of water; many poor cities have inadequate systems for collection, treatment, and disposal of waste water.

Operation

Most reformers introduced private operation under various guises – management contracts, leases, concessions, and, more rarely, outright sales to private investors. By 2004, 80 percent of developed countries and 35 percent of underdeveloped countries had some form of private participation in water and sanitation (out of 147 in total, Estache and Goicoehea 2005).[7] This may seem like a surge of private participation, but in fact private operation of water and sanitation has lagged behind other infrastructure. From 1990 to 2004 private investment in water and sanitation amounted to $41 billion, which is only 5 percent of total private investment in infrastructure in underdeveloped countries (Izaguirre and Hunt 2005).

Private operation is controversial. Many popular books and articles oppose water system privatization, and aid agencies that were proponents have become agnostics or opponents. The Millennium Development Report on water states that:

> The decline in private sector investment in water supply and sanitation for underdeveloped countries has taken place against the backdrop of an ongoing and heated debate about the appropriate roles for the private sector in this area – a debate that has been polarized around conflicting ideological positions and has led to major conflicts, especially around large-scale projects involving multinational companies. (UN Millennium Project 2005a, p. 73)

There have been several highly publicized reversals of water system privatizations. Although from 1990 to 2004 only 20 privatizations were cancelled or "became distressed," these included some of the largest, amounting to 37 percent of private investment in the sector (Izaguirre and Hunt 2005). Private investors have become wary of water and sanitation projects, and private investment has fallen from its peak in the 1990s.

Are the criticisms of water and sanitation privatization justified by the outcomes?

WHAT ARE THE OUTCOMES OF WATER REFORMS?

Based on what we know now, it is impossible to generalize about the outcomes of reform of urban water systems. There are few published studies with comparative statistics and their findings are ambiguous. Some studies find no difference. For example, using a stochastic cost frontier to analyze 28 state-owned and 22 private water companies in 19 Asian and Pacific region countries, Estache and Rossi (2002) found no statistically significant difference in cost efficiency. Higher costs were associated with better water quality and more metering, as well as with higher salaries and more inputs, so it is not clear what these findings imply, except, as the authors note, the need for better cost data (ibid.). Kirkpatrick et al. (2006) also reported no significant difference in performance in Africa. This study used data envelopment analysis and stochastic cost frontier to compare about 100 state-owned utilities with only nine private utilities and had other serious data limitations. Besides these published studies, a working paper (Clarke et al. 2004) compared privately managed and publicly managed water utilities in 18 cities in three Latin American countries and found no significant difference in the rates of expansion in connections.

Other studies have found positive benefits from private management. Galiani et al. (2005) compared Argentine cities with private and publicly operated water systems and found faster declines in child mortality rates in cities with private systems, especially in poorer areas. A comparison of private and public utilities in Chile determined that private firms invested more and kept prices lower, although rates of unaccounted-for water were higher (Bitran and Valenzeula 2003, cited in Clarke et al. 2004). A recent unpublished study (Gassner et al. 2006) compared a larger sample (973 water and sanitation utilities in 49 countries) over a longer time period (1992 to 2004), using a wider set of descriptive variables and controls. Using a variety of statistical techniques, Gassner et al. found that private sector participation had largely positive effects, including improvements in service quality, connection rates, and labor productivity, but was also associated with declines in employment, increases in price, and increases in operating expenses.

Most case studies also report positive outcomes from private operation. One comparison of cases found substantial welfare gains in three privately managed systems compared to a counterfactual based on how the same systems would have performed under continued public management

(Shirley 2002). A review of 34 studies of 22 municipal cases also determined that performance improved with private sector participation (Clarke et al. 2004). Connections increased, often substantially, in 17 of the 22 cases (ibid., Table A2). Real water prices went down in six of the cases, up in seven, stayed the same in three and increased for some customers while decreasing for others in one case (the trend in prices for the other five cases was unknown). Many case studies have defects, however; they fail to construct a counterfactual or to compare the improvement in the treatment case with a control case. It could be that performance improved equally well in the control group, as Clarke et al. (2004) found for access.

Studies of water produce these ambiguous results partly because water systems are hard to analyze with cross-country econometrics. For one thing, there are good reasons to expect that the decision to invite private sector participation in the first place is endogenous to the performance of the state-owned water and sanitation company. In other sectors governments often choose to privatize their best performing state-owned companies to raise cash, but since water system assets are seldom sold this incentive is largely absent. Instead, politicians are more likely to privatize badly performing water systems that need large cash infusions or politically difficult price hikes and lay-offs. Head-to-head comparisons that do not control for endogeneity may find that privatized systems perform the same as state-owned systems not because they are equally well managed, but because the pre-privatization utility underinvested in maintenance or expansion. Or privatized utilities may increase prices more to reach cost recovery than state-owned utilities not because they are gouging the public, but because pre-privatization prices were further below operating costs.

Local details can also invalidate econometric studies of privatization. Localities with scarce or contaminated raw water are inherently more costly than systems with abundant clean water. Water systems will also be more costly if they serve sparsely populated or far-flung service areas. Differences in raw water and service areas translate into different extraction costs, treatment costs, delivery costs, maintenance costs, and billing and collection costs, as well as different rates of sustainable use. I can illustrate this by comparing two cities, Lima, Peru, and Santiago, Chile (based on Shirley and Ménard 2002). Lima, located on the coast of Peru, has an arid climate, receiving less than 15 mm of rainfall a year. Lima depends on 53 rivers for two-thirds of its water, but 25 of them dry up entirely during the dry season, and its main water source, the Rimac River, is polluted by heavy metals when it flows through a mining region, then contaminated by Lima's raw sewage. The remaining third of Lima's water comes from wells sunk ever deeper into the city's shriveling aquifer. Many wells near the coast have had to be abandoned because they became contaminated by salt water; the aquifer itself is increasingly contaminated by the ocean as the water table falls. Only 75 percent of Lima's population is connected to the piped water system, and during the dry season almost half of these connections receive water for less than 12 hours a day. Now consider Santiago. Snowmelt from the Andes provides Santiago with an ample supply of relatively clean water. The snowmelt flows downhill into Santiago's main river, the Maipo, where part of it is diverted through a gravity-fed system of pipes into the treatment plant. During the relatively rare droughts Santiago can also draw on a large natural reservoir and deep wells. A head-to-head comparison of Lima with Santiago would find costs much higher in Lima for geographical and hydrological reasons alone. For example, in the 1990s Lima's intermediate costs per cubic meter of water production in constant dollars were twice as high as Santiago's (Shirley 2002, p. 356, Table A.14).

Knowledge of local details is required not just to identify exogenous costs, but also to determine whether outcomes are economically efficient. Higher operating costs sometimes result from quality improvements, as Estache and Rossi (2002) found in Asia, and lay-offs could be related to productivity gains as Gassner et al. (2006) found worldwide. Local details are needed even with panel data. Trends in costs and returns are affected by droughts, increases in pollution or turbidity of raw water following, for example, the opening of a mine, an earthquake, changes in population size or density, or changes in the boundary of the utility's service area. Econometric studies ignore these local changes at their peril. For instance, the number of connections can increase without an actual increase in coverage if the utility's service area expands to include areas that are already connected, as happened in Queenstown, South Africa, or if existing but unbilled connections are now billed, as happened in Mexico City (Clarke et al. 2004, Table A2). Conversely, the utility may be investing heavily yet coverage will stay the same if the population of a city is growing rapidly and coverage is already high, as happened in Santiago, Chile. From 1987 to 1997 coverage in Santiago was 100 percent of the population in the service area (Shirley et al. 2002). It would be wrong to conclude that the trend in connections was stagnant, however. Santiago's population increased, shared housing was replaced by more individual units, and several peripheral towns were incorporated into the service area. As a result, Santiago's water utility had to build over 300,000 new connections to maintain 100 percent coverage.

Local details also matter for pricing, which is a third hornets' nest for scholars. Typically much of the water system in underdeveloped countries is unmetered, and the average water price is estimated by dividing the utility's total sales revenue by its sales volume. Sales volume is calculated by subtracting an estimate of unaccounted-for water from the amount of water pumped into the pipes by the treatment plant. This price could go up because (i) water tariffs increased, (ii) production volumes declined, (iii) unaccounted-for water increased, or (iv) better billing and collection increased water revenues. Thus, average prices could increase in cases (ii)–(iv) without any bill-paying customers paying a higher price for water.

Knowledge of local circumstances is also required to determine whether a price increase was economically efficient or inefficient, socially beneficial or harmful. Was a price increase necessary to cover the costs of operating and maintaining the system, to provide a return on capital to finance future expansion, or to encourage conservation? Or should prices have gone down because costs were inflated by inefficient operation of the system? Did a price increase make water or sanitation unaffordable for some consumers? These are the sorts of questions that are answered in careful case studies but not in most cross-country or cross-city studies.

None of this discussion should be taken to mean that comparative statistical studies are useless. To the contrary, well designed cross-city or cross-country statistical analyses are badly needed. An excellent example is Galiani et al. (2005), which found that municipal water privatizations in Argentina reduced child mortality from water-borne diseases. The dependent variable in this study – child mortality – is less affected by local, non-ownership influences than the cost or productivity measures used in other comparative studies. The authors allow for heterogeneity across municipalities and control for endogeneity. The authors pair municipalities that privatized their water systems with municipalities with similar attributes that did not, and they use panel data to control for trends in child mortality independent of water system privatization. They analyze why a municipality privatized its water system to rule out reverse causality, and they check that privatization's effect on child mortality is from a reduction in water-borne diseases and not correlated with deaths from causes unrelated to water supply, such as accidents. Unfortunately such careful studies are rare in water.

In sum, the number of comparative studies on water and sanitation reform is few, the data used are sometimes misleading or flawed, and the findings are ambiguous. Although the studies cited above are careful to point out their data problems, these caveats tend to be ignored in survey papers and by proponents of particular points of view. There are strong popular beliefs about water that I discuss below, and the lack of good comparative studies has contributed to the ill-informed nature of the debate over private participation, water pricing, and water and sanitation reform in general. Water and sanitation is a sector where more informed analysis is much needed.

AN INSTITUTIONAL FRAMEWORK FOR STUDYING WATER SYSTEM REFORM

In previous chapters I argued that economic advice may be sound in principle, but will not be implemented unless it can overcome obstacles arising from beliefs, norms, and rules. To illustrate this in water and sanitation reform I first develop a framework to study obstacles on the demand and supply side of reform. Later I will apply this framework to the cases of Buenos Aires and Santiago.

Demand for Reform: Beliefs and Institutions

People hold strong beliefs about water. Since water is essential and in many forms free, some believe that all water should be provided free or at very low prices. They object to the idea that piped water is a private good or that it might be provided by private, for-profit firms. These beliefs persist even though most uses of water are not essential – washing cars, watering flowers – and much water is wasted though evaporation of irrigation water, leaks in pipes, or losses because of improperly closed taps and malfunctioning toilets. These beliefs persist despite the dismal failures of state provision in most poor countries, the waste encouraged by under-pricing, and the harm that low-cost water does to the unconnected poor.[8] The following quotes are representative of the more moderate and more extreme beliefs:

> In our view water privatization represents a troubling shift away from the conception of water as a good requiring common social management, and towards the conception of water and water management services as commodities that individuals can purchase as they can afford. Water is essential for life . . . The nature of water as a scarce, essential, monopolistic resource makes it particularly important that the government guarantee access to it. Privatization of public resources, such as water, may diminish the ability of governments to ensure that the needs of all their citizens are met, because governments are no longer directly in charge of their services. (Mulreamy et al. 2006, p. 30)
>   The moral call for us is not to privatize water. Water should be free for all. (Cassandra Carmichael, director of eco-justice programs for the National Council of Churches in the US quoted in Chu 2006)

Such beliefs are in stark contrast with economic arguments. Economists argue that, regardless of ownership, when consumers pay for a scarce and essential good they will make better use of it and demand better service. Most economists agree that the choice of public versus private provision of piped water should be driven by an empirical examination of costs and benefits, risks and rewards, rather than based on the assumption that either government or private actors will provide better service selflessly and inevitably.

It seems plausible that beliefs have had an important effect on urban water reform. Beliefs may partly explain why so few countries have implemented cost-recovery pricing or privatized ownership of their urban water systems. A survey of 136 water systems with private sector participation found that only 10 percent were outright divestitures, 66 percent were concessions, 19 percent were management contracts, and the rest were leases or affirmages (Gassner et al. 2006, p. 83).

Beliefs about how water should be priced or managed persist despite a history of poor performance. Cities such as Lima, Mexico City, and many African capitals have tolerated poor and deteriorating service for decades. When beliefs about water change it is usually in the context of a broader crisis that shakes elites' faith in the usefulness of the dominant belief system in general; something I describe in Chapter 7. The public too is more ready to accept water and sanitation system reform as part of a broader program of change. And water system reform seems more likely to endure when it is supported by a cohesive set of alternative ideas, a new paradigm that explains the rationale for changing many economic institutions, not just those governing the urban water system (see, for example, the cases in Shirley 2002). Sustained acceptance also depends on the performance of a broad set of institutions that determine how power and income are shared. Consumers reject even welfare-enhancing reforms when they feel they are part of an ultimatum game where benefits are distributed unfairly (Shirley 2005b).

Besides beliefs, demand for reform is reflected by interests and influence. Those connected and those neglected by the water system are not a single set of actors with similar beliefs and interests but many different groups often with differing beliefs and conflicting interests. An interest group's influence over reform depends partly on how effectively its members overcome their collective action problems (Olson 1965). Residents who are not connected to the water and sanitation system often face larger collective action problems than connected households; they tend to be poor, recent migrants with fewer ties to their current community. They may be fearful of confronting the political authorities over water supply if they occupy homes without title, live in illegal or peripheral settlements, or work in the informal sector. Besides collective action problems, poor, unconnected residents may live in dictatorships where their interests are ignored, or in clientelist democracies where there are few political candidates who represent their views (Keefer 2002). They also have less influence because they are less able to pay bribes or make campaign contributions.

Saliency also varies between interest groups. Notwithstanding the emotional rhetoric, access to piped water is not always the most salient issue for unconnected households. Surveys have shown that the poor sometimes place a higher value on connecting to the electrical grid than to the water system (Hanemann 2006, p. 80). Poor people have found ways, however undesirable, of providing for their basic water and sanitation needs. For example, as much as one-fourth of Lima's population has coped without direct access to piped water and one-third without connection to the sewerage system for decades (Alcázar et al. 2002b). Unconnected residents may not want piped water if they have to pay large connection charges and invest in costly household pipes and appliances. Even where their current water source is making them sick, they may still be unconvinced that piped water is superior. They may not know that their water is the cause of their illnesses since it is often impossible to determine by taste or smell whether drinking water is contaminated by micro-organisms or heavy metals. And consumers will not see health improvements from safer drinking water if their hygiene and sanitation have not improved (Esrey 1996). Even residents who gain access to safer water and better sanitation and who practice better hygiene will still become sick if their foodstuffs are contaminated by untreated sewage in irrigation waters or if they swim or fish in contaminated waters.[9] For all these reasons unconnected residents may undervalue connections to piped water and improved sewerage, and connected users may misjudge the water utility's performance in improving water quality.

No single interest group determines the political feasibility of reform; it depends on the alignment of all concerned interests. Fortunately for poor and powerless residents without connections, they are not the only groups who lobby for expanded access. Residents concerned about their health want improved water and sanitation to reduce the risk of contagious diseases such as cholera; construction companies want to bid on contracts to expand the system or to build new buildings; property owners want new construction that raises the value of their property; developers and realtors want to profit from growth in the city's building stock; and local government leaders want the votes, campaign contributions, bribes, or patronage opportunities that accompany lucrative contracts for construction of water lines, dams, and reservoirs. Foreign aid agencies and NGOs are also a powerful lobby for reform, providing money and advice to extend water and sanitation to the poor. Opposing these groups are residents who are already connected to the piped water system and fear their prices will increase to cover the cost of expansion; environmentalists, conservationists, and downstream users who want to limit development and curb pollution; and neighboring farmers who want to prevent urban encroachment on their access to water at low prices. Different local combinations of these competing interests exercise their influence through the different electoral, political party, and legislative rules and norms that determine which political actors set the agenda for change, who can veto changes, who are the powerful constituents, what are politicians' time horizons in office, and who has standing in committees or agency meetings; that is, how much sway different interest groups have over policymakers.

Jurisdictional disputes can also affect which interest groups have influence. Even though water and sanitation are supplied and used locally, municipal and state or provincial governments have little influence over major decisions in some countries. For example, the concession contract in Buenos Aires, Argentina, and the lease in Conakry, Guinea, were largely negotiated with their federal governments. Aid agencies and international NGOs typically exercise their influence at the national level, but national leaders will be less responsive to local interest group politics if their constituency is largely rural, upper class, or military, or if national politicians are at odds with the leaders of municipal and state jurisdictions. Under such circumstances, national leaders may ignore local opposition to change, or not care enough about local support to fight for reform.

So far this discussion has focused on the choice to reform; another big issue is whether reform is sustained. The design of reform has an important effect on sustainability since it determines how conflicting political interests are mediated by, for example, allocating costs and benefits across interest groups. Sustainability also depends on the extent to which the regulatory body is subject to capture by any one group or is swayed by short-term political pressures. As we will see in the case of Buenos Aires, customers' perceptions of the regulator's independence and effectiveness strongly influenced their acceptance of reform.

Supply of Reform: Investors and Government Credibility

Investors are always wary of the power of the state to expropriate them outright, tax away their returns, or impose high transaction costs through regulation. Such concerns are especially salient in a highly capital-intensive sector like water and sanitation, with its large fixed costs in assets with long useful lives and low returns. Water systems have a high ratio of fixed to variable costs so marginal costs are often below average costs, resulting in prices that allow only a small return on capital over long periods (see Noll 2002). Private investors will only sink capital into a regulated monopoly with such low returns if government can credibly commit not to expropriate or otherwise confiscate or dissipate their returns over the long payback period. Low credibility is sometimes the real reason behind expropriations such as the takeovers of private waterworks by municipal governments in the US from 1897 to 1915 (Troesken and Geddes 2003). Waterworks were taken over in those municipalities that "were unable to credibly precommit to not expropriating value from private water companies once investments were made resulting in a rational reduction in investment in water provision by private companies. Local governments, in turn, used this rational under-investment as a pretext for municipalizing private water companies" (ibid., p. 373).

Government credibility is consequential even if the utility is not priva-tized. A large literature on state-owned enterprises suggests that SOE man-agers' incentives only change if government's commitment to improved performance is credible (Shirley 1999; Shirley and Nellis 1991; Shirley and Xu 1998, 2001; World Bank 1995).

The credibility hurdle in water and sanitation is not likely to be reduced any time soon. One reason the hurdle is so high is that returns are lower and riskier than for other infrastructure. Guasch (2006) calculates the internal rate of return (IRR) including management fees for investments from 1990 to 2002 in a sample of Latin American water and sanitation concessions and sales. He estimates the IRR was only 11 percent, below the 15.5 percent estimated cost of equity at the time of the transaction, and below other infrastructure investments (see Table 6.1).

Returns in urban water and sanitation are also low because there has been little technological progress or organizational experimentation in urban water systems, unlike other infrastructure sectors where large returns have come from innovations like mobile telephony or wholesale electricity

Table 6.1   Profitability and cost of equity in privatized and concessioned firms in Latin America and the Caribbean, 1990–2002 (%)

Sector	IRR (inc. management fees)[a]	Cost of equity at time of transact.[a]
Water & sanitation	11.0	15.5
Transport	11.5	13.5
Energy	14.5	14.0
Telecommunications	21.0	14.0

Note: a. The internal rate of return (IRR) is the return earned by investors from flows of dividends minus flows of capital injections into the infrastructure over the life of the project. The cost of equity is based on a CAPEX (capital:equity) pricing model which takes the long-term return on US Treasuries, adds a general market risk premium, a market risk premium for non-diversifiable investments in that industry, a country risk premium, and a sector and regulatory risk premium (Guasch 2004).

Source: Sirtaine et al. (2005), reproduced with permission.

markets (See Ménard 2006). The main new development in water is desalination, the average cost of which has fallen about 90 percent over the last 40 years. But the cost is still too high for desalination to be widely adopted, and in any case desalination is relevant only for urban areas that have access to the ocean or other bodies of saline water.[10]

Besides credibility hurdles, water systems have information problems that create further risks for investors. Investors cannot cheaply see how well underground pipes have been maintained or even where the entire network is located. They are buying into utilities in underdeveloped countries that often have little or no reliable data on their customer base, their costs, or their resource.

Lower returns and arguably larger information gaps help explain why water and sanitation concessions are more frequently renegotiated than contracts in other infrastructure sectors. Almost 75 percent of a sample of water system concessions in Latin America were renegotiated between 1985 and 2000 compared to only 10 percent of electricity concessions and 55 percent of transportation concessions (Guasch 2004, p. 13, Table 1.7). On average, water system concessions were renegotiated only 1.6 years after signing (ibid., p. 14, Table 1.8), and usually at the instigation of the private investor.[11] Guasch argues that water and sanitation concessions are renegotiated more often than other infrastructure agreements because the sector is less profitable. He also suggests that investors may be acting opportunistically, making generous offers to win the bid in the expectation of future renegotiations, although he offers no direct evidence of opportunism. The low IRRs of water and sanitation concessions in Table 6.1 include earning after renegotiations, suggesting that if investors were acting opportunistically they were not particularly successful in recouping their investment.

Credible commitment is demanding, especially for the governments of poorer countries (see Levy and Spiller 1994; Troesken and Geddes 2003; Weingast 1993). Commitments are more credible when: (i) government officials have reason to care about the state's reputation because, for example, government depends on private investors to finance its deficit; (ii) reneging would be politically difficult because, for example, government made campaign promises to expand water coverage; and (iii) laws or norms make it hard for the government to change contracts without due process because, for example, rules and traditions impede agreements to renege or an independent judiciary would revoke such agreements.

I summarize the conceptual framework described above in Table 6.2. In the rest of this chapter I illustrate how institutions affect reform by comparing the water system reforms in Buenos Aires, Argentina, and Santiago, Chile, using this conceptual framework.

Table 6.2   Institutions affecting demand and supply of reform

---

Demand
Beliefs
- Shift in wider economic paradigm
  - Crisis
  - Alternative
  - Articulated program
Interests favoring and opposing reform
- Characteristics of conflicting interest groups
  - Ability to overcome collective action problems
  - Saliency of issue
  - Ability to mobilize
    - Votes
    - Money
- Political institutions mediating influence of interest groups
  - Electoral rules
  - Political party rules
  - Legislative rules
  - Jurisdictional rules
  - Norms vis-à-vis corruption, accountability
- Sector institutions mediating influence, attitudes interest groups
  - Contract
  - Tariff
  - Regulation

Supply
- Reputational concerns
- Costly signals
- Laws, norms making it difficult to renege
- Independent judiciary & right of appeal

INSTITUTIONS AT WORK: WATER AND SANITATION REFORM IN BUENOS AIRES AND SANTIAGO

The experience with water and sanitation reform in Buenos Aires and Santiago illustrates how a host of specific institutions influence the outcome of reform and explains why economists' advice may be irrelevant or even harmful. Their experience further shows how misleading it is to attribute differences in reform outcomes to gross differences in institutions, such as state versus private ownership, dictatorial versus democratic government, corrupt versus honest bureaucracy, or well regulated versus unregulated monopoly. Buenos Aires and Santiago tell a different story: outcomes are determined by interlocking networks of economic and political institutions that are numerous, subtle and complex. These networks of institutions are not exogenous; they are themselves the outcome of a long history of jockeying between elites groups tied to non-elites through patronage. In this section I first summarize the two reforms and then analyze the institutions that determined demand for reform and supply of investment.

Buenos Aires' and Santiago's water and sanitation systems make good comparators because they share important similarities. Both rely on abundant and low-cost river water for 90 percent of their supply, and both serve the capital city of a middle-income country. At the time of reform, both cities were expanding populations at similar rates: 1.5 percent a year in Buenos Aires and 1.8 percent in Santiago. There were also some similarities in their economic and political trends: both countries had experienced recent bouts of hyperinflation and economic crises that had increased readiness for reform. Reform conditions were thus relatively favorable in both cases; they faced fewer income, hydrological, or political hurdles than many other poor countries. As I discuss later, the designs of reforms also had important similarities.

There were also important differences between the two, however. Argentina was wealthier. When reform of the Buenos Aires water system began in 1993, GDP per capita in purchasing power parity terms was $10,384 in Argentina, compared to $4,648 in Chile when reform of Santiago's water system began in 1988 (World Bank various). The Buenos Aires water system was also larger. At the time of reform, the population in its service area was 8.6 million (1993), almost double Santiago's 4.4 million (1988), and it had 2.3 million connections while Santiago had only about 800,000. Despite its wealth and size coverage in Buenos Aires was less. Its water system reached only 70 percent of its residents and the sewerage system reached only 58 percent, while coverage of Santiago's system was about 98 percent for water and 90 percent for sewerage. Coverage was not the only problem in Buenos Aires; its system was generally more poorly run than Santiago's, with higher rates of leakages and water losses, less efficient billing and collection, and a higher rate of overstaffing. Politically, things were also different. After a long period of democracy Chile was ruled by a brutal military dictatorship when water and sanitation reform began in 1988, although democracy was restored a year later. Argentina had ended military rule and restored democracy ten years before the water reform.

Nature of the Two Reforms

The two reforms had some important similarities. For one thing they were both designed to encourage private operation under an independent regulator. Both also relied on economist and scholarly research to design their economic reforms. The main components of Santiago's reform were:

1. Changing the autonomous water agency into a state-owned enterprise, EMOS (Empresa Metropolitana de Obras Sanitarias) as a prelude to the sale of assets.
2. Creating an independent regulator with the power to set tariffs and enforce standards.
3. Setting tariffs to assure a 7 percent return on assets to an efficiently operated company.
4. Replacing cross-subsidies with means-tested subsidies.

The Buenos Aires water system reform consisted of:

1. Signing a 30-year concession with a private consortium and creating a new water company, Aguas Argentinas.
2. Creating an independent regulator with the power to set tariffs and enforce standards.
3. Setting tariffs based on a initial reduction followed by periodic cost-based increases.

Although Chile's reform was designed with the intention of privatizing EMOS, the actual sale of assets to Lyonnaise des Eaux-Dumez (now Suez) was delayed until 1999. Three groups bid on the Buenos Aires' concession and at the end of 1992 it was awarded to the group led by Lyonnaise des Eaux-Dumez who had offered the largest decrease in water tariffs, 26.9 percent. The contract required the winner, over the course of the next 30 years, to connect all of the population to water and 90 percent to sewerage; to treat 93 percent of all sewage; to renovate 45 percent of the water network; and to reduce unaccounted-for water to 25 percent of water production.

Both water system reforms were part of much larger programs of changes. Menem's administration implemented one of the largest privatization programs in the world: Argentina's government signed 154 privatization contracts in the 1990s (Galiani et al. 2005). Chile was a pioneer in privatization, shrinking state ownership from about 40 percent of GDP at the time of the coup in 1973 to 24 percent by 1983 and 13 percent by 1989 (Corbo et al. 2005, p. 17). The Pinochet government also privatized Chile's social security system, reduced the size of government, deregulated, decentralized, and liberalized trade dramatically, slashing tariffs to 10 percent across the board.

Results of the Reforms

Both reforms produced substantial benefits in their first five years as we can see in Table 6.3. Sustainability of the reforms was very different, however. Private operation of Buenos Aires' water and sanitation system did not endure; the concession did not survive a wrenching change in economic circumstances. At the time of the concession the Argentine peso was fixed at parity to the dollar; banks could offer dollar accounts and loans, and dollars were freely circulating. For reasons I discuss below, parity with the dollar became unsustainable, and the Argentine peso was devalued drastically in 2002. Aguas Argentinas and the government disagreed about whether the terms of the concession still applied and the government froze the company's prices. Efforts to negotiate a compromise failed and prices stayed frozen, culminating in the cancellation of the concession in 2006.[12] There is no way of knowing whether the concession might have survived had such a drastic change in circumstances not occurred. It is plausible that the seeds of reversal were sown in the initial design of the reform, which produced good economic outcomes for many consumers but conformed poorly to the institutional and political circumstances in Argentina, producing regulatory conflicts and feeding into a deep-seated sense of injustice among lower income groups (see Shirley 2005b). What is clear is that the circumstances that led to the devaluation and the contract cancellation are rooted in Argentina's institutions.

In contrast Santiago's water and sanitation reforms were sustained and expanded despite dramatic political changes. The water system legislation in Santiago was designed by the Pinochet dictatorship to provide a credible framework for a private system. The military government lost the 1988 plebiscite on the continuation of its rule after the water system reforms were enacted into law but before they were implemented. Democracy was restored and when the military's preferred candidate lost the election in December 1989 his opponent was allowed to assume power. Although the privatization of EMOS was put on hold by the newly elected government of President Patricio Alywin, the radical pricing reform and other major changes were implemented as planned and EMOS was sold to a private consortium nine years later. Performance of the water system continued strong, sewage treatment was expanded, and there are no signs that reforms will be reversed.

To understand why reform was sustained in one country and not in another, we need to understand their institutions. This is the subject of the rest of this chapter.

Table 6.3   Performance of the Santiago and Buenos Aires water and sewerage systems, first five years

Reform	Santiago	Buenos Aires
Water prices	Increased to cost-recovery levels & were 60% above pre-reform levels in real terms by 1993.	Declined by 26.9% in Dec. 1992 were 14% above pre-reform levels in real terms by 1997.
Access	To water by 724,000 (100% connected); to sewerage by about 964,000	To water by 1.5 million people (from 70% to 83% connected); to sewerage by 583,000 people.
Welfare[a]	By 284 million NPV in 1996 US $. 1% of gains to consumers, 85% to government.	By $1.4 billion NPV in 1996 US $. 80% of welfare gains went to consumers.
Worker welfare[a]	Higher wages; welfare went up by about $21,000 per employee NPV in 1996 $. Downsizing had occurred earlier in 1970s.	Workers received shares; welfare went up by an estimated $10,000 per employee NPV in 1996 $. No involuntary lay-offs. Voluntary severance with one year's pay.
Productivity[b]	Workers per thousand connections dropped from 2.15 to 2.02. UFW dropped from 34% to 29% of production.	Workers per thousand connections dropped from 3.4 to 1.7. UFW dropped from 44% to 34% of production.
Service	Response times and water pressure remained excellent.	Response time to water complaints dropped from 144 hours to 48 hours (by 1995); customers with acceptable levels of water pressure went from 17% to 54% (by 1996).

Notes:
a.   All welfare numbers calculated by comparing the net present value of gains from post-reform trends to pre-reform trends projected over a ten-year period. NPV = net present value.
b.   UFW = unaccounted-for water.

Sources: Author's calculations based on Alcázar et al. (2002), Shirley et al. (2002), and Shirley (2002, statistical appendix).

Demand for Reform

Paradigm shifts

In both cases, acute economic crises and dramatic political shifts challenged beliefs in the status quo and encouraged the elites and the general public to replace dysfunctional economic institutions based on import substitution with putatively better ones based on markets and free trade. These crises had their roots in the countries' political histories. The state and the economy in both Argentina and Chile had long been dominated by a few elite coalitions that alternated in power. With increasing urbanization and industrialization, new groups arose: business elites, the urban middle class, and unionized labor. When these new groups sought access to power politics became increasingly polarized.

First consider Argentina. Prior to the rise of Juan Perón in the 1940s, Argentina's economy and politics were dominated by large landholders. After a military coup, Perón amassed power by co-opting unionized industrial workers, organizing them into state sanctioned labor unions, and jailing union leaders who resisted. Union leaders became a new elite and the Peronist Party sought special privileges and benefits for union members, disregarding the rest of the labor force. For the next five decades the Peronists alternated in power with the military and with parties representing the traditional agrarian interests and the growing urban middle class.[13] Argentine politics was based on clientelism: when one party was in power it used the government to benefit its supporters, expanding the size of the state, running fiscal deficits, and reversing the actions of its predecessors. The military intervened periodically in response to what it perceived as political paralysis and radicalization; there were five military coups from 1930 until the restoration of democracy in 1983. Argentina's polarized and unstable politics contributed to rising inflation and economic decline. Shrinking real income exacerbated the divisions between the urban working classes, the agrarian elite, and the urban middle class, as well as the regional split between industrialized Buenos Aires and the agrarian hinterlands (Hill and Abdala 1996, p. 207).

Polarization and instability persisted because Argentina's political rules discouraged cross-cutting coalitions that might have made structural reforms possible. Its federalist structure and decentralized political rules elevated parochial interests over national ones, contributing to frequent paralysis on important issues (Haslam 2003). For example, until constitutional reforms in the 1990s, senators were elected by the provincial legislators. Congressional political careers were largely controlled by provincial party leaders who determined whether federal legislators were re-nominated and, by controlling candidates' positions on the ballot, controlled their chances of being re-elected. To avoid challenges to their power, party bosses would not re-nominate most incumbents or placed them low on the ballot, leading to relatively short congressional careers (Jones et al. 2000). This predominance of provincial over national political power created legislative deadlock whenever Congress was controlled by a different party from the president. Even when both branches were controlled by the same party, the executive had to cut special deals with the provincial governors to get programs enacted.

This situation changed in the late 1980s when crisis hit; hyperinflation reached 3000 percent a year and GDP fell by 1.3 percent. The economic crisis plus rising fears of another military intervention led moderates in the Peronist (now Justicialist) Party and the opposition Radical Party to compromise. After Carlos Menem won the 1989 presidential election with 47 percent of the votes, the congressional moderates passed laws that allowed him to take office five months ahead of schedule and gave him sweeping powers to implement policy by executive decree. Menem used these powers extensively: he issued 308 decrees in his first three years in office compared to only ten decrees during his predecessor's entire four-year term (de Michele and Manzetti 1996). To the surprise of the electorate, Menem abandoned his populist platform that had won the votes of most of the unions and the poor. Instead he used his decree powers to enact free-market reforms, such as privatization and government downsizing, along the lines of a program articulated by his future economic minister Domingo Cavallo (see Chapter 7). This meant that the reforms were not the result of an institutionalized process to produce compromise among competing political interests, but were based on extraordinary politics, including the suspension of legislative checks on the executive, the special powers granted the president, the extensive use of executive decrees, and presidential actions that did not just belie but actually reversed platform promises.

Hyperinflation and a sense of crisis changed many people's beliefs; Argentines were increasingly ready to accept privatization, liberalization, trade and ties with industrialized countries, and other market reforms (O'Neil Trowbridge 2001). For example, public support for privatization increased from about 57 percent in 1985 to over 75 percent in 1990. The Buenos Aires water concession had more tepid support, however. Thirty-six percent of the city's population had positive views of the privatization of the water and sanitation system in 1993 and 33 percent negative; the rest were undecided or neutral (Alcázar et al. 2002a, p. 72, Table 3.3).

Chile's reforms also arose out of a history of political polarization culminating in economic crisis. By the late nineteenth century, Chile had evolved a multi-party system based on three distinct ideological blocs, left representing unionized labor, right representing traditional agrarian interests, and center dominated by the urban middle class (Scully 1995).[14] Chile had a winner-take-all, strong presidential system with a one-term limit for presidents that provided little incentive for coalitions to survive after the elections (Valenzeula 1994).[15] Nevertheless, the parties representing the three ideological blocs had been alternating peacefully in power through most of the early twentieth century thanks to an accommodation whereby the congressional elections focused on horse trading over local issues, while the presidential races raised the more divisive national and ideological issues (Shugart and Carey 1992, see tables 1 and 2 of the Statistical Appendix).

Several changes in Chile's political institutions contributed to increased polarization and led to a crisis in the early 1970s. One was the election in 1953 of a left-leaning populist (Ibánez) who ran against politics and the traditional parties. Ibánez enacted a law prohibiting "corrupt" electoral pacts at the provincial level and requiring national electoral pacts to be promulgated more than 120 days before an election, thus reducing the scope for cross-party bargaining (Scully 1995). Polarization was exacerbated by migration of rural voters to urban centers, eroding the traditional political base of the right and strengthening the centrist Christian Democrats who became strong enough to "go it alone" instead of compromising with coalition partners. The basis for compromise was further eroded by the 1970 constitutional reform that required that no amendments be attached to legislation unless they were germane to the bill itself. By reducing the power of parties to deliver locally targeted spending, this change weakened the ability of party blocs in Congress to extract compromise (Shugart and Carey 1992).[16] The constitutional change also strengthened the presidency, raising the stakes in presidential elections and motivating the parties to focus more on divisive national issues. By 1970, party polarization contributed to a three-way split in the vote that led to the election of Socialist Salvador Allende with 36.6 percent (Scully 1995). The economic crisis that followed set the stage for the 1973 military coup in which President Allende was killed. The coup installed a military dictatorship headed by General Augusto Pinochet, which banned political parties and destroyed electoral registries; Pinochet blamed parties and political opportunism for Chile's social and economic ills (ibid.).

During the dictatorship Chile's dominant paradigm shifted. After several years of drift, the military government embraced the program of the so-called Chicago boys: privatization, trade liberalization, deregulation, less government intervention, decentralization to local governments, and the like (see Chapter 7). Rapid economic growth in the late 1980s and 1990s helps explain why the free-market paradigm of the dictatorship was sustained after democracy was restored. Subsequent democratic administrations treated privatization and trade liberalization pragmatically and simultaneously introduced new social legislation that reduced Chile's highly unequal income distribution.

Interest group politics

These political trends set the stage for reform in water and sanitation, but the detailed design was driven by interest group politics. In Buenos Aires, wealthier residents in the center were connected while poorer residents on the periphery were not. In those poorer districts where as few as 10–13 percent of the households were connected to water and sewerage, about half of all voters supported Menem. In contrast, he got only 37 percent of votes in the capital district, where 99 percent of households were connected (Alcázar et al. 2002a, Table 3.4). Thus those who would benefit from new connections were Menem's core supporters. Water reform was not the most salient issue for many of them, however, since they already had well-water and septic systems. Water politics were further complicated because another Menem constituency, unionized labor, was initially opposed to private operation in Buenos Aires. Eventually they were co-opted through promises of generous severance packages, no involuntary lay-offs, and share ownership for workers who remained employed. In any case, unionized labor had few viable alternatives to supporting Menem; his party had controlled the unions since Juan Perón's presidency.

It is curious that the concession was ultimately awarded to the bidder who offered the largest price reduction since that benefited already-connected customers the most. Why would the Menem government design a reform that rewarded those middle and upper-class customers who had not voted for him? This decision, like many of Menem's reforms, was designed to benefit his core supporters and simultaneously attract – or at least not alienate – new voters. The architects of the Buenos Aires' concession assumed, wrongly as it turned out, that since the state-owned water company had been so inefficient, a private operator could reduce prices and still finance the required expansion. It may also seem curious that Menem would care about future voters since he was constitutionally restricted to one term. But it was symptomatic of Argentina's weak rule of law that Menem began to maneuver to amend the constitution to permit him to run again almost as soon as he was elected (his maneuvers were successful and he was re-elected in 1995).

Interest groups also had an important effect on water and sanitation reform in Santiago, even though reform began under a military dictatorship. Voters in Chile were largely – but not entirely – disenfranchised. The military government held two elections. A plebiscite in 1980 approved its proposal for a new constitution by 70 percent of the vote (Shirley et al.

2002, p. 196). A plebiscite in 1988 voted to end the military government, and the military agreed to restore democracy. Even though the military's preferred candidate was defeated in the subsequent presidential election, the Pinochet dictatorship gave up office. Besides abiding by elections, the regime tolerated dissent on purely economic issues even while it suppressed opposition on all other issues, sometimes violently.

Santiago's interest group politics differed from Buenos Aires'. Most consumers in Santiago were already connected to piped water; only about 100,000 were not, compared to 5.6 million in Buenos Aires. Most unconnected consumers lived in shantytowns outside the utility's service area. In addition some poorer residents also stood to benefit even though they lived in households that had a connection. Santiago had a very high rate of shared housing and expansion would permit construction of additional units and bring down housing costs, allowing more poor people to buy their own homes. This interest group was largely irrelevant to Pinochet's decisions, however, since Santiago's lower classes were among his strongest opponents.[17] The capital had been a bastion of opposition to the military coup and had cast a large percentage of votes against the new constitution in 1980 and against the continuation of the military regime in 1988 (Shirley et al. 2002). Some interests favoring water reform were influential, however, notably developers, contractors, and business owners. This group wanted new construction that would increase their business opportunities, enhance their property values, and stimulate their city's economy. They generally supported the Pinochet government (Mèndez 1990), and eventually helped draft the new legislation governing the water sector (Shirley et al. 2002). As in Buenos Aires, unionized labor in Santiago opposed privatization of water, but legislation enacted under the military dictatorship had greatly weakened union power and the Pinochet government paid little heed to union views in any case.

Once democracy was restored in Chile, the influence of these different interest groups shifted. Developers lost and the unconnected poor gained influence after Patricio Alywin's coalition was elected in 1990 (Shirley et al. 2002, p. 199). Alywin's coalition had pledged to expand housing for poorer residents in its political platform, and planned to fund additional connections by increasing water prices. We might expect that consumers who were already connected would oppose price increases, but opposition was muted partly because poor and lower middle-class customers were shielded by subsidies, as I describe below. With these shifts in influence, privatization was put on hold. Privatization was not part of Alywin's platform, plus EMOS' workers, who opposed privatization, were important constituents (ibid.).

Jurisdictional disputes were not important in the design of either reform since the power of local politicians was minimal in both Buenos Aires and

Santiago. In Buenos Aires the mayor only became directly elected in 1994, after the concession was signed. Argentina's president set the agenda on water and, as I described earlier, he faced few checks on his discretion from the legislature, at least at the beginning of his term. As for Chile, its dictatorial executive branch controlled the design of Santiago's water reform even more tightly than Argentina's democratically elected administration.

Sector institutions and interest group politics

Contracts   Earlier I argued that a utility's contract could help mediate conflicting local interests. Buenos Aires' concession contract did the opposite, inciting conflict by providing disproportionate benefits to one group of consumers, and fueling customers' distrust of the utility. Santiago's contract, in contrast, tempered interest group politics and moderated public fears.

One way the Buenos Aires' concession contract incited conflict was through fixed charges. Political expediency produced a contract that combined price reductions and massive investment, a combination that was financed in part by an "infrastructure charge" covering the cost of extending the secondary network to new neighborhoods. This charge, combined with the usual charge for connecting the secondary network to the house, ranged from $1107 to $1528, as much as 18 percent of the annual income of poorer consumers (Alcázar et al. 2002a, p.85). Aguas Argentinas gave customers up to two years to pay these charges, the minimum time allowed under the concession contract, but the charge was probably unaffordable for the poorest consumers (ibid.). Consumers were especially aggrieved that wealthier residents who had connected under the old state-owned system had not had to pay an infrastructure charge; the cost had been incorporated into the rate base. Politicians representing poorer areas of Buenos Aires mobilized opposition to these connection charges, and even consumers who could afford the charge refused to pay it. Because of these non-payments Aguas Argentinas built up large receivables and pressured the government to renegotiate its contract. The 1997 renegotiation replaced the infrastructure charge with a fee to all users, raising rates for consumers who were already connected to the water system. In the end, even though already-connected consumers had benefited by an initial rate reduction of nearly 27 percent and newly-connected consumers had benefited by being connected, both were disgruntled with the concession.

Although Santiago's utility, EMOS, did not have an explicit contract, the new laws and regulations governing the sector were an implicit contract, one that smoothed interest group divisions as much as Buenos Aires' contract provoked disputes. Unlike the Buenos Aires concession, EMOS' contract did not treat different customers differently. All customers paid a flat monthly charge for the fixed costs of maintaining and operating the system, and the cost of expanding the secondary network was included in their variable, metered charge. New consumers were charged the cost of connecting their house to the network, but those eligible for a water and sewerage subsidy could pay this charge over two to three years, and the very poorest consumers had to pay only 5 to 10 percent of the charge (Alfaro 1996).

Pricing Earlier I argued that the way water prices are set influences how consumers view reform. Pricing in Buenos Aires contributed to public suspicion of the private operator. For one thing, most residential customers in Buenos Aires were not metered and the concession did not change that; by 1998 only 14 percent of connections had meters (Alcázar et al. 2002a). Without meters, customers paid a flat rate and had little information with which to challenge their bill, and no way to reduce it by reducing consumption. Besides lack of meters, the way prices were set in Buenos Aires was complex and obscure. Non-metered residential tariffs were based on five measures: (i) where the property was located, (ii) the area of the property, (iii) the square meters of construction on the property, (iv) the age of any buildings, and (v) the category of buildings, from low budget to luxury (ibid. 2002, p. 78). Aguas Argentinas could change customers' rates by adjusting any of these measures. The utility could also reclassify a customer from residential to non-residential; non-residential customers pay about twice as much as residential. During the first five years of the concession the utility reclassified about 11 percent of customers from residential to non-residential and recalculated the size of built areas for some 425,000 consumers (ibid.). The regulator had little information with which to decide whether to approve these reclassifications, although in one case the regulator arbitrarily disallowed Aguas Argentina's reclassification of 80,000 users from residential to non-residential.

Large cross-subsidies exacerbated interest group conflict. A customer with a newer, more luxurious home could pay up to seven times more for water than a customer on a property of similar size with an older, less luxurious home (Alcázar et al. 2002a, p. 81). Cross-subsidies gave Aguas Argentinas an incentive to connect first those customers who would pay more, and there is evidence that it did so; district-level poverty in Buenos Aires was negatively correlated with coverage (Casarin et al. 2007, p. 238).

Santiago's pricing structure was far less likely to create controversy. The city was entirely metered so poor consumers could keep their bills down by curbing wasteful consumption, and EMOS provided information to customers on how to save money by, for example, promptly repairing leaking faucets or toilets (Shirley et al. 2002). EMOS did little reclassification and since there were no cross-subsidies for water and sanitation services in Santiago, EMOS had the same incentive to serve low-income as high-income consumers. EMOS prices went up but they went up for all customers. Price hikes had less impact on Santiago's poorer consumers because of Chile's targeted subsidy program. The subsidy was paid directly to EMOS and covered up to 60 percent of the water and sewerage bill as long as the beneficiary was up to date on the balance. This gave EMOS a strong incentive to connect subsidy recipients.

The cities also differed in how they determined rate increases. The economists in Buenos Aires and Santiago who designed the contracts tried to approximate price caps, which some theorists argue are more efficient than rate of return or cost-plus pricing (for a discussion of price cap versus other tariff-setting measures see, for example, Armstrong et al. 1994). Usually price caps in water are calculated as RPI+K, the retail price index (RPI) plus a K factor calculated to provide a return on investment to a benchmark efficient firm. The RPI increases are meant to be automatic, while the K is decided infrequently by the regulator.[18] The Buenos Aires system was not really a price cap, however. After the hyperinflation Argentina had changed its constitution to make it illegal to fix prices to an index such as RPI, so the designers of the Buenos Aires concession contract tried to approximate RPI+K by allowing the water utility to petition the regulator for a rate increase whenever a composite cost index rose by more than 7 percent.[19] The 7 percent threshold produced infrequent, lumpy, and obvious price increases, as we can see in Figure 6.1. Because increases had to be instigated by Aguas Argentinas, these often led to controversy with the regulator and bad publicity, especially since the concession had been awarded for the largest tariff reduction. Opposition politicians argued that *any* price increases were a sign that the winning consortium had made its bid in bad faith.

Real water prices in Santiago rose much more steeply than in Buenos Aires over the first five years of the reform (Figure 6.2), yet water prices were far less controversial. Instead of tariffs being raised at EMOS' request, they were set annually by the regulator on the basis of a computer model designed to allow an efficiently operated, benchmark firm to earn a minimum annual return on assets of at least 7 percent. Tariff increases were thus automatic, quite unlike the messy process of negotiation and renegotiation that caused such controversy in Buenos Aires. Average prices collected in Santiago went up steadily during the period and seem to have surpassed prices in Buenos Aires (see Figure 6.2), although the two levels are not strictly comparable because water is metered in Santiago and not in Buenos Aires.[20] The increase in the average amount collected per cubic meter sold in Santiago was almost entirely the result of tariff increases dictated by the regulator's model. This is quite different from Aguas Argentinas, which raised revenues by many means other than tariff increases, including reclassifications and better bill collection.

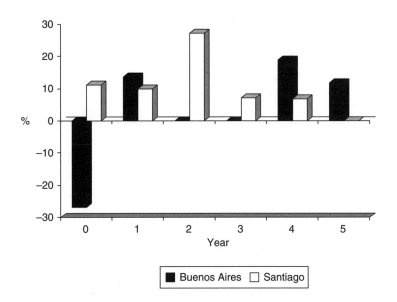

Note: The Buenos Aires numbers are changes in the K factor; the Santiago numbers are changes in the price per cubic meter of water in 1966 dollars. The 1997 increase in Buenos Aires includes the effects of the incorporation of the infrastructure charge into the rate base as a result of the renegotiation of the contract.

Source: Author's calculations based on information in Shirley (2002).

Figure 6.1　Percentage change in real water tariffs for the first five years after reform, Buenos Aires (1992–1998) and Santiago (1987–1993)

Regulation　All the issues just discussed were bad for the Buenos Aires reform, but problems with the regulator were devastating. A regulator viewed by the public as strong, nonpartisan, and expert can make up for weaknesses in the contract, but Buenos Aires' regulator made the opposite impression, and had the opposite effect. The regulator, ETOSS (Ente Tripartito de Obras de Servicios de Saneamiento), had a six-member board with two members each representing the federal government, the province of Buenos Aires, and the municipality. The executives treated their two directors as political appointees. Since the president, governor, and mayor were political rivals, ETOSS' board was often paralyzed by partisan disputes.[21] The federal government intervened often, bypassing or overturning ETOSS' decisions, usually in favor of Aguas Argentinas. Many of ETOSS' decisions also favored the utility, and they were taken in secret, without public hearings (Casarin et al. 2007). The weakness and secrecy of the regulator and the federal government's bias in favor of the investor left

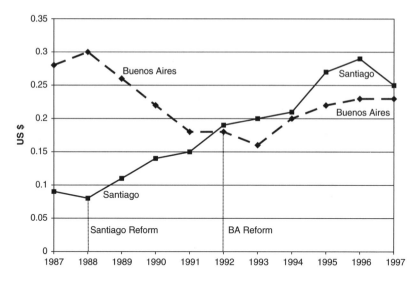

Source: Author's calculations based on data in Shirley (2002, Statistical Appendix, Table A.22).

Figure 6.2 *Average amount collected per cubic meter of water sold, Buenos Aires and Santiago (US dollars per cubic meter)*

Buenos Aires' consumers feeling unprotected before a foreign-owned utility.

Santiago's regulator was, in contrast, a politically independent, objective, and technical body, making the new rules credible to EMOS' public managers as well as to subsequent private investors. The Superintendencia de Servicios Sanitarios (SSS) was under the Ministry of Public Works, and headed by a regulator appointed by the president. The heads of SSS have been technical rather than political appointees and have served indefinite terms, rather than changing after elections as ETOSS directors did in Buenos Aires. SSS set prices, resolved disputes with consumers, and intervened actively to assure that the utility met water quality and service standards.

I have argued that the reforms in Santiago avoided many of the interest group conflicts that arose in Buenos Aires. It could be argued that Santiago's reforms were more acceptable just because EMOS was owned by the state when many reforms were implemented, while Aguas Argentinas was a private company. According to this reasoning, consumers in Santiago were reassured because government rather than the private sector benefited from the steep price increases, while citizens of Buenos Aires opposed any price increases because the company was privately run. Yet welfare analysis shows that government, not consumers, was the biggest beneficiary in

Santiago, while consumers, not the private operators, were the biggest beneficiaries by far in Buenos Aires, at least during the early years of the concession. Furthermore, the reforms in Santiago were implemented with the stated intention of privatizing the company, and, as we can see in the next section, designed to make the contract credible to private investors. Privatization was delayed in Santiago, but it was not dropped.

Supply of Reform

Building credibility through reputation and costly signals

Reforms in both cities were credible to investors, but for very different reasons. Investors were reassured by Argentina's adoption of a currency board fixing the peso to the dollar. The increasing dollarization and openness of Argentina's economy under parity made it politically and economically costly for government to devalue or renege on its obligations to foreign investors. Yet even though parity initially enhanced the government's reputation, its long-run sustainability became increasingly doubtful. As Spiller and Tommasi (2000) show, Argentina's political institutions were not compatible with a fixed exchange rate. As we have seen, the Argentine constitution gave considerable political power to the provincial governments. It also gave them considerable fiscal power as well. Revenue collection was centralized and funds were distributed to the provinces in a convoluted and discretionary fashion (Jones et al. 2000). Some provinces' claims on the federal treasury were larger than the revenues they contributed, and no individual provincial government had an incentive to be fiscally responsible (Spiller and Tommasi 2000). Quite the opposite, fiscal austerity would have forced governors to cut patronage, threatening their political power base. Argentina's Congress did not concern itself with fiscal austerity either. Most federal legislators served single, four-year terms, and showed little interest in the long-term implications of their fiscal decisions (Jones et al. 2000). Since their political careers were determined by provincial party bosses, federal legislators had no incentive to curb fiscal deficits if that meant cutting funds for their province and thereby alienating local party leaders. In such a political milieu it should not surprise us that growing fiscal deficits put increasingly unsustainable pressures on parity. Buenos Aires' concession contract was written under the assumption that the fixed exchange rate would prevail throughout the life of the agreement, and the 1997 renegotiation had even promised that Aguas Argentinas' tariff would remain dollar denominated should the exchange rate change. When parity ended in January 2002 the government froze Aguas Argentinas' tariffs and kept them frozen until it terminated the concession in 2006.

The institutions safeguarding investors in Chile were more secure and sustainable, and by the time EMOS was privatized they had operated well for nine years. The eventual buyers were protected by Chile's constitution, which specifically protected private property rights against government encroachment, and by its independent judiciary, which enforced that protection. The democratic government continued to build Chile's reputation as a market where private investors were protected from arbitrary state action. Surveys of the perceptions of business leaders suggest that they regard Chile's economy favorably; the World Economic Forum ranked Chile on a par with Portugal and Ireland on its 2005 competitiveness index (Corbo 2005, slide 17).

Credible regulation
Credible regulation strikes a delicate balance, reassuring both consumers and investors that their interests will be fairly represented. A regulatory framework that tilts toward consumers will not attract private investors in the first place, but regulation that tilts largely toward investors will not be credible either, since investors will expect a backlash eventually. Santiago's water and sewerage system was not privatized until nine years after reform began, yet its regulation was far more credible by design.

The credibility of Buenos Aires' regulation suffered from the outset from the politicization and paralysis of ETOSS. Aguas Argentinas' capacity to bypass ETOSS and go directly to the executive to resolve regulatory deadlock was helpful to the private investors in the short run, but it was bad for the long-run credibility of the concession. It held government's adherence to its part of the bargain hostage to the shifting incentives of different presidents. ETOSS' politicized board members also lobbied for politically motivated decisions that harmed Aguas Argentinas' reputation with its customers. For example the municipality's representatives on the board pushed Aguas Argentinas to provide water and sewerage to a new town because the mayor had promised to resettle a shantytown dislocated by a highway. Aguas Argentinas agreed to this request only when ETOSS agreed in turn to increase water rates to cover the additional costs, the sort of deal that alienates consumers and worries investors (Alcázar et al. 2002).

Santiago's regulatory agency was more credible than ETOSS because it was less politicized. The military government and its democratic successors established the norm that regulators were apolitical experts. This norm was reinforced by the computer model used to set tariffs; by reducing regulatory discretion, the model reduced the political pay-off from intervening in regulatory decisions. The computer model was also complex, technical, and not easily manipulated, further deterring political interference.

Credibility is also enhanced by investors' confidence that rules will endure over the life of the contract. The rules supporting water and sewerage reform were more vulnerable to reversal in Argentina than in Chile. Argentina's laws were easily changed; as I mentioned above, each time a new party took power it reversed much of the legislation of its predecessor. We can also see this legal fragility in Menem's cavalier attitude towards constitutional term limits. By comparison, Chile's institutions made it very difficult to reverse legislation. The constitution required an absolute majority in Congress to change laws. Since Chile's electoral rules assured minority party representation, it was hard to get enough votes in Congress to change course without widespread agreement. In addition, Chile had unelected senators appointed by the previous president, the military, and the judiciary, who would be likely to oppose change (Baldez and Carey 2000).

Judicial appeal

Both Argentina and Chile allowed their water and sanitation companies to appeal to the judicial branch in the event of a conflict with the regulator. The chance to appeal the regulator's decisions to the courts can increase government's credibility by allowing utilities to protest politically motivated decisions that violate the contract. Appeal only enhances credibility, however, if the judiciary is itself independent of political interference. The credibility of appeals in Argentina was weak because its judiciary was subject to political manipulation. Argentine courts had not been an independent check on executive discretion since Perón impeached and replaced four of the five supreme court justices in 1949 (Alston and Gallo 2005). Subsequent presidents regularly intervened in the courts, including Menem. Menem increased the size of the supreme court in order to appoint his allies, and also appointed his supporters to a large number of positions as federal judges and state prosecutors (Iaryczower et al. 2000). Judges in Argentina opposed the executive branch's position only when they were political opponents of the current regime (Iaryczower et al. 2000). The judiciary's partisan tendencies made long-term contracts such as the Buenos Aires concession vulnerable to the next president's legal reshuffling.

Chile's judiciary was generally regarded as more honest and independent than Argentina's, although slow. Moreover, Chile's regulation allowed the utility to appeal tariff decisions to an arbitration panel of three people, one appointed by the regulator, one by the company, and one jointly agreed (Shirley et al. 2002). Arbitration had two advantages over the courts. First, decisions could be reached much more quickly: by law the panel must decide in 37 days. Second, arbitrators would be more likely than judges to be expert in the complexities of the tariff legislation. Even when EMOS was still operating as a state-owned enterprise, it could and did appeal to the arbitration panel, which found in its favor on occasion.[22]

CONCLUSION

While the Buenos Aires and Santiago reforms in water and sanitation were notionally similar, the two cases differed in their contractual rules and regulations. The contract and regulation governing the Buenos Aires concession fed interest group conflict and failed to protect and inform consumers or properly motivate investors. Some critics have attributed the failure of the Buenos Aires concession to the venality of the investors or to a basic incompatibility of profits and basic needs, but there is little evidence of that. Others have rightly blamed the weak regulator, corruption in the Menem administration, and the adverse macroeconomic circumstances that destroyed the currency board. But these were proximate causes; the ultimate cause was the persistence of institutions that characterize a weak state and unresolved social struggles (see de Ferranti et al. 2004 on this point).

Changes in Chile's fundamental institutions allowed reforms in water and sanitation to be implemented, expanded, and sustained from dictatorship to democracy. The 1980 constitution and regulations produced more cooperative coalition politics and better protection of property rights. The democratic administrations retained these protections and simultaneously reduced Chile's historically high levels of inequality through social welfare programs.

I hope this chapter has illustrated how comparative case studies can capture the complexity, diversity, and persistence of institutions and the underlying regularities of human behavior across cases and even across disciplines (see also Ostrom 2005). In arguing that institutions are complex, diverse, and persistent, I am not arguing that they cannot be studied scientifically and, eventually, statistically. Nor am I arguing that development is impossibly difficult. As I discuss in the next chapter, progress can occur and it can be propelled and sustained through new ideas.

NOTES

1. Data on prices must be treated with caution for reasons I explain later in the chapter. The combination of lower tariff rates plus lower rates of metering, billing, and connection suggests that the effective price of water in Mexico City was much lower than in Santiago. Mexico City's profligate water system depended on large subsidies from the federal government.

2. The idea that water is a private good with some public characteristics is controversial, as I explore later. This led the Dublin conference to proclaim that water is an economic good with "economic value in all its competing uses" (Dublin Statement from the International Conference on Water and the Environment, 1992, quoted in Boland 2004, p. 530). This vague proclamation did not reduce the controversy since "economic good" is a very broad term, referring to any good or service that has a scarcity value to people; both public and private goods are economic goods.

3. Noll (2002) notes that because a water system has a high ratio of fixed to variable costs, the private marginal costs of supply may be below the average costs. He suggests an optimal, two-part tariff where one part is a usage price based on private marginal cost and the other is a capacity charge that recovers any costs not covered in the usage charge.

4. Larger pipes have a capacity to carry more than proportional larger volumes of water, because of lower turbulence and engineering scale economies. See Noll (2002).

5. A few urban systems do rely on multiple independent sources (Roth 1987, cited in Noll 2002).

6. Perhaps metering would not have made a difference since water customers behaved in many ways that economists consider irrational and ill-informed. Water customers objected to nominal rate increases even when marginal water rates stayed low, real rates were below historic levels, average rates were below those of comparable cities, and performance improved (see my description of the Buenos Aires water and sanitation concession below). Elsewhere I have argued that a general and perhaps justified suspicion of the rules of the game in utility privatization and politics more broadly may be responsible for this attitude (Shirley 2005b).

7. Private participation among underdeveloped countries varied by income: almost half of the 72 middle-income underdeveloped countries in the sample had some private involvement in their water sector compared to only 18 percent of the 55 low-income underdeveloped countries (Estache and Goicoehea 2005).

8. Sanitation has never had the cachet of water, even though it too is crucial to preventing disease. Connecting households to clean, piped water does not make children healthier unless sanitation is also improved, from no facilities to pit latrines or from pit latrines to flush toilets. Based on an epidemiological study of diarrhea prevalence, height for age, weight for age, and weight for height scores of 5000 urban and 12,000 rural children aged 3–36 months in eight underdeveloped countries (Esrey 1996).

9. Cholera transmission in Lima in the mid-1990s has been attributed to undercooked fish from ocean waters contaminated by the city's sewage, as well as contaminated water from tanker trucks and contaminated food sold by street vendors (US Government 1995).

10. The cost of desalination depends upon the type of technology used and whether the raw water is brackish or seawater. The average cost of desalinating seawater by the so-called MSF process fell from $9.00 per cubic meter in 1960 to about $0.90 in 2000 (Zhou and Tol 2003).

11. Guasch finds that renegotiation in all sectors is largely instigated by the operators. Further, contracts that are bid competitively are renegotiated more frequently than those awarded through bilateral negotiation. Contracts that are awarded to the bidder who offers the lowest tariff are renegotiated more frequently than those awarded to the bidder who offers the highest transfer fee. Contracts that set prices based on a cap that is increased according to inflation are renegotiated more frequently than contracts that set prices based on rate of return. Contracts where the regulator is created after the concession agreement is signed are renegotiated more frequently than those where a regulatory body existed before the contract is signed (Guasch 2004, 2006).

12. A new state-owned enterprise, Agua y Saneamientos Argentinos, S.A., was created and took over the water system in March 2006. Although there had been some evidence of deterioration in service (for example, complaints about service tripled and construction of high-rise buildings had to be delayed), there is no way of knowing if this is due to the transition or to more ingrained problems. The state announced a new investment plan, but there is not enough evidence to know if expansion will continue.

13. The information on Argentina draws on Alcázar et al. (2002), Alston and Gallo (2005), de Ferranti et al. (2004), Gallo (2002).
14. These were: left (Communist and Socialist); center (Radical, Christian Democrat, Agrarian Labor); and right (Conservative, Liberal, National) (see Scully 1995). (See Haggard and McCubbins 2000, for a summary of the literature on the effects of open versus closed lists on party politics.)
15. The president did not need to compromise with his/her coalition to govern, while his/her coalition was not motivated to compromise by the prospect of the president's re-election (see Valenzuela 1994).
16. Similar to the situation described by North (1990, p. 90), the constitutional reform limited the degrees of freedom of political entrepreneurs to bargain and still maintain the loyalty of their constituent groups, setting the stage for a discontinuous change in Chile's institutions.
17. Pinochet's strongest supporters were rural or upper class (Mèndez 1990).
18. During this interval the company has an incentive to improve its efficiency because it will reap any additional profits. Subsequently the regulator will capture these efficiency gains for the consumer. (See, for example, Armstrong et al. 1994, chapter on water.)
19. More precisely, the composite price index is used to adjust the K factor that is multiplied times the tariffs paid by individual consumer groups. When the concession was won with a bid to reduce water rates by 26.9 percent, the K factor was set at 0.731.
20. Buenos Aires should be the cheaper supplier thanks to economies of scale. The cost of raw water should not be very different.
21. The mayor of Buenos Aires was from the party in opposition to Menem and the governor of the province was Menem's chief rival in his own party.
22. EMOS was still allowed to appeal decisions even though it was state owned, and EMOS did appeal when it was under state ownership and the decisions were largely in its favor (Shirley et al. 2002, p. 210).

7. The role of scholars and scholarship in economic development

Institutional change ultimately depends on the decisions of a country's citizens and the individuals who govern them. Under ordinary circumstances neither the general public nor their leaders favor radical change in their society's institutional framework. This is understandable since an institutional framework provides the basic constructs for human interaction (North 2005b). Radical change in such basic constructs would require not merely changing the rules of the game, but what Shepsle described as replacing one game form with another, transforming the current institutional regime into something substantially different (Shepsle 2001). This does not happen easily. As we saw in Chapter 3, a society's institutional framework is molded through a long history of ruling groups structuring rules and promoting and enforcing norms that perpetuate their interests. This explains why durable institutional frameworks are self-enforcing in Greif's sense – no one with the power to change them has an incentive to do so. The ruling elites may be overthrown by non-elites, but the institutional framework will endure as long as it serves to perpetuate the power of the new ruling group as much as it did the old ones. The rhetoric and the actors may change, but the rules and norms that limit access and competition do not.

It is not surprising that those who stand to lose if an institutional framework is altered resist change and are usually powerful enough to prevent it. It is more surprising that those who are not benefiting from the status quo also resist change. As we saw in Chapter 2, institutional frameworks are congruent with shared beliefs about how the world operates. Radical change in institutional frameworks requires changing shared beliefs, values, and practices, overturning society's shared conceptual paradigm. Changing shared systems of beliefs and assumptions is usually a wrenching process, which helps explain why most people conform to the dominant paradigm. Conformity is crucial to self-enforcing institutions. The expectations of how others will act, how others expect us to act, and how others will react if we do something unexpected have a powerful influence on human behavior. In early societies myths, superstitions, and religion helped establish order and conformity (North 2005b, p. 42). Myths, sagas, and legends also served to record and explain early societies' agreed history, a shared view of "what really happened" in the past (Huizinga 1960b, p. 41). Radical institutional change is rare because it is not just a matter of simply declaring new rules and establishing new organization forms, but of changing beliefs and values inherited from the past (Greif 2006, pp. 210–11).

Conformity explains why rules and norms persist under unstable and adverse circumstances. I recall walking through a square in Accra, Ghana, in 1983 shortly after a massive devaluation. The economy was hitting rock bottom; gasoline was rationed; and few goods and services were available. When we went to one of the few restaurants still open and asked what soft drinks they had, the waiter replied, "Boiled water and beer." The economy was in shambles, yet the square in Accra was filled with long, orderly queues of women, babies on their backs and bundles on their heads, patiently waiting hours for one of the few buses able to get fuel. This sight was a striking contrast to the chaotic, pushy mob that jockeyed to board buses during snowstorms in Washington, DC. Clearly the norm to queue was powerful in Ghana despite the shortage of buses with fuel – and of just about everything else.

Despite the persistent, self-enforcing nature of institutional frameworks, under the right circumstances changes do occur, changes that over time transform societies. We understand very little about how societies' shared beliefs and institutions change. History suggests that when circumstances are ripe, as they were in Europe in the seventeenth and eighteenth centuries during the Enlightenment, ideas and learning are powerful forces for overcoming the beliefs and norms that inhibit radical change in institutional frameworks (North 2005b). A great deal has been written about how the Enlightenment transformed thinking in Europe, but most of these descriptions do not explore how such transformations might occur in other regions at other times. There have also been few comparisons of similar intellectual transformations in newly developed countries. In this chapter I have tried to provide some preliminary insights into the puzzle of how shared beliefs shift in ways that permit self-enforcing and persistent institutions to change radically. My descriptions of the transformations in Enlightenment Europe and in newly developed countries are highly abbreviated; I cannot do justice to the rich literature on these topics in one chapter. My hypotheses about intellectual change are preliminary; much further research is needed to understand how ideas and scholars affect institutional change. I hope this chapter will be a helpful starting point.

The next two sections examine the role of scholars and scholarship during the Enlightenment in Europe and analyze the marketplace for ideas today. The chapter then proposes hypotheses about how scholars influence policies, beliefs, and institutions and applies them to six case studies. The cases focus on scholars who acted as intellectual entrepreneurs, promoting a new set of assumptions about the way the world functions and designing a program of policies that followed logically from this new economic paradigm.

SCHOLARS AND THE EUROPEAN ENLIGHTENMENT

The change in attitudes that we call the Enlightenment was a gradual process whereby a fortuitous combination of circumstances and individuals fostered a new way of thinking. The Enlightenment spawned new ideas that prompted new norms and rules and changed beliefs about the world, the economy, and the state among the literate members of European societies. Before the Enlightenment scholarship in early medieval Europe was dominated by the clergy, who were among the few persons able to read and write. Medieval thought adhered strictly to doctrinal authority, viewing the Church as "the living embodiment and organization of the immediate revelation of God" (Huizinga 1960a, p. 269). As Huizinga describes it, "the Middle Ages set a binding authority and authoritative norms for everything intellectual" (ibid., p. 271). Cosmology and theology were "deeply intertwined" and any views of the universe that questioned orthodoxy were blasphemy (Mokyr 2006, p. 19). Medieval theology supported the dominant social hierarchy and discouraged changes in the social or economic status quo. Thus Catholic dogma warned against the pursuit of wealth beyond one's social order and opposed the development of capital markets by treating money lending as improper or worse for Christians and charging interest or usury as unequivocally sinful (Muller 2002).

The Church's iron grip on ideas was threatened in the fifteenth and sixteenth centuries by the rise in trade and the growth of cities described in Chapter 3, as well as the development of printing and an increase in literacy. Before the invention of the printing press in the mid-fifteenth century, manuscripts were few and expensive, laboriously hand copied, usually in monasteries. The spread of the printing press, the increasing use of paper, and economies of scale in printing and paper production contributed to a drastic fall in the price of books, by as much as 85 to 90 percent between 1455 and 1485 (Zanden 2004). Literacy was increasing rapidly in the late Middle Ages; in Amsterdam, for example, literacy rose from about one-third in 1500 to almost 50 percent by 1600 (ibid., Figure 7). Thanks to these two trends Western European per capita consumption of books soared from the latter half of the fifteenth century to the first half of the seventeenth century, growing from an annual average of only about 3.1 per thousand inhabitants to over 40 per thousand (Buringh and Zanden 2006, p. 45, Table 3).[1]

Literacy was not the only factor eroding orthodoxy. The Protestant Reformation in the early sixteenth century created competition in the realm of beliefs, not just between Protestants and Catholics, but also between sects, such as Lutheran, Calvinist, and Anglican. Make no mistake, the early Protestant sects were at least as doctrinaire as Catholicism and as – if not more – opposed to amassing wealth or charging interest. Nonetheless, the clash of dogmas had an important effect on intellectuals. The competition between differing religions and sects for control of the state, and the use of the military power of the state to repress opposing doctrines produced two centuries of religious civil wars. This prolonged and bloody violence prompted intellectuals to question the justification for using the state as a tool to promote one dogma and brutally suppress all opponents (ibid., p. 24).

At the beginning of the sixteenth century, when university education was still largely dominated by clergy teaching Catholic dogma to future priests, a few curious minds began to question orthodoxy. For example, a group of young scholars in Paris who called themselves *philosophes* shared a new way of seeing the world that relied on empirical observation and included a "sharp point of view on such topics as freedom of thought, social equality, and religious toleration" (Huppert 1999, p. 3). They also developed their own secular schools teaching students who were not destined for the clergy to question authority. The *philosophes* translated the works of classical authors into French so that students would not have to learn Latin to read them, and new publishing houses made these and other texts more widely available (ibid., pp. 76–81). The large number of colleges and publishing houses established in the Latin Quarter of Paris created a "testing ground" for new ideas (ibid., p. 24) and broke the stranglehold of orthodoxy over the channels of knowledge transmission. Secular education gradually spread throughout France as municipal authorities who wanted to emulate "the style of Paris" supported a growing number of local colleges (ibid.). Thanks to these free municipal colleges, exceptionally bright young men were able to move out of poverty, to attend university, and even to end up teaching others. For example, Pierre La Ramée went from a "charcoal burner's cottage in Picardy to a Royal Chair of Philosophy" in Paris (ibid., p. 37). Although increasingly repressed by alarmed clergy and crowned heads, this sort of new critical reasoning and individualism spread among the intelligentsia in Europe, laying fertile ground for the radical and innovative ideas that emerged in the seventeenth and eighteenth centuries.

The expansion of trade, consumerism, urbanization, and wealth also created a growing, literate middle class. A proliferation of coffee houses, reading clubs, salons, and Masonic lodges, combined with the rise in book markets and journals, made it possible for new ideas to reach increasingly larger numbers of people (Muller 2002). For example, social clubs for stonemasons evolved into Masonic lodges that freely discussed science and new ideas, held frequent elections, and "placed great emphasis on living by laws and constitutions, on voting and oratory, and on charitable works" (Jacob 2001, p. 21). These sorts of new social organizations chipped away at the old social order, worldview, and dominant belief system. The new urban commercial class in the sixteenth and seventeenth centuries was "interested in increasing economic openness, monetary stability, more secure property rights, enforceable contracts, a state that solved obvious problems of coordination, and fiscal commitments that were subject to consent" (Mokyr 2006, p. 32). Faith in reason and in scientific knowledge based on empirical observation became their new conceptual paradigm. Social organizations began to demand greater participation in politics. Such groups created new channels for the spread of Enlightenment ideas; indeed the Freemasons were even accused of having caused the French Revolution, "a charge that grew out a deep conviction that the enlarged public sphere had done irretrievable damage to the absolutist political order" (Jacob, 2001, p. 22).

Political fragmentation in Europe was another important force in the Enlightenment, because fragmentation allowed dissident opinions to emerge and spread (Mokyr 2006). Mokyr describes how reactionary power in Europe was divided into rival camps (Hapsburg, Bourbons, and Papacy), as was Protestantism, while, within countries, universities, boroughs, and guilds exercised their own sovereignty (ibid., p. 24). Without a single centralized government to defend the intellectual status quo, dissidents and heretics could find havens in which to pursue their ideas and persuade powerful individuals to protect them. Mokyr argues that in the seventeenth and eighteenth centuries the intellectual community was less fragmented than the political structures. Norms and rules emerged in the intellectual community that promoted competitive behavior among scholars, a market for ideas in which acceptance of competing theories and evidence was based on "logic, rigor, experimental evidence, and observation" (ibid., p. 21). Simultaneously, the costs of diffusion of new ideas among scholars was declining, not just because of cheaper printing, but also cheaper paper, postal services, and cheaper personal transportation, along with the development of schools and universities, academies, and scientific societies (ibid., p. 30).

Important new discoveries about the world and the universe reinforced Enlightenment ideals of tolerance for heterodox ideas and persuasion by evidence. The discoveries of Columbus, Copernicus, Galileo, and others inspired intellectuals to analyze the properties of the world and the universe objectively and empirically. For example, the observation that humans were all one species led naturalists to conclude that humans are biologically the same, giving a scientific basis to the proposition of social equality (Huppert 1999, p. 16).

Enlightenment thinkers created the intellectual arguments to justify and explain the introduction of competitive markets and politics. They attacked the institutions that promoted rent-seeking, such as barriers to trade and entry and the special privileges and monopoly rights enjoyed by elite groups and individuals (Mokyr 2006). Voltaire, for example, popularized a number of ideas that proved to be fundamental to the logic of open access markets and polities, such as "the pursuit of happiness, the expansion of individual freedom, the rule of law, and the use of human reason modeled on the methods of the natural sciences to challenge the nonrational claims of religious faith" (Muller 2002, p. 22).

Adam Smith's writings went even further in revolutionizing thinking about the economy. At a time when classical and Christian teaching regarded the pursuit of wealth as evil, Smith argued that pursuit of wealth was inevitable and, through commerce, could be made beneficial. Smith described the market economy as the best mechanism to improve people's lives, to allow most people to escape the moral degradation of poverty, to liberate people from serfdom and service to aristocrats, to foster self-control and industry, and to channel base desires into actions that benefited society (ibid.). Smith explained the workings of the market to decision-makers who had the power to enhance or destroy the developing capitalist system. Moreover he described it so persuasively that, as Walter Bagehot wrote on the centennial of the publication of the *Wealth of Nations*, it fastened his ideas on the imagination; "he has put certain broad conclusions into the minds of hard-headed men, which are all which they need know and all which they for the most part will ever care for, and he has put those conclusions there ineradicably" (quoted in Muller 2002, p. 83).

Smith and other Enlightenment thinkers helped transform attitudes toward work and wealth (Porter 2000, p. 384), and these new attitudes fed back into changes in consumption, production, and institutions. New thinking also emerged about the role of the state, with John Locke and others proposing a new form of political order in which the state's power would be divided, limited, and shared, and many religions would be tolerated. These new worldviews supported the new institutions that fostered the industrial revolution in England.

As this very brief history suggests, a number of developments fortuitously combined to challenge the dominant views of the world during the Enlightenment, including the rise of new scholarly attitudes towards learning and dogma, a growing understanding of market mechanisms, an increase in wealth that spawned a growing middle class, the spread of ideas through greater literacy and social clubs, the invention of the printing press and the publishing house, political fragmentation, and the clash of religious dogmas. Religious wars eroded confidence in doctrines and systems of thought that demanded slavish devotion to state-sponsored religions and meek submission to existing social hierarchies. An emerging belief that the universe could be understood through the use of reason and empirical observation rather than through appeal to religious doctrine and authority helped foster scientific discoveries, which in turn changed people's understanding of the physical world. These same attitudes towards rationality and religion were applied to human understanding more broadly, with a new emphasis on tolerance and the search for truth through empirical observation. Some scholars in this period played the role of intellectual entrepreneurs, challenging existing dogmas, promoting new learning, and explaining the economy and polity with a new analytical framework that condemned the barriers to competition. Competition in ideas before a much wider audience of opinion than had existed in the past spread these new concepts among the literate members of European society. In a lengthy and complex process, rulers, opinion leaders, and the growing literate public began to change their views, allowing new policies and institutions to be put in place, and laying the basis for modern, open access polities and economies.

Why do such intellectual transformations not occur more frequently today? A number of middle-income countries, such as those in Latin America and Asia, have a large literate population, a growing middle class, and exposure to new ideas through trade, travel, and the global media. Yet the sort of intellectual ferment and search for objective knowledge that occurred in Europe during the Enlightenment is far less common today. The circumstances may not be ripe, as I describe in the case studies below, but there are also factors within the intellectual community that may reduce the supply of intellectual entrepreneurs. The next section of this chapter considers possible explanations why the current marketplace for scholars may not be encouraging iconoclastic scholarship in developing countries.

THE MARKETPLACE FOR SCHOLARS IN DEVELOPED AND UNDERDEVELOPED COUNTRIES

Scholars are not typically prone to challenge status quo paradigms within their academic discipline. As described by Kuhn (1962), there is a strong tendency for scholarly ideas to become intellectual dogmas and for scholars to adopt pedantic attitudes and jargon, behaving as a secular clergy preaching received wisdom. In some countries iconoclastic scholarship is actively prohibited, but even in modern democracies there are rules that direct finance and fame to those whose research and teaching supports the status quo, discouraging independently-minded scholars. Empirical research is expensive, and scholars whose findings might seriously challenge agreed wisdom are deterred if money and academic positions go only to those whose views are in accord with orthodoxy or only to trivial and irrelevant inquiries that pose little threat to dominant belief systems. Knowledge that might threaten the status quo is also quarantined when mainstream conferences and journals are controlled by proponents of status quo paradigms; under these circumstances avenues for communicating nonconforming research become marginalized.

Economics as a discipline may be less prone to challenging dominant assumptions among policymakers because it is less policy-oriented than in Adam Smith's day. Many economists today do not aspire to make discoveries that might have a useful impact on public debate. Bruno Frey even asserts that:

> Economics has increasingly become the analysis of formal and self-defined problems within a closed academic field. Economics tends not to be used in order to meet the challenges posed by reality, but to engage in an academic discourse following accepted intellectual standards. No contribution to economic policy is intended . . . the social influence of economics is neither seen nor considered to be relevant. (Frey 2000, p. 17)

While Frey may overstate the case, economics' focus on techniques such as cross-country growth regressions yields few discoveries specific enough to interest local decision-makers or to inform their actions. Neoclassically trained economists also tend to ignore or dismiss the institutions and beliefs that constrain their own and their fellow citizens' behavior, making their analyses less relevant to many policy discussions.

Not all economists fit this mold, and economic ideas still produce powerful policy changes, as we can see with the example of the impact of economic research on US regulatory policy over the last 50 years.[2] As Roger Noll has pointed out, economists' research and advice on public policy helped propel major changes in US regulatory policies and institutions (Noll 2006). For example, a large economics literature called for deregulation of competitive markets, which subsequently occurred in the 1980s. Winston (1993) has documented huge cost savings from deregulation of sectors such as transport and telecommunications. A more specific example of the influence of scholarly work is the seminal 1959 article on the Federal

Communications Commission in which Ronald Coase argued that defining property rights and making them easily tradeable would likely be more efficient than government allocation of rights to the radio spectrum. He also argued that this would eliminate what amounted to government interference in freedom of the press (Coase 1959). Coase specifically proposed that rights to the radio spectrum be auctioned off, and this eventually began to happen in the US in 1993.

Developed countries have advantages over underdeveloped countries in generating new knowledge. First, they have more mechanisms to foster scholarly research and discovery than poorer countries. There are also more funds available for research and a sizeable share of those funds are allocated through competitions, so that scholars in large numbers of universities and research institutes can vie for funds from many different public and private sources. Scholars get first-hand knowledge of real-world priorities when they are asked to serve on government councils and on private sector boards, to testify before legislatures and courts, and to contribute to popular media. The ideological leanings of the funding source can bias researchers and distort their findings, but this tendency is partly offset by other incentives inherent in the process. In particular, the openness of the process creates the possibility that biases will be revealed when researchers present their results for challenge by peer reviewers in conferences and at journals, or when they make their data available for others to replicate or reverse their results. Second, research findings are more widely disseminated in wealthier countries: economists in universities and institutes are encouraged to present their findings at scholarly conferences and publish their results in one of the many peer-reviewed journals. The competitiveness of the process and the large numbers of scholars vying for recognition creates the possibility that mainstream paradigms will be increasingly challenged by revolutionary, heterodox thinkers, similar to the process that Kuhn (1962 [1996], p. 144) described for the hard sciences:

> Any new interpretation of nature, whether a discovery or a theory, emerges first in the mind of one or a few individuals. It is they who first learn to see science and the world differently, and their ability to make the transition is facilitated by two circumstances that are not common to most other members of their profession. Invariably their attention has been intensely concentrated upon the crisis-provoking problems; usually in addition, they are men so young or so new to the crisis-ridden field that practice has committed them less deeply than most of their contemporaries to the world view and rules determined by the old paradigm.

Moreover, the internet has reduced the cost of entry for new researchers and increased the circulation of working papers, making challenges to dominant paradigms faster and more transparent – and more chaotic.

In most underdeveloped countries the hurdles to scholarly ideas are higher and the market less competitive. Universities are few and underfunded. Professors are not paid a living wage and often hold several fulltime teaching jobs. Money for research is scarce and allocated in an uncompetitive fashion.[3] Most insidiously, research funding is largely dominated by foreign donors who determine the research questions, decide the design and management of the research, and hire the best researchers to work for them as staff or consultants. Many research institutes are equivalent to consulting firms, bidding on research projects designed and monitored by government or donors. Although researchers in developed countries are also sometimes captured as consultants to governments or other funding sources, there are more scholars in wealthier countries and they have many more opportunities to fund their own, independently-designed research projects, opportunities that are largely absent in poorer countries.

Scholars living in poor countries who challenge the dominant mainstream paradigm are often repressed and discouraged; many depart. It is obvious that objective scientific inquiry cannot flourish in oppressive dictatorships or countries ruled by ideological or religious fanatics. It is less obvious when ideas that challenge the dominant viewpoint and assumptions are subtly suppressed in nominally democratic societies. I am not referring here to rebellious thinkers writing vitriolic polemics against the government who are easily identified, isolated, and ignored by the ruling groups. I refer instead to well-trained scholars doing serious empirical research whose findings could fuel a debate about basic concepts and assumptions within the elite and among the wider public. The internet has made this suppression more difficult, but access to computers in many underdeveloped countries is still so limited or internet communication so censored that ideas communicated on the internet have less chance of affecting public debate or even the policy dialogue among ruling elites. I am not suggesting that subtle suppression of heterodox views does not also occur in wealthy countries; as I described above, it does. The difference is one of degree. Because there are more channels for funding, more avenues for dissemination, and more university positions, iconoclasts are not so easily stifled or discouraged in richer countries. Thanks to sheer numbers they are less isolated and more able to form a critical mass of like-minded peers to support organizations, conferences, and journals or newsletters.

Scholars in poorer countries may also be isolated because they work in universities or research institutes suffering from systemic problems that have nothing to do with the suppression of unpopular ideas. In countries dominated by patronage systems and mismanagement, the organizations responsible for higher education and research often fall victim to the same corrupt and inefficient practices. Powerful academics and heads of research organizations reward loyalty over merit, hoard funds for their own use, and waste scarce resources in inefficient activities. Younger scholars and new ideas are stifled by a feudal system of selection and reward with no clear standards by which performance is judged. State-run universities are often starved for cash and overcrowded with students. Merit-based competition between universities or scholars may be minimal if it is allowed at all. These conditions help explain why a recent draft report for the Ford Foundation on the activities of private foundations supporting higher education in Russia found that merit-based assistance to individual scholars and networks accomplished a lot, while costly institutional support to universities and research institutes was largely wasted (Kotkin 2007). Again, similar problems arise in wealthy countries, but the larger size of the scholarly community and the larger number of funding sources and career prospects provide iconoclastic scholars with more options.

Many of the financial and career challenges faced by scholars in poor countries are similar to those confronting Enlightenment scholars, but there are several significant differences. In many poor countries the most serious threat to local scholarship is brain-drain. When Enlightenment scholars fled to different world capitals, they remained in the European intellectual community. Scholars in developing countries today are a prime recruitment target for aid agencies and consulting firms in an increasingly global market for knowledge skills. Many study abroad and top foreign students in Western universities often do not return to their home countries. This may not matter if they continue doing research that is relevant to their country's economic problems and their findings are communicated and influential in their home countries. But often they switch to other, less relevant topics, leave research entirely, or lose influence over local debates because they are outside their own country. Another difference from Enlightenment Europe is the influence of foreign aid funding, which encourages local researchers to adopt donor orthodoxy and to adhere to outsiders' priorities.

These adverse circumstances are not the only reasons why scholarship may be uninfluential. Fault also lies with scholars themselves. Some researchers are poor communicators who refuse to use accessible language or popular modes of communication or to explore the policy relevance of their findings. Some researchers prefer abstract analyses of esoteric topics to toiling over data in order to answer more mundane but more pressing questions. Some researchers disdain their knowledge of local institutions and prefer to apply conventional wisdom and sophisticated methodologies, however inappropriate. Researchers such as these are found in both developed and underdeveloped countries, but researchers' preferences matter less in wealthy countries where there are large numbers of scholars. Within a large scholarly community there will likely be some researchers who prefer to address the most immediate problems, to translate and popularize the otherwise inaccessible discoveries of their colleagues, or to interpret and apply esoteric findings to real-world issues. In poor countries with small numbers of scholars, researchers' preferences for jargon, abstraction, and irrelevancies can preclude scholars from having much influence.

Age also matters. As Kuhn (1962 [1996]) asserted, younger scholars tend to be more open-minded and have less of a stake in status quo institutions. But they are also susceptible to peer pressures and the weighty authority of their academic advisers. These pressures prompt some young researchers to adopt inappropriate or irrelevant models and ignore contradictory evidence. Young researchers in poorer countries are especially vulnerable to conformist pressures since they are often more isolated, with less feedback and fewer opportunities for scholarly discourse with those who would challenge their assumptions than their peers in wealthy countries.

Even scholars making relevant new discoveries and writing their conclusions clearly and persuasively will still have little impact on decision-makers if the circumstances that favor new ideas, new policies, and institutional change do not exist. The next section develops some hypotheses about when scholars have an influence.

WHEN DO SCHOLARS INFLUENCE CHANGE IN POLICIES, PARADIGMS, AND INSTITUTIONS? SOME HYPOTHESES[4]

In this section, which is based on joint work with Jessica Soto, I argue that change in deeply-rooted institutions and beliefs begins with a series of policy reforms explained and supported by a new set of assumptions about the way the economy functions – a new economic paradigm. Cognitive paradigms have been described by Campbell as "taken-for-granted descriptions, and theoretical analyses that specify cause and effect relationships, that reside in the background of policy debates and limit the range of alternatives policy makers are likely to perceive as useful" (Campbell 2002, p. 22). The process of changing the economic paradigm begins with a felt need for reform among those powerful enough to enact new policies and to change institutions. Their desire for change may be triggered by an external threat such as foreign competition for trade or military dominance, or by economic upheavals such as hyperinflation or abrupt economic decline, problems that are not remedied by status quo policies and institutions. This situation creates the potential for radical change in economic paradigms even though elite actors may only be seeking to change policies in the first instance.

A threat or shock does not mean that interest group politics can be ignored. Not all powerful elites will be ready to change their assumptions in response to threats or crises. Some will oppose any change in policies or paradigms, no matter how dysfunctional, if such a change would threaten their power base. Meaningful change is only feasible, therefore, when those with the power to effect change are in a position to ignore, overpower, or buy out those who oppose them. Such an opportunity could arise because the usual power relationships have been undermined by crisis, or weakened or overturned through a political change such as a revolution, coup, or election.

Even if opposition can be overcome, an external threat or economic shock only creates an opening for change; change is not inevitable. The elite must first accept the new policy program and its corresponding rationale, its paradigm. Hall (1993) argues that new ideas influence policy when they are persuasive enough to offer an alternative to the worldview or paradigm of those in a position to provoke change. This alternative paradigm must be seen as relevant to the perceived problem, different from previous failed models, and internally coherent. Significant changes in policies may be more likely when there is a role model to emulate that provides evidence that the new policy program will work. A role model is not sufficient, however. The economic paradigm and its broader ramifications must also be accepted. There are many failed attempts to emulate a role model's policies and laws without adopting the necessary supportive institutions. For example, Keefer and Stasavage (2003) find that efforts to create monetary stability by mandating the independence of the central bank largely fail without effective institutions to check the discretion of political actors.

North et al. (forthcoming) suggest a further set of "doorstep" conditions that must be present for scholars to influence change towards more open access economies and polities. More mature natural states, such as those in Latin America, have civilian control over the military, a greater array of complex organizations in civil society, business, and the state, and some property rights for non-elites. Elites in such states are more prepared to accept and more able to implement reforms without provoking disorder and instability. In fragile limited access states, in much of Sub-Saharan Africa for example, the structure of society is not conducive to change, and reforms promoting greater openness are likely to cause dominant elites to respond with violence, repression, or other unanticipated consequences. In North et al.'s view, the most that reformers in fragile states can expect to accomplish is to stabilize the state, promote civilian control over military force, and foster more complex organizations and expanded property rights.

A new paradigm is more likely to be accepted when it is advocated by individuals who are perceived to be credible experts. Haas (1992) suggests that experts gain credibility when their ideas are shared by a community of recognized fellow experts who are seen as professionals with similar normative and causal beliefs and similar criteria for evaluating the validity of knowledge in their area of expertise. Lupia and McCubbins (1998) have shown through experiments that those receiving new information will trust the information when the proponent is viewed as knowledgeable and seen as either having the best interests of the audience at heart or as operating in an institutional context that creates incentives to be truthful. People see advocates as motivated to be truthful when lying would be costly to the proponent, because truth can be verified and lies can be punished. People are also more likely to believe proponents who are observed to exert costly effort by, for example, spending money and time to show that their ideas will work (ibid.).

Proponents of new ideas will be more effective at changing a society's economic paradigm if they understand the constraints and opportunities created by shared assumptions and inherited institutional frameworks. Shared beliefs and institutional frameworks differ vastly in different societies, giving experts with local knowledge a strong advantage. Experts will also be more persuasive if they present the argument for change as part of an empirical analysis of current economic and institutional problems. Enlightenment thinkers such as Smith were not only influential because their arguments were erudite and persuasively written, they were also influential because their ideas were useful for tackling current problems, and, as Mokyr (2006) points out, congenial to some interests.

Local experts also must have channels – books, TV, conferences, conversations – to communicate their shared vision to decision-makers and the public. Outside experts, such as aid agency staff, foreign consultants, and other foreign advisers often have the channels without the local knowledge, while local scholars often have the knowledge without the access.

In our conceptual framework we are focusing on one kind of expert, scholars, particularly economists. Although scholars share beliefs and mental models with the rest of the population in their own country, they tend to have more exposure to new or contradictory ideas because they have been educated overseas, attend conferences outside their own country, or engage in debates or collaborations with foreign researchers. Economics training prepares scholars to develop coherent models to explain their observations of regularities and anomalies, to use accepted methodologies to test theory against evidence, and to follow coherent assumptions in imagining change and predicting its effects. We might also expect, as Kuhn suggests, that advocates for change are more likely to be younger scholars

(Kuhn 1962). Younger scholars typically have fewer stakes in status quo institutions and are in the process of forming peer groups with like-minded colleagues.

So far we have focused on what it takes for experts to convince the elite to accept a new economic vision and overcome elite opposition to change, but North (2005b) argues that for sustained institutional change, new ideas must eventually gain the confidence of a broader public, to the point of changing their beliefs about the world. As Greif (2005, p. 210) puts it, new ideas must alter what people believe and "what people believe others believe." Repressive dictatorships may be able to alter the official ideology by fiat and require conformity with the new worldview, but if public sentiments do not change, then reforms will not endure over the long run even in dictatorships. Indeed, as we will see later, an important force for change in dictatorships such as China today or South Korea under Chun Doo Hwan was the fear of public backlash if the failed status quo policies and paradigm were allowed to continue.

The sociological literature argues that public acceptance of new ideas is more likely when the political leaders advocating change are prestigious, the proposed changes are the leaders' consensus view, and the leaders command high levels of media attention (see Strang and Soule 1998, for a review). Such leaders have been credited with promoting rapid institutional change in Eastern Europe (for example, Murrell 2005). Empirical evidence on diffusion is thin and many important questions have yet to be answered, including how the process of diffusion occurs, how to measure changes in deeply-rooted beliefs as opposed to changes in ephemeral opinions, and what proportion of the public needs to accept the new paradigm for change to be sustained.

Change begins when, in response to an external threat or economic shock, the ruling elites introduce a new policy program proposed by a group of expert scholars and justify reform in the language of the new paradigm. If the ruling group views the outcomes from these early changes as largely positive, they may enact additional, more fundamental reforms, including changing rules and permitting new forms of organizations to enter. This is where the process often stalls, however. The crisis that created the impetus for change has been resolved by the new policies. Inflation (or some other problem) has been curbed and growth has resumed: why go further? The new economic paradigm promises continued stability and even higher rates of growth, but the risks for the ruling groups of fully implementing the new paradigm are becoming increasingly evident. (Indonesia is an example of this; see the next section.)

In rare cases, elites may continue to enact changes even after the crisis abates, including changes in fundamental institutions. Beneficiaries of the new policies have a stake in promoting further institutional changes and pre-venting back-sliding, and begin to demand not just economic power but political power. Often the new policies expand the middle class, who become a lobby against elite privilege and oppose the institutions that support rent-seeking. New policies and institutions also create opportunities for beneficiaries to form new organizations that further increase their influence. I describe this process in detail for six case study countries in the next section.

I can summarize these hypotheses as follows:

1. *Change is seen as necessary*: those who have the power to make radical changes (a) face serious threats or economic shocks, and (b) perceive that previous reforms failed to solve these problems; and,
2. *There is a viable alternative*: an alternative economic vision exists that is internally coherent and different from previous failures; and,
3. *There is a role model*: the alternative vision is supported by a role model, that is, some applicable experience elsewhere; and,
4. *The alternative is the consensus of a group of experts*: the alternative vision is the consensus proposal of a group perceived as experts by those who have the power to make radical changes and seen as trust-worthy because the proponents are believed to be:
    (a)   disinterested,
    (b)   motivated to be truthful, and
    (c)   knowledgeable about the constraints and opportunities provided by local history and local institutions; and,
5. *The alternative is known by the elite*: the expert group has channels to make their alternative vision known to those with the power to effect change; and,
6. *The alternative is feasible*: those in a position to effect change have the ability to co-opt, compensate, or coerce interest groups who might oppose radical changes; and,
7. *The alternative is diffused*: expert proponents and political leaders have the prestige, persuasive power, and media access to diffuse the new vision to those interest groups whose beliefs need to change for the new institutions to become self-enforcing; and,
8. *Early outcomes are successful and create beneficiaries who support further change*: early attempts to enact the new policies and institutions proposed by the experts are successful in eliminating or reducing the economic problem and create beneficiaries who organize to prevent retreat and to promote further change.

We hypothesized that these circumstances make it more likely that the process of change in policies and paradigms will cause changes in

Figure 7.1   Policies, paradigms, and institutional change

institutional frameworks. This process is presented graphically in Figure 7.1. The next section compares these hypotheses with the experience of selected underdeveloped countries.

WHEN DO SCHOLARS INFLUENCE CHANGE IN POLICIES, PARADIGMS, AND INSTITUTIONS? CASE STUDIES

This section compares the roles scholars played in six underdeveloped countries based on the hypotheses summarized above; the cases are summarized in Table 7.1 at the end of the chapter. It is impossible in this brief chapter to do justice to the complex histories of these six countries. Instead

I focus the discussion on those few components that are relevant to the earlier hypotheses, and look for patterns or regularities that support or refute them. Much more detailed analysis will be needed to test these hypotheses against full case studies.

The sample of cases is not random. It represents cases of development success (Taiwan, South Korea), rapid economic growth and political transition (Chile, China), and counterfactual cases where scholars had influence but reforms were not sustained (Argentina) or where scholars' influence was circumscribed (Indonesia). Taiwan and, to a lesser extent, South Korea have become politically and economically open access societies in North et al.'s terms (forthcoming), while Chile has become increasingly open access politically in line with its open access economy. The fourth case, China, is out of equilibrium with an increasingly open access economy and a closed access political system. Argentina is an example of how a nominally open access society has not been able to sustain reform despite highly influential scholars. It is a counterfactual case that seemed to meet all the requirements for development yet failed to sustain reforms. Indonesia is a second counterfactual case. Despite some scholarly influence and two decades of growth, the Indonesian economy imploded and the economy and polity are largely closed to non-elites.

The sample focuses on countries that pursued market-oriented paradigms, although with many local adaptations. Scholars have sometimes influenced countries to pursue a different route, of course. In India, for example, the dominant intellectual elites largely rejected free markets and global liberalization (Cameron and Ndhlovu 2001; Mukherji 2002; Tendulkar and Bhavani 2005). A long and influential tradition of Indian scholarship stresses economic interdependence, social values, the beneficial role of government, and the importance of uniquely "Indian solutions" to economic problems. The experiences of China and other rapidly growing East Asian economies have been characterized by such scholars as not especially relevant to India. Although some prominent Indian economists do favor deregulating markets and liberalizing trade (for example, Jagdish Bhagwati, Deepak Lal, T.N. Srinivasan), many of them are outside India and until recently their views have not represented mainstream thinking in the Indian academy. Some attribute the slow pace of Indian economic liberalization to this deep-seated intellectual opposition (see, for example, Mukherji 2002). In the mid-1980s an increasing number of scholars began to favor reforms that had been proposed by Bhagwati and others in the mid-1960s (Khatkhate 1994). The gradual deregulation and increased openness introduced after Prime Minister P.V. Narashimha Rao came to power in 1991 was partly a response to these increasing intellectual arguments for deregulation, but also a response to public sentiment that increasingly favored reform, and to concerns over India's marginalization in world economic affairs (Bhagwati 1993).

The sample excludes cases from Central Europe, despite recent development successes in the Czech Republic, Estonia, Hungary, Slovenia, and Slovakia. Confounding factors make these countries *sui generis*. The dominant paradigm, communism, was not part of shared beliefs in most of these societies. Arguably, communism was viewed by the public and many elites as a foreign ideology imposed and sustained by outside force and outside financial incentives. Scholars in Central Europe labored to keep the memory of their past economic system alive and teach it to subsequent generations. For example, the Vice Dean of the Prague Higher School of Economics, Helena Kotrbova, told me in May 1990 that the economics faculty had secretly circulated photocopies of Western economics texts, such as Samuelson's *Economics*, for that very reason.[5] Thus, Central European scholars proposing a return to a market economy were able to use powerful nationalistic and historic arguments that seem to be irrelevant to other regions.

The case studies focus on periods when there was a bright-line turning point in the official policy program. The goal is to learn why some policy changes culminated in sustained changes in institutions, while others did not, and what role scholars played in winning acceptance of a new economic paradigm. Although much further research and additional cases are needed to refine and test our premises, several regularities are evident in Table 7.1 (at the end of the chapter) that support some of the earlier hypotheses about the circumstances that allow scholars to influence economic institutions.

Change is Seen as Necessary

In all of the cases economic shocks or external threats, often combined with political changes, created the opening for new policy ideas. Previous efforts to solve economic problems had failed and the ruling elites were searching for new ideas. Four of the countries, Argentina, Chile, Indonesia (Phase I), and South Korea faced a crisis.

The first crisis case was a democracy, Argentina. When Carlos Menem was elected president in 1989, inflation had reached the astronomical annual rate of almost 5000 percent and the economy was in recession. Even before Menem took office he had become convinced of the need for change (Stokes 2001) and, as we saw in Chapter 6, once elected he adopted a program of reform very different from his populist campaign. Menem devalued, privatized key enterprises, and introduced an austerity program, yet inflation persisted and began to accelerate in 1989. The continued crisis set the stage for further reforms.

The other three countries where crises created opportunities for change were military dictatorships. In Chile, Indonesia I, and South Korea a military dictatorship had taken power in a coup and proved unable to curb inflation or maintain growth. In Chile, President Salvador Allende's government had pursued a socialist program of nationalization and agrarian reform, imposed wage increases and price controls, and frozen prices on public services. By 1973 inflation had soared to an annual rate of 500 percent, the fiscal deficit had climbed to 25 percent of GDP, and Chile had depleted its international reserves (Bosworth et al. 1994, pp. 4–5). As described in Chapter 6, the military deposed Allende in a bloody coup in 1973 and installed a junta headed by General Augusto Pinochet. Initially the economic team was composed of military officials and technocrats associated with the Christian Democratic and National parties who pursued a moderate program of reforms. When oil prices rose sharply and Chile's export earnings fell in 1975, the military government began looking for new solutions.

In Indonesia, when Suharto took over in a 1966 military coup the economy was in a "shambles" (Kuncoro and Resosudarmo 2005, p. 1). Inflation had accelerated to an annual rate of 600 percent, and production and trade were stagnant. Suharto wanted to win public support by restoring growth and curbing inflation. Reforms abated when the crisis abated, setting the stage for a later phase of reforms in 1980 (Indonesia II) when oil revenues fell and Suharto was again amenable to following scholars' advice.

Although South Korea's economic stagnation in 1980 was far less severe than the declines in Chile or Indonesia, it was a shock compared to South Korea's past economic performance. The previous autocrat, President Park Chung Hee, had promoted large investments in heavy and chemical industries financed by directed credit from state–owned banks; Park's government also gave monopoly privileges and subsidies to large conglomerates known as *chaebol*. These economic policies contributed to rising shortages of skilled labor, an increase in inflation to an annual rate of 26 percent (considered high in comparison to past inflation in South Korea), and a fall in the rate of growth from 10 percent a year to 2 percent (Haggard and Moon 1990, pp. 217–18). South Korea's economic stagnation coincided with a new and unpopular dictator, General Chun Doo Hwan, who took power in 1980 after the 1979 assassination of Park. Chun was unpopular because of his brutal suppression of a civil uprising in Kwangju in May 1980 (Kim, Yoon-Hyung 1994), and he was eager to restore growth and stability in the hopes of increasing his government's legitimacy and quieting the democratization movement.

There was not a crisis in China but economic problems were accumulating. The post-Mao leaders of the Communist Party were convinced that accelerated economic development was essential to maintaining the Party's power (Qian and Wu 2003). China had experienced a series of economic successes, but by 1992 tensions between the degree of central planning and the decentralized economy were increasingly evident. At the same time the debts of state enterprises continued to spiral upward. Although the special enterprise zones were doing well, China's township and village enterprises (TVEs), which had been highly successful engines of growth, were beginning to have problems in China's increasingly competitive product and factor markets. Rising inflation, rampant corruption among government officials, the collapse of the Soviet Union, and the rapid development of Japan and the East Asian tigers further spurred China's leaders to reconsider the centrally planned economy.[6] Deng Xiaoping famously made an inspection tour of the south in 1992, visiting the special economic zones, and asking "regardless of whether you call it capitalism or socialism, does it raise productivity?" (quoted in Brahm 2002, p. 13).

Taiwan faced moderate economic problems, but important external threats. In the 1950s and 1960s the ruling elite in Taiwan were members of the Kuomintang or KMT who had followed Chiang Kai-shek from mainland China to the island after their defeat by the Communists. Initially Taiwan grew rapidly, spurred by heavy state investment and ownership, policies that were financed in large part by US foreign aid. By the mid-1950s, however, growth was slowing, inflation was rising, and the US was pressuring the country to reduce its dependence on aid. President Chiang Kai-shek also wanted to reduce Taiwan's aid dependency and curb the influence of US advisers (Haggard and Pang 1994; Wu 2005). This created the conditions for the first round of reforms in 1958–91 (Taiwan I). In the 1980s a second phase of reforms (Taiwan II) was also triggered by external threats, including the rapid growth and widening recognition of China, Taiwan's growing isolation, continued military threats from China, pressures from the US to reduce its trade deficit with Taiwan, and Taiwan's desire to join the WTO. The second phase was also spurred by internal challenges to elite dominance. The island's expanding private business sector and its native Taiwanese population were demanding more freedoms, both economic freedom, demanded by business people who wanted to invest in China and elsewhere, and political freedom, demanded by the democratization movement.

There is a Viable Alternative and Role Model

In all of the cases a group of local scholars advocated an economic paradigm different from previous economic models. The economic policies promoted by these scholars generally called for deregulation, lower barriers to trade, less government intervention, more fiscal discipline and tax reform, and some privatization of state-owned business. These policies were justified by an underlying economic paradigm that assumed that market forces combined with more credible protection of private property rights and freer trade – or at least with an orientation towards export promotion rather than import substitution – would generate faster growth, more employment, and greater efficiency. In each case the scholars proposed changes that were adapted to their country's local history and circumstances, taking existing policies and institutions as their starting point. With the possible exception of Chile, the scholars were not advocating broad, abstract blueprints, such as the Washington Consensus, but heterodox packages of policies based on empirical analysis of their economy's specific circumstances. As I mentioned earlier the elites did not necessarily subscribe to all of the scholars' assumptions at the outset, but they found it convenient to adopt the new policies and rhetoric.

The cases provide less support for our hypothesis that reform is more likely when there is a role model. Chile did not have an obvious contemporaneous role model, although clearly the US had a significant impact on the thinking of Chile's US-educated scholars. Chile did become something of a model for Argentina. Indonesia, South Korea and Taiwan were influenced by the US, although it is not clear that they saw the US as a role model. Although too small to be models, the "four little tigers" were influential in China's views about the desirability of markets.

The Alternative is the Consensus of Perceived Experts

In most of our cases the scholars advocating change formed an identifiable team. Who were these scholars? In Argentina, the "Cavallo Boys" were part of Domingo Cavallo's think tank: "young, highly trained and internationally trained. Loyalty to anti-statist ideas was a requirement for recruitment" (Corrales 1997b, p. 56). Cavallo (1984) had written a widely-read book, *Volver a Crecer* (*Return to Growth*), laying out his economic ideas in 1984, and had personally delivered a copy to Menem's predecessor, President Raúl Alfonsín (Corrales 1997b). He was a personal friend of Menem, and Menem was familiar with his ideas before he was elected.

In Chile the "Chicago Boys" had PhDs in economics from the University of Chicago and other US universities, and were advocating the free-market views of Milton Friedman as early as 1970, although they gained power only in 1975 under the Pinochet military dictatorship. When a member of the Chicago Boys asked one of the generals why they had taken the advice of the free-market economists the general replied, "Because you agreed with each other and gave us simple answers to our questions" (Pinera 1994,

p. 225). The Chicago Boys proposed to liberalize markets, promote free trade, encourage private initiative, sell public enterprises, shrink the government bureaucracy, and reduce political discretion over economic decisions (Silva 1992). They had both influence and power. One source identifies 26 economists who supported the Chicago approach and served in important government positions during the military government, including six ministers of finance, specifically Sergio de Castro, Sergio de la Cuadra, Rolf Lűders, Carlos Cáceres, Jorge Cauas, and Hernán Bűchi (Dèlano and Traslaviña 1989, pp. 32–6 cited in ibid., p. 3).[7]

China had a large cadre of young Chinese scholars who had been educated in universities abroad and returned to China to staff the universities and the bureaucracy. Sending scholars to study abroad and bring back "fresh knowledge" was a practice used by the Qing Dynasty in the nineteenth century (Antal and Wang 2003). Deng Xiaoping adopted a "strategy of strengthening China through human capital" in 1978 and by the end of 2003 a total of 700,200 Chinese nationals had studied abroad and some 172,800 of them had returned (Li 2004, p. 2). Since 1988 China has also had a policy of establishing world-class universities. This was combined with intentional policies to increase turnover in mid-level and top positions in the provincial governments, including age limits on some positions (Li 2002), allowing younger people to rise to positions of power. What the Chinese call "western economics" replaced Soviet style economics in education and research over the course of the 1980s (Qian and Wu 2003). The intellectual roots of the decision to build market socialism in 1992 dates back to debates in the 1980s among economists over the virtues of an integrated approach to establishing a market system. These ideas, advocated by the "integrated reform" school (Wu et al. 1988, cited in Qian and Wu 2003), were rejected in the 1980s but had an impact in 1992 (Qian and Wu 2003). Cai cites a number of publications in which Chinese economists "ruthlessly criticized the traditional economic system, expounding the necessity of reform" and analyzing the problems of current reforms based on their empirical research (Cai 1998, pp. 4–5). He argues that economists were not involved in the initial "bottom up" reforms in agriculture or the initial efforts to reform SOEs, but were influential in the design of the special economic zones along the coast and the issue of plan versus market.

> It was through the efforts of economists after Deng Xiaoping's inspection to the southern cities of China and a series of talks in the early 1992 [sic] that a reform target of socialist market economy in China was explicitly adopted at the 14th session of the Communist Party of China National Congress held in 1992 . . . since the 1980s economists have participated in the formulation and drafting of all important documents, regulations, and programs concerning the economic

> reform and the economic development issued by the Party and the government. (ibid., p. 10)

Once the idea of market socialism became the ideology, it was implemented by Premier Zhu Rongji, who had connections to Tsinghua University and was especially influenced by Zhou Xiaochuan, whose PhD was from Tsinghua, as well as by Li Jiange, and Lou Jiwei, Wu Jinglian from the Chinese Academy of Social Science, and Wang Qishan (a graduate of Northwestern University) (Brahm 2002, pp. 19, 164).

The "Berkeley Mafia" in Indonesia were largely students at the Faculty of Economics at the University of Indonesia who went on to get PhDs from the University of California at Berkeley and other US universities. The Berkeley Mafia, particularly Widjojo Nitisasro, impressed Suharto at a seminar in August 1966, and that led to their appointment as a "Team of Experts" in economics and finance (Ford Foundation 2003). They advocated free trade, limited state intervention in the economy, and conservative fiscal and monetary policies. This group had considerable longevity and some (Widjojo Nitisasro and Ali Wardhana) were key advisers in both phases I and II of reform.

In South Korea, Kim Jae Ik, who had a PhD from Stanford, became the chief economic adviser to President Chun, and he and like-minded colleagues prepared a set of reforms in macroeconomic policy (Lee 2005). Other influential economists (who also had PhDs from US universities) were academics, Park Yong Chul and Sakong Il, and EPB bureaucrats, Kang Kyong Shik, Kim Ki Hwan, and Kim Man Jae. Their agenda called for a reduction in government deficits, tight monetary policy, trade liberalization, reduced control over foreign direct investment, privatization of commercial banks, and a phase-out of subsidies to heavy and chemical industries (ibid., p. 13). The new military regime under Chun decided to abandon the old idea of a developmental state and ally itself with these economists, who had been influenced by the "emerging ideologies of marketization and privatization" (Kim 1999). The mottos of the Chun regime's free-market ideology were "self-control," "trade liberalization," and "free competition" (Kim, Yoon-Hyung 1994, p. 52).

The most influential scholars in Taiwan were originally from mainland China and were living in the US and teaching in US universities. In the late-1950s S.C. Tsiang (Rochester and Cornell) and T.C. Liu (Cornell) shaped a vision of a market economy and became influential government advisers. They proposed a shift from import substitution to export promotion and argued that a market-oriented approach would be more effective than the command economy as a way to achieve rapid industrialization. In the mid-1980s they were joined by scholars from Yale (John Fei), Michigan State

(Anthony Koo), and Princeton (Gregory Chow), as well as Chinese University Hong Kong (Hsing Mo-huan). In September 1986, S.C. Tsiang joined with John Fei, Anthony Koo, and two other prominent economists (Wang Tsoyung and Yu Tsong-hsien) to author the "Five economists' paper" proposing concrete policies to liberalize Taiwan's economy (Hsueh et al. 2001, p. 73).

Experts are Seen as Trustworthy with Local Knowledge

The influence of these scholars was partly based on their credibility as highly trained, technical experts with no ties to business and no corrupt motivation for their economic views. Most were considered apolitical. Even Cavallo, who was elected to Congress, was never seen as wedded to any one political party. The status of the scholars was high; they were viewed as prominent persons with reputations to protect, and as such, motivated to take positions based on their research or their convictions rather than their personal self-interest.[8]

The scholars' connections with top government policymakers were also crucial to their influence. Indeed, in two cases the scholars had few constituencies other than top policymakers. One was Taiwan, where the influential scholars initially were Chinese from mainland China who were largely isolated from Taiwanese society. The other case was Indonesia, where the Berkeley Mafia did not have a large domestic constituency outside the university and state offices they controlled. They had joined Suharto's power circle partly as a way of gaining political influence (Kuncoro and Resosudarmo 2005, p. 10).

Except possibly in Taiwan, the scholars understood local conditions and constraints, as we can see in Table 7.1. This local knowledge came from living, studying, and teaching in their countries as well as from prior efforts to try to persuade political leaders. Even the influential scholars in Taiwan, although they lived and worked in the US, had close ties with top leaders, held prominent advisory positions in Taiwan, and were affiliated with local universities and scholarly institutes.

Scholars did not always value or employ their local knowledge. The most prominent example of this is the Chicago Boys in Chile, who initially followed a free market model with little regard for local norms and rules that might cause unintended consequences.[9] For example, when the government privatized the banks and industries nationalized under President Allende, the Chicago Boys were largely unconcerned about the resulting concentration of financial and economic power in the hands of a few large groups. The team belittled the risk that these powerful groups would direct their banks to make unprofitable loans to bail out the groups' money-losing industries.[10] The Chicago Boys were convinced that the conglomerates would be disciplined by the free market, which would force them out of business if they tried to keep unprofitable subsidiaries afloat. This attitude ignored the real constraints on Chile's market as well as the traditional behavior of groups with monopoly power in Chile. A flood of cheap international and domestic credit to unprofitable firms contributed to a banking crisis in 1983, and the government had to place many of the conglomerates' banks in receivership or liquidate them.

The support of international aid agencies, particularly the World Bank and the International Monetary Fund, has been cited as a reason for the influence of scholars advocating liberalization, but this is questionable. Since aid agencies provide funds regardless of whether the beneficiaries seriously adopt liberalization policies or merely "aspire" to liberalize, their imprimatur has limited effect on decision-makers, as we saw in Chapter 4.

Argentina's experience illustrates that aid-givers may support intellectual entrepreneurs, but that support is seldom the main reason for their influence. Cavallo had the support of aid-givers such as the World Bank and the IMF, but he was valuable to President Menem for many other reasons. Funds from private financial organizations were far more important to Argentina's economy than aid, and Cavallo's presence in the government gave credibility to Argentina's commitment to liberal policies and particularly to parity with the US dollar in the eyes of the private international financial community. Cavallo's credibility was based on his long advocacy of free-market ideas, his role as architect of the government's liberalization programs, and his past history as the chief negotiator of Argentina's foreign debts in the early years of the Menem administration, not solely on the support of agencies such as the World Bank or the IMF.[11]

The backing of foreign aid agencies was clearly insignificant to the prestige of the Chicago Boys in Chile. Aid agency influence in Chile was low in the 1970s and 1980s because most had suspended new aid to Chile after Pinochet took power in a coup. Additionally the World Bank had cancelled an ongoing loan to Chile's electricity company in response to the government's decision to privatize the utility. The Chicago Boys welcomed this cancellation since they saw the World Bank as advocating "statist" policies that they explicitly rejected (based on the author's participation in discussions with the Chilean economic team in the 1980s). After foreign aid to Chile resumed, the government routinely refused donor-driven projects that it considered unnecessary or ill-advised.[12]

I have already described the limited role foreign aid played in motivating reforms in China. Qian and Wu (2003) assert that China's reform never relied on foreign economic advisers, but was heavily influenced by Chinese economists who were themselves influenced by the academic exchange with the West and with Eastern European countries. Aid was useful in financing scholarships for Chinese economists to study in Western universities and for funding conferences with Western academics, and World Bank economic research was influential in China, but foreign aid projects and policy advice had little sway over government decisions.

The one case where support of international and US aid agencies was important to policy choices seems to have been Indonesia. Suharto put scholars on his economic team and followed their macroeconomic policies in part to win the support of the donor community (Kuncoro and Resosudarmo 2005). Indonesia became a large recipient of foreign aid, and its pursuit of macroeconomic orthodoxy may explain why aid-givers overlooked the regime's systemic corruption. Aid agencies continued to support Suharto despite growing problems in the financial sector, which had become a conduit for channeling funds to industries connected to Suharto's cronies (World Bank 1999).

Scholars in Taiwan and South Korea were influenced by advisers from US AID, but their governments did not implement reforms in order to win more foreign aid. Quite the contrary, an important early impetus for reform was to reduce dependence on US aid (Haggard and Moon 1990; Haggard and Pang 1994). US pressures to deregulate the South Korean financial system during the 1960s and 1970s illustrate the problem of trying to get rulers to shift their economic paradigm by using aid and advice.

> During this period a host of U.S. advisors (E.S. Shaw, John Gurley, Hugh Patrick, and others) visited Korea frequently under the auspices of USAID and international organizations. Their recommendations were put into practice with much fanfare and had an apparently dramatic effect for a while. These experiments, imbued with American ideas and implemented by officials more susceptible to U.S. influence, made ripples on the surface of Korea's financial structure. *In most cases, these experiments were short-lived, distorted, ignored, and eventually overwhelmed by the main currents flowing steadily under the surface.* (Kim, Pyung Joo 1994, p. 278 cited in Lee (2005), p. 259; original italics)

The Alternative is Known by the Elite

It's not enough for scholars to have a coherent new vision, they must also have ways to reach the ruling elite and persuade them of the merits of their point of view. The scholars in our case studies used think-tanks, academic societies, and universities to disseminate their ideas to other young scholars, build a peer group, and influence policy. To reach a wider audience, they published books and monographs, such as Cavallo's book. Personal ties to a powerful leader were important in Argentina and Taiwan. As mentioned, conferences between scholars and powerful autocrats were significant in Chile and Indonesia. For example, Chile's Chicago Boys held a conference attended by their former professors, Milton Friedman and Arnold Harberger among others, that attracted wide publicity for their ideas (Silva 1992). The Chicago Boys also bombarded the leadership with arguments that freeing markets would be the most efficient method, and that the resurging inflation could be controlled through "shock" therapy (Valdivia Ortiz de Zarate 2001). Conferences, as well as research and debates among Chinese economists in the 1980s, had an important intellectual impact on the leadership's 1992 decision to build market-supportive institutions (Qian and Wu 2003) and on the subsequent approach to managing the market (Brahm 2002). Korean scholars spread their ideas through the Korean Development Institute, a semi-autonomous government think-tank under the Economic Planning Bureau.

Once the alternative is known, key decision-makers have to be persuaded that it is in their interest to adopt the new program. It is impossible to know whether and to what extent policymakers personally believed in the reform paradigms (see Campbell 2002, on the problems of ascertaining the beliefs of political actors). It seems clear in several cases that the ruling elite saw the new policy program as a way to restore stability and growth, gain legitimacy with the public, and serve the interests of their main supporters. Much of the literature portrays Pinochet in Chile, Suharto in Indonesia, and Chun in South Korea as largely uninterested in the economic paradigm, focused rather on how well the new policy program could help them retain power (see country cites in Table 7.1). In Argentina and Taiwan I the new policy programs were seen as the only alternative, although Menem and key technocrats in Taiwan's economic bureaucracy also seem to have been convinced of the merits of the paradigm (Stokes 2001; Wu 2005). In China and Taiwan II the intellectual debate seems to have been much more important in the reform decision, arguably because in both cases there had been experimentation with market reforms for some time. The Communist Party leaders in China were fearful that if they did not keep growth rates high they could face a revolt as part of a backlash against the Cultural Revolution (Guo et al. 2005; Shirk 1993).

In all the cases scholars ended up as top advisers or controlling key cabinet positions. In Argentina, Cavallo dominated economic policy once he became Minister of Finance in 1991 (Corrales 1997b), while in Chile in the 1980s almost the entire economic team was made up of fellow PhDs from the University of Chicago, including the Minister of Economy, the President of the Central Bank, and the Budget Director (Silva 1992).

Chinese scholars also became influential advisers and filled such positions as Vice Minister of Commerce, Chairman of the China Banking Regulatory Commission, Vice President of the Supreme Court, and Mayor of Shenzhen (Li 2004). In Indonesia the Berkeley Mafia dominated the Ministry of Planning and National Development and Widjojo Nitisasro was appointed to head the Ministry of Planning and National Development in 1967 (Shiraishi 2006). In South Korea, Kim Jae Ik was the chief economic adviser and under his leadership "the Economic Planning Board forged a policy consensus within the bureaucracy by drawing on the work of a group of young, foreign-trained economists" as early as 1978 (Haggard and Moon 1990, p. 219). According to Kim (1999) the military gave Kim Jae Ik the "unhindered right" to govern the economy. In Taiwan, the scholars did not take government positions but became key advisers and teachers of the influential bureaucrats who shaped Taiwan's economic policy. For example, in the 1950s S.C. Tsiang (Tsiang Sho-chieh), T.C. Liu (Ta-Chung Liu), and Hsing Mo-huan persuaded Yin Zhongron and other powerful bureaucrats to introduce market reforms (Kuo and Myers no date; Wu 2005). In the 1960s John C.H. Fei influenced many key reformers, including Li Kuo-Ting, a reform-minded Minister of Finance sometimes termed the "architect" of Taiwan's miracle (Yu 2006).

The Alternative is Feasible

Once the ruling groups know about the scholars' new vision and are persuaded that it is in their interest to implement change, they need to overcome opposition. Most of these regimes were autocratic at the time of interest; the exception was Argentina. We should not read too much into the autocratic nature of most of the sample; there is far less difference between poor autocracies and poor democracies than the labels imply, as I argued in Chapter 5. Even in autocracies the rulers have to retain the backing of their main supporters and reduce the threat of unrest or revolt from disaffected groups in the population. The scholars argued that the reforms they advocated would accelerate growth, and growth was seen by autocrats as a way to reduce unrest and demands for democracy. The dictatorships in our sample were able to overcome potential opposition from their supporters by maintaining or increasing military spending and allowing military and business constituencies to share disproportionately in the benefits of faster growth. In democratic Argentina, President Menem was given extraordinary powers when he first took office and also enjoyed a honeymoon period with the public as we saw in Chapter 6. The main opponents of his free-market reforms came from the left wing and organized labor, but these groups had few political alternatives to Menem since his political party was their traditional party. Menem solidified his position by rewarding groups who supported his policies and punishing those who opposed him, as I describe in more detail below (Acuña et al. 2004).

In the initial years after the coup in Chile the military junta was united in its commitment to controlling inflation and restoring social order and growth, but disagreed about methods. Specifically, they were divided over how much they should reduce the size and role of the state and who should bear the social costs of adjustment (Valdivia Ortiz de Zarate 2001). General Pinochet was the Chicago Boys' strongest supporter because "he was well aware of the fact that for the definitive consolidation of his personal rule he needed the continuous achievement of successes on the 'economic' front" (Silva 1992, p. 395).[13]

In China provincial party elites played an important role in policy implementation and one way the central leaders won their support was to allow them to benefit from the growing market economy, giving them control over local resources and revenues generated from township and village enterprises (Chhibber and Eldersveld 2000, p. 361). Draconian measures were also used. In the early 1990s the government ordered the Great Wall Corporation to shut down as part of its program to stop banks from corrupt self-dealing. When the head of the corporation refused he was investigated and, when massive fraud was revealed, "promptly executed" (Brahm 2002, p. 19). The Communist Party also avoided opposition from the military or labor by directing state banks to prop up large money-losing state enterprises, many of them owned by the military, which employ massive numbers of workers.

Suharto solved the problem of keeping his support by implementing enough change to restore growth, spur exports, and generate a stream of rents to enrich his allies, while not implementing any more fundamental market reforms that might threaten his cronies' monopoly powers (Kuncoro and Resosudarmo 2005; Temple 2003). In Indonesia, Suharto's government gave protection, monopolies, credit, and government contracts to key industries owned by his cronies and family, including steel, oil refineries, and petrochemicals (Kuncoro and Resosudarmo 2005). Chun Doo Hwan did something similar in South Korea by instituting reforms that did not threaten the rent-seeking activities of the military. He also never seriously threatened the powerful *chaebols*. Although Chun introduced measures to reduce economic concentration, such as the compulsory sale of non-essential affiliates and non-business real estate, these never went far enough to curb the extensive economic power and political influence of the large conglomerates (Kim, Yoon-Hyung 1994, p. 56; Kim 1999).

From the 1950s until the late 1970s the government in Taiwan only concerned itself with opposition from the supporters of the ruling KMT and
the military; opposition from all other interest groups was repressed. The
KMT's main constituents were well rewarded as employees of the large
government and state-owned sector (Haggard and Nobel 2001; Haggard
and Pang 1994). Also, throughout this period the government kept military
spending high. The 1986 shift in strategy in Taiwan II was possible because
of changes in the KMT's constituency as private business and the middle
class had become increasingly powerful. International trade and the influx
of large numbers of students returning from abroad introduced new value
systems, new ways of thinking, and new patterns of behavior, creating a
more pluralistic society ill-suited to the KMT's "monolithic authoritarian-
ism" (Hsu 1993, p. 15). As restrictions were eased new organizations also
emerged, including consumer movements, women's movements, and a
vocal environmental movement. The number of civic organizations grew
from 2560 with about 1.3 million individual members in 1952 to 10,482
with 6.5 million individual members by 1985 (ibid., p. 21). The military still
had to be appeased, and President Lee, who introduced direct elections in
Taiwan in 1991, chose a prominent general as his premier to reassure them
(Cheng and Haggard 2001).

Early Outcomes are Successful and the Paradigm is Diffused

Except in Indonesia, the early success of their policy prescriptions helped
solidify the scholars' reputations and the acceptance of their paradigms, as
we can see in Table 7.1.[14] Indonesia differed from the rest of the sample
because Suharto never adopted the entire vision; specifically, he never implemented the scholars' advice to promote deconcentration and greater domestic competition. In Chile, China, South Korea, and Taiwan leaders of the
then autocratic states spread the ideas widely as part of the official ideology.
In the one democracy in our sample, Argentina, diffusion was spurred by
wide press coverage and a vigorous public debate between proponents and
opponents of the new vision. Cavallo and Menem made numerous speeches
promoting the reform program and, as I mentioned earlier, public support
for privatization, for example, climbed from 57 percent in 1985 to over 75
percent in 1990 (Manzetti 1993, p. 152, cited in Acuña et al. 2004, p. 18).

Long-run Effects of Reform

The new economic paradigms had unintended consequences, which in
some cases went far beyond the original intentions of the elites who
enacted the early changes. One reason for this was that economic reforms

created beneficiaries who pressed for greater political power in order to protect their gains. This did not happen in Argentina or Indonesia, however.

Argentina's reforms were increasingly distorted by partisan politics and never resolved its underlying institutional contradictions. Although Menem's government instituted sweeping policy and institutional changes, as we saw in Chapter 6, the changes never tackled the constitutional, electoral, and party rules that gave disproportionate power to provincial party bosses. Nor did they address the norms that compromised the independence of the judicial system. Menem engineered the reform program to assure his own and his party's electoral success, sparing some politically useful, small provinces from paying their share of the costs of adjustment. Instead he put most of the costs on the large urban provinces of Santa Fe, Cordoba, and Mendoza, where 70 percent of the population and 80 percent of economic activity are located (Acuña et al. 2004, p. 12). Menem also used privatization to reward his political allies in large business conglomerates (ibid., p. 15), giving some of them monopolistic or oligopolistic positions (Bambaci et al. 2002). The partisan bias of Menem's reforms undermined the market economy, heightened poverty and economic inequality, reduced confidence in the reforms, and helped propel the economy towards crisis. Cavallo resigned as Minister of Finance in 1996 after accusing members of the cabinet and other government officials of serious corruption and abuse of power.[15] Menem's second administration (1995–99) enacted few serious reforms, continuing past policies of deficit spending and political maneuvering (Acuña et al. 2004). As we saw in Chapter 6, parity with the dollar collapsed in 2002 and some of the previous reforms were reversed, although some reforms have been sustained, including improved infrastructure and a more globally competitive business sector (ibid.). Nevertheless, damaging core institutions remained unchanged, including Argentina's malleable constitution and laws, its subservient judiciary, its independent and still menacing military, and its dysfunctional federalism. The federal institutions are especially harmful, fostering polarized, parochial, and patronage-driven incentives in both the legislative and executive branch.

Indonesia is the second case where reforms never instigated a sustained process of institutional change. Western-educated scholars gained influence during the economic crisis in 1966 and the revenue shortfall in 1980, when their advice on macroeconomic policies was implemented (Azis 1994; Cho 1994; Kuncoro and Resosudarmo 2005). But their proposals to increase domestic competition and reduce monopoly power were never adopted, and their influence waned whenever crises eased. Any proposed policies or ideas that might threaten the power or wealth of Suharto's family and cronies or his support from the military were ignored (Kuncoro and Resosudarmo 2005). Instead the scholars were used to enhance Suharto's image as a liberalizing technocrat with aid donors and foreign investors. Some market-oriented reforms were implemented, such as balanced budgets, limits on the public debt, trade liberalization, and devaluation. These reforms contributed to Indonesia's rapid growth, which averaged 7 percent a year from 1979 to 1996, dramatically reducing poverty (World Bank 1999, p. 1).[16] These good outcomes had a "halo effect" with aid donors, prompting them to downplay the corruption in Suharto's regime and the inconsistencies in Indonesia's performance.[17] Eventually, however, this corrupt system became unsustainable. The president's family and cronies used the state banks to obtain large amounts of foreign funds. When devaluation became unavoidable and foreign funds dried up, the economy collapsed (Shiraishi 2006, p. 23). Donors were "taken by surprise" by the severity and depth of the crisis (World Bank 1999, p. 1).

In contrast to Argentina and Indonesia, the reforms in Chile had a sustained effect on the country's economic policies and transformed its institutions. Interestingly, some of the most prominent opponents of the Pinochet government ended up in charge after democracy was restored. The success of earlier economic reforms convinced these new leaders of the merits of continuing the economic paradigm, but prior success was not the only determinant. Among other influences, Chile has a tradition of bureaucratic competency and programmatic political parties rather than parties based principally on clientelism and patronage (de Ferranti et al. 2004, p. 15). In the Pinochet era, when the parties were deprived of power and patronage, they managed to overcome their past polarization and develop a more pragmatic approach (ibid., p. 136). In addition the constitutional changes described in Chapter 6 encouraged compromises among political parties and protection of property rights. The democratic leaders did not just implement and consolidate much of the Chicago Boys' program, they also improved social welfare and lowered Chile's historically high levels of inequality and poverty. Since the early 1990s Chile has seen a 16 percentage point reduction in the proportion of the population living below the poverty line (ibid., p. 47). Chile has enjoyed rapid economic growth and a strong reputation among international investors. Although international indices are subject to all the problems I described in Chapter 5, it is nonetheless striking how strongly and consistently Chile ranks across measures of government effectiveness, low corruption, rule of law, and protection of civil liberties, as well as on economic measures of openness, protection of property rights, economic freedom, and the like. Public opinion polls suggest that progress is still uneven, however. A surprisingly large proportion of Chile's population believe that the country is run for the benefit of a few large groups, that competition is harmful, that democracy is not the best system of government, and that government ownership should be increased (World Values Survey various).

China's adoption of a socialist market economy in 1992/93 supported continued rapid economic growth and private sector expansion. Although official data make it hard to measure the size of the non-state sector, Dougherty and Herd (2005) estimate that the private sector share of industrial output increased from about one-quarter in 1998 to more than half by 2003. Tensions between China's increasingly open access economy and its closed access political system have propelled a process of continued institutional reforms. The emergence of an independent civil society and the freedom for ordinary citizens to organize are important moves towards an open access political system, and there is some evidence that this is happening in China. The Communist Party "encouraged the formation of a wide array of new business and professional societies with strong ties to the state. It also transformed the membership of the CCP, bringing into its fold the technocratic leaders of business, social, and intellectual life" (Fogel, Robert William 2006, p. 16). These business and professional societies are still controlled by the state and there is some debate over how much they can act independently. According to one source,

> If one looks beyond the national level, beyond the lack of popular national elections and the regime's treatment of dissidents, to the grass roots, to China's villages and cities, one sees modes of interest articulation and pursuit of interests that suggest significant political change has occurred in China. Citizens cannot elect their national leaders, but a new range of *other* activities and channels have become open to citizens to articulate and pursue their interests that were never before possible in China. (Oi 2000, p. 4; original italics)

Another source argues, however, that there is no evidence that the reforms have produced independent interest groups acting as significant political actors; local party cadres continue to exercise major influence over policy implementation (Chhibber and Eldersveld 2000, p. 356). An example of this tension between local interests and the local political elite is the 2007 law on private property. The dynamism of the economy, the lack of enforceable property rights, and the absence of a functioning legal system made it possible for locally powerful party cadres to earn huge rents by taking land from villagers and otherwise extorting less powerful citizens. This led to a surge of protests, including 26,000 "mass incidents" in 2005 (*The Economist* 2007, p. 24). In response the party leaders added a clause to the constitution that private property was "not to be encroached upon" in 2004 and drafted a law to that effect that was passed in 2007 (*The Economist* 2007, p. 23). In an unusual move, a 2005 draft of this law had been unveiled to the public and an open debate had been allowed. The new law was greeted by rare public opposition from the left wing of the CCP to the point where the law had to be withdrawn and reissued in 2007 with little fanfare and no debate permitted. Although debate was suppressed and enforcement of the law will likely be weak, the emergence of vocal opposition from both sides of the political spectrum in China shows how far the reform process has affected politics there. As one analyst describes it, the Chinese leadership is trying to bend the political system without breaking it (Oi 2000).

South Korea's reforms gradually increased economic and political access, although the market power of the large conglomerates continually threaten this process. In the early 1980s, General Chun followed scholars' advice to reduce direct state intervention and end the massive program of state investment in heavy and chemical industries. Growth accelerated, but the already strong democracy movement was not appeased. Student groups, labor, environmental organizations, and intellectuals challenged the legitimacy of Chun's government and pressured for full election of the president, which was finally enacted in 1987. Arguably, the economic reforms fed this democracy movement by creating more wealth and more middle-class students prepared to demonstrate for democracy. The success of the reforms also served the democracy movement by feeding grievances, especially those of labor groups who felt the new wealth was unfairly distributed. New political interests emerged on both sides of the spectrum. The retreat of the state from direct control over credit allocation and the increasing independence of the *chaebols* gave big business increased political leverage (Lee 2005). "In fact, the 1980s saw an increasing politicization of the government-business risk partnership as political connections rather than economic fundamentals appeared to play a more important role in the survival of firms. These tendencies were reinforced after South Korea's democratization in 1987 as competitive elections were held without adequate checks on campaign financing and spending" (Kim and Lee 2004, p. 30). Besides their political influence, *chaebols'* weight in the economy made it too costly for the government to allow them to go bankrupt even as they used their control over banks and their subsidiaries to build up unsustainable levels of debt (Lee 2005). The over-indebtedness of the *chaebols* culminated in a financial crisis in 1997 that finally spurred the government to enact long overdue reforms in financial regulation, corporate restructuring, competition policy, and labor market regulations (ibid.). Since the 1997 crisis political access has also opened further, creating a counterweight to business interests and a more competitive system. Civic organizations and interest groups grew to 6000 in 2000 and have become "formidable players in the policy process" (Shin and Park 2003, p. 8). By 2003, 82 percent of Koreans viewed the current regime as democratic, a big change from the previous regime, which 72 percent rated as undemocratic (ibid., p. 17). As Lee describes it, "reforming institutions in Korea has been a long drawn-out process involving, first a change in the political-economic paradigm and then an ever-present struggle among competing interest groups. The post-crisis reforms are the culmination of this reform process that started in the early 1980s when a shift in paradigm took place" (Lee 2005, p. 272).

Taiwan is another good example of how initial policy reforms can gradually induce increasingly open access to economic and political power. Although the initial reforms were modest they fostered continued rapid growth of the private sector. The business sector was predominantly native Taiwanese and the KMT was suspicious of them and of private enterprise in general, so businesses were discouraged from concentrating and business organizations were tightly controlled. New interest groups had few formal channels for representation since opposition parties were outlawed (Haggard and Nobel 2001). Nonetheless by the 1980s the growing middle and entrepreneurial class had become too economically important to ignore. The rules against concentration had produced a highly competitive business sector composed of relatively small firms, so Taiwan avoided the *chaebol* problem plaguing South Korea. Businessmen began to support non-mainstream politicians within the KMT and to enter politics themselves. Under these new influences factions formed within the KMT that developed into political parties after 1986 when opposition was legalized (Cheng and Haggard 2001). Pressure from increasingly numerous business interests for more commercial freedom was combined with US pressure to reduce its trade deficit with Taiwan, and the rising political and economic threat/ opportunity posed by mainland China (Cheng 2001; Cheng and Chang 2003; Cheng and Haggard 2001; Haggard and Pang 1994; Hsiao and Hsiao 2001). In the mid-1980s scholars were again influential in arguing for a more dramatic shift toward market-oriented policies (Hsueh et al. 2001).[18] An increasingly open access economy was combined with increasingly open access to political activity as the KMT leaders gradually yielded to pressures for democratization. As Cheng and Chang describe it, "democratization unfolded in tandem with economic liberalization in Taiwan providing the private sector with incentives to participate in the economic policy making process, lest its interests slip rather than advance" (2003, p. 12).

CONCLUSION

This chapter has suggested that under the right circumstances institutional change is stimulated by a new policy program based on a coherent economic paradigm, articulated, coordinated, and promoted by a cohesive group of local scholars. The new policies and paradigm created more open and competitive markets and also launched a process of reform that in some cases transformed political and economic institutions. A scholarly group and a coherent program and paradigm are not sufficient conditions for sustained progress, as we saw in the case of Indonesia. Even when a new vision is implemented, it may still be undermined if long-lived institutional failures are not addressed, as in Argentina. It is also possible that scholars successfully promote a paradigm that does not spur growth, as in India. In four of the cases, however, scholars played a significant part in launching changes that propelled the transformation of policies, paradigms, and institutions. In Taiwan the reform process gradually moved society from a dictatorship promoting heavy industry and import substitution into an open access democracy with a rich array of civil organizations and a vibrant and competitive market economy. Although the transformation of South Korea is not as far along, the progress there is also striking. Chile has also evolved toward economic and political openness, although the extent of popular dissatisfaction suggests that the process is still fragile. Finally, despite impressive economic change, China's political openness is still in its infancy and its future direction is uncertain.

These transformations were long and gradual, which makes it harder to discern the contribution of scholars in instigating the process. More research is needed to improve our understanding of how scholarship, learning, and ideas change beliefs in contemporary societies.

Table 7.1 Case studies of scholarly influence on change

	Argentina	Chile	China	Indonesia	South Korea	Taiwan
Start period	1989 election Menem; 1991 appt. Cavallo Minister Economy.	1975 appointment Chicago Boys to cabinet posts.	1993 decision to adopt "Socialist Market Economy".	I. Post-1966 reforms. II. Post-1983 reforms.	1980 stabilization & other reforms.	I. 1958–61 shift from ISI to exports. II. 1986 liberalization.
Change seen as necessary (a) serious economic problems or external challenges	Hyperinflation & economic crisis. Newly elected, Menem introduces stabilization & fiscal austerity program similar to Cavallo's program.	Economic & political crises, hyperinflation under socialist president. Military coup in 1973 brings Gen. Pinochet to power. Economic crisis due to increase in price of oil, drop in export commodity prices.	Increasing decentralization incompatible with degree of central planning, increasing problems with state enterprises, rampant corruption. Collapse of USSR.	I. Suharto-led military coup in 1966. Economic crisis; inflation rose to 600%. II. Fall in oil prices 1980 led to revenue shortfall.	Military coup in 1980, 3.7% drop in GDP, rising inflation, falling growth in exports. Pressures for democracy led autocrats to emphasize growth. Pressure from US to reduce trade surplus. Purge of 8000 civil servants created vacuum.	I. mid-1950s slowing growth, inflation, rising, inc. corruption & shortages forex. Pressure US & desire to be less dependent on US aid. II. Pressure US to reduce trade surplus. Pressure businesses, native Taiwanese for more freedom. Challenge of

(b) failure past reforms	Menem rejects his own populist campaign program as unable to curb inflation or restore growth.	Protection & nationalistic program under military failed to restore growth & control inflation 1973–75.	Township & village enterprises, prior engines of growth, facing problems competing. Fear of unrest from backlash to Cultural Revolution and Tiananmen Square if growth slows.	I. Previous government intervention had left economy & trade stagnant by 1965. II. 1980s govt. industries unable to generate sufficient revenues.	Strong government intervention had contributed to inflation, slower growth, & inequality.	China. Desire to join WTO. I. Partial reforms of command economy failed to reduce dependence on US or improve balance of payments. II. Partial reforms fail to satisfy US or reduce threat from China's growth.
Viable, coherent alternative, different from past reforms	Coherent plan for liberal market economy, including privatization, smaller government, free trade, fixed exchange rate. Proposed to previous president & rejected.	"Chicago Model" coherent plan for liberal market economy, small government, free trade, based on teachings of Milton Friedman.	Coordinated move to market system, liberalization prices, monetary & financial reforms, market-oriented tax & fiscal system, property rights.	I. 1960s ad hoc approach focused mainly on macro stabilization combined with trade liberalization, smaller role for government, balanced budget. II. 1980s partial reforms again	Coherent neo-liberal model, supporting reduction state intervention, privatization, deregulation, financial liberalization, and trade liberalization. Some also challenged	I. Coordinated incremental approach to export-led market-oriented growth. II. Five economists' paper calling for sustained growth through economic liberalization.

Table 7.1 (continued)

	Argentina	Chile	China	Indonesia	South Korea	Taiwan
				focused mainly on macro policy with some efforts to liberalize banking.	authoritarian regime (Kang Kyong Shik e.g.).	
Different from past reforms	Differed from both Peronist populism and previous short lived, ad hoc austerity programs.	Radical change from military's moderate reforms & its protection of "strategic" industries.	Radical change from previous reforms allowed private investment & market forces.	Not radically different.	Major shift from economic nationalism and focus on heavy industry.	I. Gradual shift from import substitution & emphasis on economic planning & state control of industry. II. Faster, deeper shift to markets.
Role model	Chile under Chicago Boys.	US influence.	Asian tigers, Japanese examples of market-led growth.	US influence.	US influence.	US influence.
Alternative is consensus view of	Domingo Cavallo wrote *Volver a Crecer*	Most of so-called "Chicago Boys" got PhDs	Growing number of returnees from studies abroad	"Berkeley Mafia" group of graduates of	US educated economists most in monetary	I. US educated S.C. Tsiang & T.C. Liu in US

experts	laying out coherent program. "Cavallo Boys," technocrats who shared his belief in market economy.	from University of Chicago & other US universities in same period. Team had shared belief in market economy. Put together program to present to politicians.	shared belief in market economy. "Integrated reform" school promoting market system.	faculty of economics at University of Indonesia (FEUI) who got PhDs from Berkeley. Led by Widjojo Nitisastro. Shared belief in market reforms.	economics; appointment Kim Jae Ik (Stanford PhD) as senior adviser. Dominated Economic Planning Board (EPB).	universities shared belief in market economy. II. Above, plus additional US educated economists working overseas. Authored joint papers supporting liberalization.
Experts are not self-interested	No ties to business; highly trained; Cavallo had been Congressman but not seen as tied to any party.	No ties to business, highly trained, considered apolitical.	No ties to business. Highly trained, most with PhDs from US universities. Long tradition of sending scholars abroad to bring back ideas for local adaptation.	Seen as objective with no ties to business. No domestic constituency outside Suharto government. Most influential during crises. Used to win approval of foreign aid donors.	No ties to business, highly trained, considered apolitical.	Apolitical without business ties. Influence through economic bureaucrats with no political ambitions, free of military & party control. Prestigious economists. Professors at major foreign universities.

Table 7.1 (continued)

	Argentina	Chile	China	Indonesia	South Korea	Taiwan
Incentives to be truthful	Cavallo's strong local & international reputation; negotiator of Argentina's debt.	Links to prominent professors at University of Chicago & strong local & international reputation. International interest in "Chilean" model.	Scholars seen as elite. Strong local and international reputations. Links to prominent US universities.	Strong reputation with foreign aid agencies. Strong local & international reputation. Links to prominent universities in US.	Strong local & international reputation. Links to prominent universities in US.	Employed by foreign universities. Strong local & international reputation.
Local knowledge	All Argentines. Experience trying to persuade prior president.	All Chileans. Experience selling program to prior presidential candidate.	All Chinese. Tradition of sending students abroad to gain fresh knowledge dating back to 1847; reintroduced by Deng Xiaoping in 1978.	All Indonesian with local ties and long experience as government advisers.	All Korean with considerable experience trying to influence government.	Chinese scholars isolated from Taiwanese society & living overseas, but working closely with local technocrats in bureaucracy & local universities.
Alternative is known	Cavallo's book, personal contacts with Menem.	Think–tank (CESEC). Access media	Chinese Economists' Society (CES) &	I. Lecturers at Army Staff & Command	Influence through EPB, became close advisers to	I. Educated local technocrats &

	Think–tank (IEERAL). High-level seminar with prominent academics and Chilean "Chicago Boys" widely covered by press.	(*El Mercurio*), first conference with prominent academics (Milton Friedman, Arnold Harberger) widely covered by press.	later another 24 research institutes. Dominate higher education. Top advisers, hold key government positions.	College. Seminar with Suharto in August 1966 led to appointment "Team of Experts". II. Controlled Ministry Finance & Planning (BAPPENAS).	president. Government-funded, autonomous think-tank (KDI).	became trusted advisers. Also US aid mission pushed. II. Joined govt. think-tank Academia Simica & formed private think-tanks (e.g. TIER in 1976). Position paper widely debated.
Change is feasible	Menem given broad powers by legislature. Extensive use of decrees. Menem able to neutralize opponents in military (weakened by Falklands War) & unions (lost power in crisis, no alternative to Menem).	Opposition repressed. Pinochet govt. popular with rural Chileans & wealthy. Military & supporters shared sense of need to reduce size and scope of government.	Party leaders successfully ousted "Gang of Four" because of backlash to Cultural Revolution. Shared sense that growth required if Communist Party to stay in power. Gave party cadres & military share in benefits.	Suharto manipulated technocrats to boost his international image; only ideas that did not threaten Suharto cronies were adopted. Military & economic nationalists also influential.	Authoritarian government able to impose policies on labor, farmers, & bureaucracy, but not on powerful conglomerates (*chaebols*) or military.	I. Chiang Kai-shek held autocratic control. Military did not oppose reforms that did not threaten military spending. II. Increasing power & political role of Taiwanese businessmen.

Table 7.1 (continued)

	Argentina	Chile	China	Indonesia	South Korea	Taiwan
Alternative is diffused	Cavallo's think-tank, newsletter, book. Vigorous public debate with opponent think-tanks, politicians. Early success in reducing inflation, spurring growth.	Vigorous public debate with opposition think-tanks, esp. CIEPLAN. Extensive coverage TV, newspapers, books. Strong growth performance of "Chilean model" after mid-1980s recession.	Socialist Market Economic Structure adopted by Communist Party Congress, became part of party dogma. Strong new business entry in some cities helped build support.	Not widely diffused. Opposition from economic nationalists in Ministry of Industry & Trade who promoted state investment heavy industry & infrastructure.	Early success in establishing stability, restoring growth, exports gave new model credibility. Support from think-tanks, US agencies. Economic policy centered in EPB.	I. Early success in controlling inflation & inc. exports. Won support Chiang Kai-shek, US advisers. II. Success inc. growth rate. Economic liberalization combined with democratization & rising power Taiwanese natives.
Institutional changes	Shrank size of government, extensive deregulation, reduction trade barriers. Electoral structure & constitution gave provincial	Decentralized government, reduced size of government & privatized SOEs, liberalized trade, deregulated, changed electoral laws to	Private ownership & rule of law incorporated into constitution in 1999. Tax reform fixed roles local & national government. New	Scholars' macroeconomic policies adopted (balanced budget, limits on public debt, trade reform and devaluation), but no real structural	Privatization banks, liberalization trade, removal some restrictions on FDI, less state intervention & greater room for market forces.	Modest shift from import substitution in 1960s allowed small, local businesses to expand into important interest group.

leaders power to undermine fiscal policy. Dependent judiciary, malleable constitution. Polarized, parochial, patronage-driven incentives in executive & legislature. Corruption & abuse of power, benefits unevenly distributed. Crisis 2002.	encourage coalition politics, provided constitutional protection private property rights. Most new economic & political institutions sustained through transition to democracy. Reduced poverty & inequality, but still high.	budget law & independent auditing. Failed to privatize or improve large SOEs, establish rule of law, develop independent banking system. Problems of corruption, abuse of power by local officials, uneven distribution of benefits of growth.	changes. Suharto gave government protection, monopolies, credit, & govt. contracts to cronies. Steel, oil, aircraft, & other strategic industries under govt. control. Systemic corruption. Crisis in 1998.	However, proposals to liberalize financial system and reduce concentration not implemented. Power of *chaebols* increased & continued to receive directed credit until financial crisis in 1997. Increasingly open access economy & politics.	Growing wealth led to rise of middle class. Their demands for more freedom & political power led to increasingly open access political sector. Past history of government repression of business left no concentrated economic groups, assured open access economic sector.

Sources: Argentina: (Acuña et al. 2004; Balze 1995; Bambaci et al. 2002; Cavallo 1997; Corrales 1997a, 1997b, 1998; O'Neil Trowbridge 2001; Public Broadcasting Television (PBS) 2002; Stokes 2001).
Chile: (Biglaiser 1999; Bosworth et al. 1994; Chumacero et al. 2005; Fontaine 1993; Pinera 1994; Silva 1992; Velasco 1994).
China: (Antal and Wang 2003; Guo et al. 2005; Hope et al. 2003; Li 2002, 2004; Qian and Wu 2003).
Indonesia: (Azis 1994; Kuncoro and Resosudarmo 2005; Shiraishi 2006; Temple 2003).
South Korea: (Cho 1994; Haggard and Moon 1990; Kim and Lee 2004; Kim, Yoon-Hyung 1994; Kim 1999; Lee et al. 2005; Noland 2005; Wonhyuk Lim 2003).
Taiwan: (Chen 2001; Cheng and Chang 2003; Cheng and Haggard 2001; Haggard and Nobel 2001; Haggard and Pang 1994; Hsiao and Hsiao 2001; Hsueh et al. 2001; Tsai 2001, Wu 2005).

NOTES

1. Excludes Russia, includes Poland, Hungary, and Czech Republic. In comparison, annual average per capita consumption of manuscripts in Western Europe went from 6.5 per *million* inhabitants in the sixth century to 929 per million by the fifteenth century (Buringh and Zanden 2006).
2. This discussion draws on remarks by Roger Noll, "Still Reforming Regulation," the AEI-Brookings Joint Center 2006 Distinguished Lecture on 14 November 2006.
3. This discussion is based on the author's own experience teaching in a university in Bogotá, Colombia, as well as her many conversations with university professors and researchers in underdeveloped countries over the last 30 years.
4. The rest of this chapter is based on "The Role of Scholars and Scholarship in Institutional Change" with Jessica Soto (Shirley and Soto 2007).
5. In a conversation with Mary Shirley on 16 May 1990 in Prague, Czechoslovakia during a World Bank mission to Czechoslovakia.
6. The "four little tigers" in East Asia were Hong Kong, Taiwan, Singapore, and South Korea (Qian and Wu 2003).
7. Three of them were not graduates of the University of Chicago but shared the belief in the model.
8. Silva (1993) presents an opposing point of view for Chile. He argues that many of the Chicago Boys had close ties to some of the large groups that dominated the Chilean economy in the early 1980s and this influenced their policy recommendations, contributing to the economic crisis in 1983. After 1983 a more pragmatic approach was followed by a different group of intellectuals (ibid.).
9. This description of Chile is based on the author's observations and conversations with the economic team in Santiago in the early 1980s when Mary Shirley was economist for Chile in the World Bank. Note that Silva (1993, p. 547) gives a different reason for the Chicago Boys' policies at this time. He argues that they were influenced by their business ties and friendship with heads of large Chilean conglomerates that stood to benefit from radical policies freeing trade and from privatization.
10. Based on Mary Shirley's conversations with Chilean officials and others during this period; at the time she was World Bank Economist for Chile.
11. Based on Mary Shirley's participation in the first World Bank structural adjustment mission to Argentina. After Menem took power it was apparent that the government was ahead of the World Bank in pushing for reform.
12. Based on Mary Shirley's conversations with Chilean officials and others during this period; at the time she was World Bank Economist for Chile.
13. Others have argued that Pinochet believed that businessmen favoring radical liberalization of markets were also less opposed to continued military dictatorship than those favoring gradual reforms (Silva 1993).
14. Measuring the extent to which beliefs changed in response to the new vision will require more in-depth study than is possible here.
15. Cavallo claimed in a later book that he had spent much of his time as Finance Minister fighting corruption (Cavallo 1997). A number of high officials were convicted of corruption by the courts.
16. The dramatic reduction in poverty seems to have been real, even though the Indonesian government's official statistics overstate the extent of poverty (World Bank 1999, p. 49).
17. Prior to the financial crisis World Bank staff working on Indonesia argued in conversations that corruption under Suharto was not as damaging in Indonesia as in other countries because it was predictable and reliable. Bribes in Indonesia were akin to US campaign contributions in their view. (Conversations between Mary Shirley and Indonesia country and mission staff in the World Bank, various years.)
18. In 1974 six prestigious economists submitted a paper to the government that dealt with macroeconomic policy changes that had an influence on government thinking about the appropriate role of the government in the economy. Although the six were employed by US universities they were also active members of Academia Sinica (Hsueh et al. 2001).

8.   Where do we go from here?

Enormous funds have been spent to spur development, and major increases in aid have been pledged. Yet recent research shows no correlation between aid and growth in per capita GDP, and no correlation between aid and policy reform. Both the history of foreign aid and economic research suggest that the largest barriers to development arise from institutions – the norms and rules of the game. When existing institutions are inappropriate or hostile to beneficial reforms, institutional change is a prerequisite to success. Yet little research currently exists on the dynamics of institutional change, and most analyses treat institutions at a high level of abstraction. Foreign aid does not promote sustainable institutional change, and little is known about what does. Although new institutional economics has added realism to economic models, far more specific analysis is needed to understand how countries overcome the institutional barriers to development.

Where do we go from here? Comparative case studies are one way to discover the determinants of reform without sacrificing necessary institutional details. The case studies of reform in the Buenos Aires and Santiago water systems in Chapter 6 suggest that the extent of detail required to understand institutional dynamics is considerable, but manageable. Unfortunately case studies have a bad and not entirely undeserved reputation as *sui generis*, unscientific, devoid of theory, and unworthy of publication in top academic journals. Comparative case studies that overcome these faults are costly and require disciplined team commitment so it's not surprising that there are only a few efforts by serious scholars to do comparative cases. Even rigorous comparative cases will likely suffer from small sample problems, selection biases, and the difficulty of constructing a convincing counterfactual. Nevertheless, comparative case studies are worth the effort if we want to begin to unravel the determinants of institutional change. It seems unlikely that cross-country econometric studies can begin to develop more nuanced measures of institutions until they are informed by comparative case studies.

Local scholars have a comparative advantage in understanding the subtle barriers to institutional change in their own countries, and their research will be crucial. But beyond research, local scholars sometimes play a pivotal role in designing and promoting new ideas and policies that permit market-supportive reforms. Are local scholars a necessary condition for development? There is not enough evidence to be sure, but it is hard to envision a change in deeply held ideas and attitudes about economic policy and institutions without a group of intellectual entrepreneurs able to articulate the reasons for reform, adapt foreign ideas and programs to local conditions, devise new solutions to local problems, and persuade policy-makers and the public of the merits of a new conceptual paradigm and policy program. Could outside advisers perform the same function? There may have been foreign experts who learned the language, built the contacts, and understood the culture, beliefs, and history of the society well enough to play the role that local scholars played in our cases. I have never known a foreign adviser who fits this type, however. Even foreign experts who are well integrated and influential rely on local collaborators to help them to understand subtle norms and complexities and to persuade leaders and the public. In a broader sense it may not matter if scholars are a necessary condition or not. Under the right circumstances for reform, the presence of scholars promoting market-oriented paradigms seems to have been manifestly beneficial.

Scholars seem to have been important in the adoption of market supportive reform in the cases presented in Chapter 7. This is not to suggest that they were the only significant cause. Interest group politics, external threats and opportunities, even good or bad luck played a part. Some will dispute this focus on the role of scholars and ideas, arguing that policy reform is largely or entirely a matter of interest group politics. In this view, new economic paradigms are merely window dressing used by cynical political actors to convince their allies and the public of the merits of change, when the leaders' sole motivation for reform is to retain their power and reward themselves and their supporters (see, for example, Silva (1993) on Pinochet's reforms in Chile). This point of view seems too simplistic, but even if correct it does not overturn the argument for the importance of scholars and ideas. Even if decision-makers do not personally believe in the vision they are selling, the policies they enact, and the institutional changes they put in place start a process of incremental change that can go beyond their expectations or desires.

Intellectual capital of the kind described in Chapter 7 has not been a central focus of foreign aid. Aid-givers have emphasized primary education and have trained policymakers and bureaucrats; but intellectual leaders have received less attention, except as potential staff or consultants. Increasing the skills of bureaucrats and policymakers through aid-sponsored training could be beneficial, but only if they are rewarded for innovation and reform. Yet it is precisely the lack of such incentives that keeps most countries poor and makes reforms so hard to sustain.

That is why the individuals who will challenge a society's damaging institutions and beliefs are more likely to come from outside the bureaucratic or political system. Young scholars are not only outsiders; they have been exposed to new ideas and have an incentive to distinguish themselves by discovering new solutions and doing research outside the mainstream.

There have been a few large-scale donor efforts to build intellectual capacity through support to universities or research institutes, such as the Global Development Network or the support from private foundations such as the Ford Foundation or the MacArthur Foundation. But support to universities and research institutes can be undermined by the same institutional flaws that defeat other forms of development assistance. In damaging institutional settings, universities and research institutes often divert research funds into overhead or inappropriate uses. Pay and perks are often monopolized by the heads of departments and research institutes, while research is done by poorly paid and poorly motivated junior scholars who are not rewarded on the basis of merit alone – or even primarily. Aid recipients follow the wishes of donors by selecting politically correct or fashionable topics. A great deal of funding goes into bureaucratic oversight structures designed to assure that donor requirements for a balance of nationalities, gender, and intellectual pursuits are met. Merit-based support to individuals would avoid these structural problems but most donors are not equipped to select and support individuals doing self-motivated research; the scale at which they operate makes efforts targeted at individuals prohibitively expensive. To the contrary, by offering large amounts of funds for topics favored by donors, aid-sponsored research may undermine the sort of intellectual curiosity that leads researchers to put time and effort into investigating important problems despite little immediate personal reward.

In the case studies in Chapter 7, well-trained and highly motivated local scholars became advisers, bureaucrats, teachers, and opinion leaders. They had the local knowledge to design and help implement sustainable reforms and to convince policymakers of the merits of their program. They bridged the gap between outside advice about global best practice and the demands of local circumstances and interest groups. Scholars such as these need funding, but it takes more than money to give young scholars the wherewithal to remain in their country and have an impact. They need mentors, collaborators, outlets to publish and disseminate their work, and certification of the quality of their research against world standards by objective outsiders. This requires scholar-by-scholar support and hands-on training and mentoring linked to skilled researchers, such as the support provided by the Ronald Coase Institute.[1] Intellectual capacity alone is not enough to forge meaningful reforms; a political opening for change will also be needed. But without intellectual capacity there will be little chance of sustained improvement.

NOTE

1. See www.coase.org.

References

Acemoglu, Daron (2005), "Constitutions, Politics, and Economics: A Review Essay on Persson and Tabellini's *The Economic Effects of Constitutions," Journal of Economic Literature*, **XLIII**(4), 1025–48.

Acemoglu, Daron and Simon Johnson (2005), "Unbundling Institutions," *Journal of Political Economy*, **113**(5), 949–95.

Acemoglu, Daron and James A. Robinson (2005), *Economic Origins of Dictatorship and Democracy*, New York: Cambridge University Press.

—— (2006), "De Facto Political Power and Institutional Persistence," *American Economic Review*, **96**(2), 325–30.

Acemoglu, Daron, Simon Johnson, and James A. Robinson (2001), "The Colonial Origins of Comparative Development: An Empirical Investigation," *American Economic Review*, **91**(5), 1369–401.

—— (2002), "Reversal of Fortune: Geography and Institutions in the Making of the Modern World Income Distribution," *Quarterly Journal of Economics*, **117**(4), 1231–94.

Acemoglu, Daron, Simon Johnson, James A. Robinson, and Pierre Yared (2005), "From Education to Democracy?" *American Economic Review Papers and Proceedings*, **95**(2), 44–9.

Acuña, Carlos, Sebastian Galiani, and Mariano Tommasi (2004), "Understanding Reform: The Case of Argentina," Global Development Network Understanding Reform Project, final draft, December, see www.gdnet.org.

Alcázar, Lorena, Manuel A. Abdala, and Mary M. Shirley (2002a), "The Buenos Aires Water Concession," in *Thirsting for Efficiency: The Economics and Politics of Urban Water System Reform*, Mary M. Shirley (ed.), Oxford: Elsevier Science, pp. 64–102.

Alcázar, Lorena, Colin L. Xu, and Ana Maria Zuluaga (2002b), "Institutions, Politics, and Contracts: The Privatization Attempt of the Water and Sanitation Utility of Lima, Peru," in *Thirsting for Efficiency: The Economics and Politics of Urban Water System Reform*, Mary M. Shirley (ed.), Oxford: Elsevier Science, pp. 103–39.

Alfaro, Raquel (1996), "Linkages between Municipalities and Utilities: An Experience in Overcoming Urban Poverty," Unpublished report for the World Bank.

Alston, Lee and Andres A. Gallo (2005), "The Erosion of Checks and Balances in Argentina and the Rise of Populism in Argentina. An Explanation for Argentina's Economic Slide from the Top Ten," Institute for Behavioral Science, Research Program on Political and Economic Change, University of Colorado at Boulder, Working Paper PEC2005-0001.

Anheier, Helmut, Marlies Glasius, and Mary Kaldor (eds) (2004), *Global Civil Society 2004/2005*, London: Sage.

Antal, Ariane Berthoin and Jing Wang (2003), "Organizational Learning in China: The Role of Returners," Wissenschaftszentrum Berlin fur Sozialforschung Discussion Paper SP III 2003-103.

Armstrong, Mark, Simon Cowan, and John Vickers (1994), *Regulatory Reform: Economic Analysis and British Experience*, Cambridge, MA: MIT Press.

Arndt, Christiane and Charles Oman (2006), "Uses and Abuses of Governance Indicators," Paris: OECD, Development Center, available at http://www.sourceoecd.org/development/9264026851.

Aron, Janine (2000), "Growth and Institutions. A Review of the Evidence," *World Bank Research Observer*, **15**(1), 465–90.

Arruñada, Benito and Veneta Andonova (2005), "Market Institutions and Judicial Rulemaking," in *The Handbook for New Institutional Economics*, Claude Ménard and Mary M. Shirley (eds), Dordrecht, The Netherlands: Springer, pp. 229–50.

Ayyagari, Meghana, Thorsten Beck, and Asli Demirguc-Kunt (2003), "Small and Medium Enterprises across the Globe. A New Database," World Bank Policy Research Working Paper 3127, Washington, DC.

Azis, Iwan J. (1994), "Indonesia," in *The Political Economy of Policy Reform*, John Williamson (ed.), Washington, DC: Institute for International Economics, pp. 385–416.

Baietti, Aldo, William Kingdom, and Meike van Ginneken (2006), "Characteristics of Well-Performing Public Water Utilities," The World Bank, Water Supply & Sanitation Working Notes No. 9, May 2006, available at www.world.org/watsan.

Baldez, Lisa and John M. Carey (2000), "Budget Procedure and Fiscal Restraint in Post-Transition Chile," in *Presidents, Politics, and Policy*, Stephan Haggard and Mathew McCubbins (eds), Cambridge: Cambridge University Press.

Balze, Felipe A.M. de la (1995), *Remaking the Argentine Economy*, New York: Council of Foreign Relations Press.

Bambaci, Juliani, Tamara Saront, and Mariano Tommasi (2002), "The Political Economy of Economic Reforms in Argentina," *Journal of Policy Reform*, **5**(2), 75–88.

Banks, Arthur (ed.) (various), *Political Handbook of the World*, Boston, MA: McGraw Hill.

Bardhan, Pranab K. (2002), "Decentralization of Governance and Development," *Journal of Economic Perspectives*, **16**(4), 185–205.

Bates, Robert H. (2001), *Prosperity and Violence: The Political Economy of Development*, New York: W.W. Norton & Company.

Bauer, Peter (1991), *The Development Frontier: Essays in Applied Economics*, London: Harvester Wheatsheaf.

Beck, Thorsten and Ross Levine (2005), "Legal Institutions and Financial Development," in *Handbook of New Institutional Economics*, Claude Ménard and Mary M. Shirley (eds), Dordrecht, The Netherlands: Springer.

Beck, Thorsten, George R.G. Clarke, Alberto Groff, Philip Keefer, and Patrick P. Walsh (2001), "New Tools in Comparative Political Economy: The Database of Political Institutions," *World Bank Economic Review*, **15**(1), 165–76.

Beck, Thorsten, Asli Demirguc-Kunt, and Ross Levine (2003), "Law, Endowments and Finance," *Journal of Financial Economics*, **70**(2), 137–81.

Berggren, Niclas (2003), "The Benefits of Economic Freedom: A Survey," *The Independent Review*, **VIII**(2) (Fall), 1086–653.

Bhagwati, Jagdish (1993), *India in Transition. Freeing the Economy*, New York: Oxford University Press.

Biglaiser, Glen (1999), "Military Regimes, Neoliberal Restructuring, and Economic Development: Reassessing the Chilean Case," *Studies in Comparative International Development*, **34**(1), 3–26.

BIMILACI (2001), "Bimilaci 2001 Report," Biennial Meeting between International Lending Agencies and the Consulting Industry, World Bank, Washington, DC.

Bitran, Gabriel A. and Eduardo O. Valenzeula (2003), "Water Services in Chile: Comparing Private and Public Performance," Public Policy for the Private Sector Working Paper, Washington, DC.

Bogart, Dan and Gary Richardson (2006), "Property Rights, Public Goods, and Economic Development in England from 1600 to 1815: New Evidence from Acts of Parliment," paper presented at the annual meeting of the International Society for New Institutional Economics, Bolder, CO, September 21–24.

Boland, John J. (2004), "Perspective Paper 9.1," in *Global Crises, Global Solutions*, Bjorn Lomborg (ed.), Cambridge: Cambridge University Press, pp. 528–34.

Bosworth, Barry P., Rudiger Dornbusch, and Raul Raul Laban (1994), *The Chilean Economy: Policy Lessons and Challenges*, Washington, DC: The Brookings Institution.

Boudreaux, Karol (2007), "Paths to Prosperity: Creating Property Rights in Africa," paper presented at Mont Pelerin Regional Meetings, Nairobi, Kenya, February.

Brahm, Laurence J. (2002), *Zhu Rongji and the Transformation of Modern China*, Singapore: John Wiley & Sons.

Braudel, Fernand (1986), *Civilization and Capitalism. 15th–18th Century. Volume 2: The Wheels of Commerce*, New York: Harper and Row.

Brumm, Harold (2003), "Aid, Policies, and Growth: Bauer was Right," *Cato Journal*, **23**, 167–74.

Buchanan, James M. (1977), "The Samaritan's Dilemma," in *Freedom in Constitutional Contract*, James M. Buchanan (ed.), College Station: Texas A&M University Press.

Buringh, Eltjo and Jan Leiten van Zanden (2006), "Charting the 'Rise of the West'. Manuscripts and Printed Books in Europe. A Long Term Perspective from the Sixth through Eighteenth Century," International Institute of Social History, paper available at: http:www.isg.nl/bibliometrics/books 500-1800.pdf.

Burnside, Craig and David Dollar (2000), "Aid, Policies, and Growth," *American Economic Review*, **90**(4), 847–68.

—— (2004), "Aid, Policies, and Growth: Revisiting the Evidence," World Bank Policy Research Working Paper 2834, Washington, DC.

Cai, Fang (1998), "The Roles of Chinese Economists in Economic Reform," *China Economy Papers*, 2, available at http://ncdsnet.anu.edu.au/online/.

Cameron, John and P. Ndhlovu Tidings (2001), "Cultural Influences on Economic Thought in India: Resistance to Diffusion of Neo-Classical Economics and the Principles of Hinduism," *Economic Issues*, **6**(2), 61–77.

Campbell, John L. (2002), "Ideas, Politics, and Public Policy," *Annual Review of Sociology*, **28**, 21–38.

Casarin, Ariel A., Josè A. Delfino, and Maria Eugenia Delfino (2007), "Failures in Water Reform: Lessons from the Buenos Aires's Concession," *Utilities Policy*, **15** 234–47.

Cavallo, Domingo (1984), *Volver a Crecer*, Buenos Aires: Editoral Sudamerica/Planeta.

Cavallo, Domingo (1997), *El Peso De La Verdad*, Buenos Aires: Planeta.

Center for Global Development, MCA Monitor (2006), "Actual vs. Estimated MCA Annual Compact Disbursements," www.cgdev.org/ accessed 8 September, 2006.

Chaudhury, Nazmul, Jeffrey Hammer, Michael Kremer, Karthik Muralidharan, and F. Halsey Rogers (2006), "Missing in Action: Teacher and Health Worker Absence in Developing Countries," *Journal of Economic Perspectives*, **20**(1), 91–116.

Chen, Shaohua and Martin Ravallion (2004), "How Have the World's Poorest Fared since the Early 1980s?," World Bank Policy Research Working Paper 3341, Washington, DC.

Cheng, Tun-jen (2001), "Transforming Taiwan's Economic Structure in the 20th Century," *The China Quarterly*, **165**, 19–36.

Cheng, Tun-Jen and Peggy Pei-chen Chang (2003), "Limits of Statecraft: Taiwan's Political Economy under Lee Teng-Hui," in *Sayonara to the Lee Teng-Hui Era: Politics in Taiwan, 1988–2000*. Wei-chin Lee and T.Y. Wang (eds), Lanham, MD and Oxford: University Press of America, pp. 113–48. Information cited here has been obtained from an early version, see http://www.la.utexas.edu/research/cgots/Papers/52.pdf.

Cheng, Tun-Jen and Stephan Haggard (2001), "Democracy and Deficits in Taiwan. The Politics of Fiscal Policy 1986–1996," in *Presidents, Parliaments, and Policy*, Stephan Haggard and Mathew McCubbins (eds), Cambridge: Cambridge University Press, pp. 183–225.

Chhibber, Pradeep and Samuel Eldersveld (2000), "Local Elites and Popular Support for Economic Reform in China and India," *Comparative Political Studies*, **33**, 350–73, available at http://cps.sagepub.com/cgi/content/abstract/33/3/50.

Cho, Lee-Jay (1994), "Culture, Institutions, and Economic Development in East Asia," in *Korea's Political Economy: An Institutional Perspective*, Lee-Jay Cho and Yoon-Hyung Kim (eds), Oxford: Westview Press, pp. 3–41.

Chu, Rebecca U. (2006), "Groups Hope to Make Bottled Water a Moral Issue," Religion News Service, reproduced at www.beliefnet.com/story/206/story_20645.html.

Chumacero, Rómulo A., Rolf Luders, Rodrigo Fuentes, and Joaquín Vial (2005), "Understanding Chilean Reforms," Global Development Network Understanding Reform Project, draft March.

Clarke, George R.G., Katrina Kosec, and Scott Wallsten (2004), "Has Private Participation in Water and Sewerage Improved Coverage? Empirical Evidence from Latin America," World Bank Policy Research Working Paper 3445, Washington, DC.

Clemens, Michael A. and Todd J. Moss (2005), "Ghost of 0.7%: Origins and Relevance of the International Aid Target," Center for Global Development, Working Paper No. 68, Washington, DC.

Clemens, Michael A., Steven Radelet, and Rikhi Bhavnani (2004), "Counting Chickens When They Hatch: The Short Term Effect of Aid on Growth," Center for Global Development, Working Paper No. 44.

Coase, Ronald H. (1937), "The Nature of the Firm," *Economica*, n.s. (4), 386–405.

—— (1959), "The Federal Communications Commission," *Journal of Law and Economics*, **2**(October), 1–40.

Coase, Ronald H. (1992), "The Economic Structure of Production," *American Economic Review*, **82**(September), 713–19.

Collier, Paul (1997), "The Failure of Conditionality," in *Perspectives on Aid and Development*, Catherine Gwyn and Joan M. Nelson (eds) Washington, DC: Overseas Development Council Policy Essay 22, pp. 51–78.

Congleton, Roger D. (2006), "America's (Neglected) Debt to the Dutch, an Institutional Perspective," Working Paper, 19 January, available at SSRN, http://ssrn.com/abstract=884257.

Corbo, Vittorio (2005), "The Chilean Investment Climate," Central Bank of Chile, Powerpoint presentation (March), available at http://www.bcentral.cl/esp/politicas/exposiciones/miembrosconsejo/pdf/2006/vcl06032006.pdf.

Corbo, Vittorio, Leonardo Hernandez, and Fernando Parro (2005), "Institutions, Economic Policies and Growth: Lessons from the Chilean Experience," Central Bank of Chile Working Paper No. 317, April, Santiago, Chile, available at http://www.bcentral.cl/eng/stdpub/studies/workingpaper.

Corrales, Javier (1997a), "Do Economic Crises Contribute to Economic Reform? Argentina and Venezuela in the 1990s," *Political Science Quarterly*, **112**(4), 617–44.

—— (1997b), "Why Argentines Followed Cavallo: A Technopol between Democracy and Economic Reform," in *Technopols. Freeing Politics and Markets in Latin America in the 1990s*, Jorge Dominguez (ed.), University Park, PA: Pennsylvania State University Press, pp. 49–93.

—— (1998), "Coalitions and Corporate Choices in Argentina, 1976–1994: The Recent Private Sector Support of Privatization," *Studies in Comparative International Development*, **32**(4) (winter), 24–51.

Coviello, Decio and Raumeen Islam (2006), "Does Aid Help Economic Institutions?," World Bank Policy Research Working Paper 3390, available at SSRN, http://ssrn.com/abstract=923296.

Curtin, Philip D. (1984), *Cross-Cultural Trade in World History*, Cambridge: Cambridge University Press.

Dam, Kenneth W. (2006), "Legal Institutions, Legal Origins, and Governance," University of Chicago Law and Economics Ohlin Working Paper No. 303, available at Social Science Research Network Electronic Paper Collection, http://ssrn.com/abstract_id=932694.

de Ferranti, David, Guillermo E. Perry, Francisco H.G. Ferreira, and Michael Walton (2004), *Inequality in Latin America: Breaking with History?*, Washington, DC: The World Bank.

de Michele, Roberto and Luigi Manzetti (1996), "Legal Security and Market Reforms: The Case of Argentina," Judicial Security and Markets Working Paper, University of Maryland at College Park.

de Vries, Jan and Ad van der Woude (1997), *The First Modern Economy. Success, Failure, and Perseverance of the Dutch Economy, 1500–1815*, New York: Cambridge University Press.

Dèlano, Manuel and Hugo Traslaviña (1989), *La Herencia De Los Chicago Boys*, Santiago, Chile: Ornitorrinco.

Disease Control Priorities Project (2006), "Improving Quality of Clinical Care. Incentives for Health Care Workers," DCCP Technical Note, July, available at http://www.dcp2.org/page/main/InBrief.html.

Djankov, Simeon, Jose Garcia Montalvo, and Marta Reynal-Querol (2006), "The Curse of Aid," Working Paper, March, available at SSRN, http://ssrn.com/abstract=893558.

Dollar, David and Aart Kraay (2003), "Institutions, Trade, and Growth," *Journal of Monetary Economics*, **50**(1), 133–62.

Dougherty, Sean and Richard Herd (2005), "Fast-Falling Barriers and Growing Concentration: The Emergence of a Private Economy in China," OECD, Economics Department Working Papers No. 471, available at www.oecd.org/eco.

Durlauf, Steven N., Paul A. Johnson, and Jonathan R.W. Temple (2005), "Growth Econometrics," in *Handbook of Economic Growth*, Philippe Aghion and Steven N. Durlauf (eds), Amsterdam, The Netherlands: Elsevier Science, pp. 555–677.

Easterly, William (2002a), "The Cartel of Good Intentions: Bureaucracy Versus Markets in Foreign Aid," Center for Global Development Working Paper No. 4, Washington, DC.

—— (2002b), *The Elusive Quest for Growth. Economists Adventures and Misadventures in the Tropics*, Cambridge, MA: MIT Press.

—— (2003), "Can Foreign Aid Buy Growth?", *Journal of Economic Perspectives*, **17**, 23–48.

—— (2006), *The White Man's Burden: The Wacky Ambition of the West to Transform the Rest*, New York: Penguin.

Easterly, William, Ross Levine, and David Roodman (2003), "New Data, New Doubts: A Comment on Burnside and Dollar's 'Aid, Policies and Growth' (2000)," NBER Working Paper No. 9846, Cambridge, MA.

The Economist (2007) (March 10-16), "Caught between Right and Left, Town and Country," 10–16 March, pp. 23–5.

Engerman, Stanley L. and Kenneth L. Sokoloff (2002), "Factor Endowments, Inequality, and Paths of Development among New World Economies," *Economia*, **3** (fall), 41–109.

—— (2005a), "The Evolution of Suffrage Institutions in the New World," *Journal of Economic History*, 65(December), 891–921.

—— (2005b), "Institutional and Non-Institutional Explanations of Economic Differences," in *Handbook of New Institutional Economics*,

Claude Ménard and Mary M. Shirley (eds), Dordrecht, The Netherlands: Springer, pp. 639–63.

Esrey, Steven A. (1996), "Water, Waste, and Well-Being: A Multicountry Study," *American Journal of Epidemiology*, **143**(6), 608–23.

Estache, Antonio and Ana Goicoehea (2005), "How Widespread Were Private Investment and Regulatory Reform in Infrastructure Utilities During the 1990s?," World Bank, Policy Research Working Paper 3595, Washington, DC.

Estache, Antonio and Martin A. Rossi (2002), "How Different is the Efficiency of Public and Private Water Companies in Asia?," *World Bank Economic Review*, **16**(1), 139–48.

Faccio, Mara (2006a), "The Characteristics of Politically Connected Firms," Working Paper, October, available at SSRN, http://ssrn.com/abstract=918244.

—— (2006b), "Politically Connected Firms," *American Economic Review*, **96**(1), 369–86.

Faccio, Mara, Ronald Masulis, and John J. McConnell (2005), "Political Connections and Corporate Bailouts," 1 March 2005, paper presented at the AFA 2006 Boston Meetings, available at SSRN, http://ssrn.com/abstract=676905.

Fogel, Kathy (2006), "Oligarchic Family Control, Social Economic Outcomes, and the Quality of Government," *Journal of International Business Studies*, **37**(September), 603–22, available at http://www.palgrave-journals.com/jibs/journal/v37/n5/pdf/8400213a.pdf.

Fogel, Robert William (2004), *The Escape from Hunger and Premature Death, 1700–2100. Europe, America, and the Third World*, Cambridge: Cambridge University Press.

—— (2006), "Why China is Likely to Achieve its Growth Objectives," NBER Working Paper No. 12122, available at: http://www.nber.org/papers/w12122.

Fontaine, Juan Andrés (1993), "Transición Económica y Política en Chile: 1970–1990," *Estudios Públicos*, **50**(autumn), 230–79.

Ford Foundation (2003), "Celebrating Indonesia. Fifty Years with the Ford Foundation, 1953–2003," Ford Foundation, available at http://www.fordfound.org/elibrary/documents/5002/050.cfm.

Fox, J. (2000), "Applying the Comprehensive Development Framework to U.S. Aid Experiences," World Bank Operations Evaluation Department, Working Paper Series No. 15, Washington, DC.

Fraser, Julia M. (2005), "Lessons from the Independent Private Power Experience in Pakistan," World Bank, Energy and Mining Sector Board Discussion Paper No. 14, Washington, DC.

Frey, Bruno S. (2000), "Does Economics Have an Effect? Towards an

Economics of Economics," University of Zurich, Institute for Empirical Research in Economics, Working Paper No. 36, February.

Galiani, Sebastian, Paul Gertler, and Ernesto Schargrodsky (2005), "Water for Life: The Impact of the Privatization of Water Services on Child Mortality," *Journal of Political Economy*, 113(February), 83–120.

Gallo, Andres A. (2002), "The Political Economy of Property Rights: Rural Rent Legislation in Argentina, 1912–1960," working paper presented at the annual meeting of the International Society for New Institutional Economics, Cambridge, MA, 27–29 September.

Gandhi, Jennifer (2003), "Dictatorial Institutions and their Impact on Economic Growth," working paper presented at the Comparative Politics Workshop, Department of Political Science, Stanford University, 24 October 2005.

Gary, Ian and Nikki Reisch (2005), "Chad's Oil: Miracle or Mirage? Following the Money in Africa's Newest Petro-State," Catholic Relief Services, available at http://www.crs.org/get_involved/advocacy/policy_and_strategic_issues/chad_oil_report.pdf.

Gassner, Katharina, Alexander Popov, and Nataliya Pushak (2006), "An Empirical Assessment of Private Sector Participation in Electricity and Water Distribution in Developing Countries," unpublished draft paper; a subsequent draft was published by the World Bank and is available at http://go.worldbank.org/TEBY2W5X40.

Gauri, Varun and Anna Furuttero (2003), "Location Decisions and Nongovernmental Organization Motivation: Evidence from Rural Bangladesh," World Bank Policy Research Working Paper 3176, Washington, DC.

Geddes, Barbara (1994), *Politician's Dilemma*, Berkeley and Los Angeles: University of California Press.

Girishankar, Navin (2001), "Evaluating Public Sector Reform. Guidelines for Assessing Country-Level Impact of Structural Reform and Capacity Building in the Public Sector," World Bank, Operations Evaluation Department, Washington, DC.

Glaeser, Edward, Rafael La Porta, Florencio Lopez-de-Silanes, and Andrei Shleifer (2004), "Do Institutions Cause Growth?," NBER Working Paper No. 10568, Boston, MA.

Gomanee, Karuna, Sourafel Girma, and Oliver Morrissey (2003), "Searching for Aid Threshold Effects," University of Nottingham, Centre for Research in Economic Development and International Trade (CREDIT) Research Paper No. 03/15.

Greif, Avner (1993), "Contract Enforceability and Economic Institutions in Early Trade: The Maghribi Traders' Coalition," *American Economic Review*, 83(3), 525–48.

Greif, Avner (1994), "Cultural Beliefs and the Organization of Society: A Historical and Theoretical Reflection on Collectivist and Individualist Societies," *Journal of Political Economy*, **102**(5), 912–50.

—— (2005), "Commitment, Coercion, and Markets: The Nature and Dynamics of Institutions Supporting Exchange," in *Handbook of New Institutional Economics*, Claude Ménard and Mary M. Shirley (eds), Dordrecht, The Netherlands: Springer, pp. 727–86.

—— (2006), *Institutions and the Path to the Modern Economy. Lessons from Medieval Trade*, Cambridge: Cambridge University Press.

Guasch, J. Luis (2004), *Granting and Renegotiating Infrastructure Concessions. Doing it Right*, Washington, DC: The World Bank Institute.

—— (2006), "The Infrastructure Challenge: Increasing Investments and Better Performance: Contracting out and Concessions," Microsoft Power Point Presentation to Fundacion del Pino Workshop on Government Restructuring: Privatization, Regulation and Competition, 29 June, available at http://www.ub.es/graap/concession-fundacion%20del%20pino-6-06%20WORSHOP.ppt.

Guo, Rongxing, Kaizhong Yang, Renwei Zhao, and Eui-Gak Hwang (2005), "How to Reform a Centrally Planned Economy: The Case of China," Global Development Network Understanding Reform Project, draft.

Haas, Peter M. (1992), "Knowledge, Power and International Policy Coordination," *International Organization*, **46**(1), 1–35.

Hadfield, Gillian (2005), "The Many Legal Institutions that Support Contractual Commitments," in *Handbook of New Institutional Economics*, Claude Ménard and Mary M. Shirley (eds), Dordrecht, The Netherlands: Springer, pp. 175–204.

Haggard, Stephan and Mathew McCubbins (eds) (2000), *Presidents, Politics and Policy*, Cambridge: Cambridge University Press.

Haggard, Stephan and Chung-In Moon (1990), "Institutions and Economic Policy: Theory and a Korean Case Study," *World Politics*, **42**(2), 210–37.

Haggard, Stephan and Gregory W. Nobel (2001), "Power Politics: Elections and Electricity Regulation in Taiwan," in *Presidents, Parliaments, and Policy*, Stephan Haggard and Mathew McCubbins (eds), Cambridge: Cambridge University Press, pp. 256–90.

Haggard, Stephan and Chien-Kuo Pang (1994), "The Transition to Export-Led Growth in Taiwan," in *The Role of the State in Taiwan's Development*, Joel D. Aberbach, David Dollar and Kenneth L. Sokoloff (eds), Armonk, NY: M.E. Sharpe, pp. 47–89.

Haggarty, Luke, Penelope J. Brook, and Ana Maria Zuluaga (2002), "Water Sector Service Contracts in Mexico City, Mexico," in *Thirsting for Efficiency: The Economics and Politics of Urban Water System Reform*, Mary M. Shirley (ed.), Oxford: Elsevier Science, pp. 139–87.

Hall, Peter A. (1993), "Policy Paradigms, Social Learning and the State: The Case of Economic Policymaking in Britain," *Comparative Politics*, April, 275–96.

Hanemann, W. Michael (2006), "The Economic Conception of Water," in *Water Crisis: Myth or Reality? Marcelino Botin Water Forum 2004*, Peter P. Rogers and M. Ramon Llamas (eds), London: Taylor & Francis, pp. 61–91.

Harms, Philipp and Matthias Lutz (2003), "Aid, Governance, and Private Foreign Investment: Some Puzzling Findings and a Possible Explanation," Study Center Gerzensee Working Paper No. 03.04.

—— (2004), "The Macroeconomic Effects of Foreign Aid: A Survey," Universität St Gallen Discussion Paper No. 2004-11.

Haslam, Paul Alexander (2003), "Argentina: Governance in Crisis," Canadian Foundation for the Americas, Policy Paper FPP-03-02, available at www.focal.ca.

Heckelman, Jac and Stephen Knack (2005), "Foreign Aid and Market-Liberalizing Reform," World Bank Policy Research Working Paper 3557, Washington, DC.

Herbst, Jeffrey I. (2000), *States and Power in Africa*, Princeton: Princeton University Press.

Hill, Alice and Manuel A. Abdala (1996), "Argentina: The Sequencing of Privatization and Regulation," in *Regulations, Institutions, and Commitment*, Brian Levy and Pablo T. Spiller (eds), Cambridge: Cambridge University Press, pp. 202–49.

Hoffman, Philip T. and Jean-Laurent Rosenthal (1997), "The Political Economy of Warfare and Taxation in Early Modern Europe," in *The Frontiers of the New Institutional Economics*, John N. Drobak and John V.C. Nye (eds), San Diego, CA: Academic Press, pp. 31–55.

Hope, Nicholas C., Dennis Tao Yan, and Mu Yang Li (2003), "Economic Policy Reform in China," in *How Far across the River? Chinese Policy Reform at the Millennium*, Nicholas C. Hope, Dennis Tao Yan and Mu Yang Li (eds), Stanford: Stanford University Press, pp. 1–28.

Hsiao, Frank S.T. and Mei-chu W. Hsiao (2001), "Economic Liberalization and Development – the Case of Lifting Martial Law in Taiwan," in *Change of an Authoritarian Regime: Taiwan in the Post-Martial Law Era*, Taiwan Studies Promotion Committee of Academia (SINICA) (ed.), Taipei, Taiwan: Taiwan Studies Promotion Committee of Academia, pp. 353–79.

Hsu, Cho-yun (1993), "Historical Setting for the Rise of Chiang Ching-Kuo," in *Chiang Ching-Kuo's Leadership in the Development of the*

Republic of China on Taiwan, Shao-Chuan Leng (ed.), Lanham, MD: University Press of America and the Miller Center, University of Virginia, pp. 1–30, available at www.millercenter.virginia.edu/scrippts/ digitalarchive/mcpubs/mcpapers/asian.

Hsueh, Li-min, Chen-kuo Hsu, and Dwight Perkins (2001), *Industrialization and the State. The Changing Role of the Taiwan Government in the Economy, 1945–1998*, Cambridge, MA: Harvard University Press.

Huizinga, Johan (1960a [1959]), "The Problem of the Renaissance," (originally published as "Renaissancestudiën, I: Het Probleem" in 1920), in *Men and Ideas. History, the Middle Ages, the Renaissance*, Johan Huizinga (ed.), New York: Meridian Books.

—— (1960b [1959]), "The Task of Cultural History," (originally published as "*De Taak Der Cultuurgeschiedenis*" in 1929, in *Men and Ideas. History, the Middle Ages, the Renaissance*, Johan Huizinga (ed.), New York: Meridian Books.

Huppert, George (1999), *The Style of Paris. Renaissance Origins of the French Enlightenment*, Bloomington, IN: Indiana University Press.

Hyde, J.K. (1973), *Society and Politics in Medieval Italy: The Evolution of the Civil Life 1000–1350*, London: Macmillan.

Iaryczower, Matias, Pablo T. Spiller, and Mariano Tommasi (2000), "Judicial Decision Making in Unstable Environments, Argentina, 1935–1998," paper presented at the annual meeting of the International Society for New Institutional Economics, Tübingen, Germany, 22–24 September. Subsequently published in *American Journal of Political Science*, **46**(4), October 2002, 699–716.

Inter-American Development Bank (2003), "Modernization of the State, Strategy Document," Inter-American Development Bank, Washington, DC.

International Monetary Fund (2003), *World Economic Outlook, April 2003: Institutions and Growth*, Washington, DC: International Monetary Fund.

—— (2005), *World Economic Outlook, September 2005: Building Institutions*, Washington, DC: International Monetary Fund.

Izaguirre, Ada and Catherine Hunt (2005), "Private Water Projects," World Bank, Private Sector Development Viewpoint Note 297, available at http://rru.worldbank.org/publipolicyjournal.

Jacob, Margaret C. (2001), *The Enlightenment. A Brief History with Documents*, Boston, MA: Bedford/St Martin's.

Jaramillo Baanante, Miguel (2004), "Transaction Costs in Peru: How Much Does It Cost to Start a New Garment Firm in Lima," Ronald Coase Institute Research Report 1, St Louis, MO.

Jones, Mark P., Sebastian Saiegh, Pablo T. Spiller, and Mariano Tommasi (2000), "Professional Politicians–Amateur Legislators: The Argentine Congress in the 20th Century," paper presented at the annual meeting of the International Society for New Institutional Economics, Tübingen, Germany, 22–24 September. Subsequently published in *American Journal of Political Science*, **46**(3), July 2002, 656–69.

Joskow, Paul L. (2000), *Economic Regulation*, Cheltenham, UK and Northampton, MA, USA: Edward Elgar Publishing.

Kanbur, Ravi (2000), "Aid, Conditionality and Debt in Africa," in *Foreign Aid and Development: Lessons Learnt and Directions for the Future*, Fred Tarp (ed.), London: Routledge.

—— (2005), "Reforming the Formula: A Modest Proposal for Introducing Development Outcomes in Ida Allocation Procedures," January, available at www.people.cornell.edu.pages.sk145.

Kaufmann, Daniel and Aart Kraay (2002), "Governance Indicators, Aid Allocation, and the Millennium Challenge Account," World Bank Institute Working Papers Series, Washington, DC.

Kaufmann, Daniel, Aart Kraay, and Massimo Mastruzzi (2005), "Governance Matters IV: Governance Indicators for 1996–2004," World Bank Policy Research Working Paper 3630, Washington, DC.

Keefer, Philip (2002), "Clientelism and Credibility," paper presented to the annual meeting of the International Society for New Institutional Economics, Cambridge, MA, 27–29 September.

—— (2004), "All Democracies are not the Same: Identifying the Institutions that Matter for Growth and Convergence," paper presented at the conference "Successes and Failures of Real Convergence," National Bank of Poland, Warsaw, 23–24 October, available at http://www.nbp.pl/konferencje/radisson/Mowcy/keefer/keefer_paper.pdf.

—— (2005), "Programmatic Parties: Where do they come from and do they Matter?" paper presented at the 2005 meetings of the International Society for New Institutional Economics (ISNIE), Barcelona, Spain.

—— (2007), "The Poor Performance of Poor Democracies," in *Oxford Handbook of Comparative Politics*, Carles Boix and Susan C. Stokes (eds), Oxford: Oxford University Press.

Keefer, Philip and Mary M. Shirley (2000), "Formal versus Informal Institutions in Economic Development," in *Institutions, Contracts, and Organizations: Perspectives from New Institutional Economics*, Claude Ménard (ed.), Cheltenham, UK and Northampton, MA, USA: Edward Elgar, pp. 88–107.

Keefer, Philip and David Stasavage (2003), "The Limits of Delegation: Veto Players, Central Bank Independence, and the Credibility of Monetary Policy," *American Political Science Review*, **97**(3), 407–23.

Khatkhate, Deena (1994), "Intellectual Origins of Indian Economic Reform: A Review of Jagdish Bhagwati's *India in Transition: Freeing the Economy* (1993)," *World Development*, **22**(7), 1097–102.

Kim, Hong-Bum and Chung H. Lee (2004), "Post-Crisis Financial Reform in Korea: A Critical Appraisal," University of Hawaii at Manoa, Department of Economics Working Paper No. 2004-10.

Kim, Pyung Joo (1994), "Financial Institutions," in *Korea's Political Economy: An Institutional Perspective*, Lee-Jay Cho and Yoon-Hyung Kim (eds), Boulder, CO: Westview Press, pp. 273–320.

Kim, Yoon-Hyung (1994), "An Introduction to the Korean Model of Political Economy," in *Korea's Political Economy: An Institutional Perspective*, Lee-Jay Cho and Yoon-Hyung Kim (eds), Oxford: Westview Press, pp. 45–62.

Kim, Yun-Tae (1999), "Neoliberalism and the Decline of the Developmental State," *Journal of Contemporary Asia*, **29**(4), 441–61.

Kingdom, William, Aldo Baietti, and Meike van Ginneken (2006), "Reforming Public Utilities," presentation to IWA Congress, Beijing, available at http://www.wsp.org/IWA/Public%20sector%20reform%20V090606.pdf.

Kinross, Lord (1977), *The Ottoman Centuries. The Rise and Fall of the Turkish Empire*, New York: Morrow Quill Paperbacks.

Kirkpatrick, Colin, David Parker, and Yin-Fang Zhang (2006), "An Empirical Analysis of State and Private-Sector Provision of Water Services in Africa," *World Bank Economic Review*, **20**(1), 143–63.

Knack, Stephen (2000), "Aid Dependence and the Quality of Governance: A Cross-Country Empirical Analysis," World Bank Policy Research Working Paper 2396, Washington, DC.

—— (2006), "Measuring Corruption in Eastern Europe and Central Asia: A Critique of the Cross-Country Indicators," World Bank, Policy Research Working Paper 3968, Washington, DC.

Komives, Kristin, Jonathan Halpern, Vivien Foster, and Quentin Wodon (2006), "The Distributional Incidence of Residential Water and Electricity Subsidies," World Bank, Policy Research Working Paper 3878, available at http://econ.worldbank.org.

Kotkin, Steven (2007), "Innovation: Individuals, Networks, Patronage," draft, cited by InsideHigherEd.com, "Lost Opportunity in Russia," available at http://insidehighered.com/set/print/news/2007/01/31/russia.

Kuhn, Thomas S. (1962), *The Structure of Scientific Revolutions*, 3rd edn 1996, Chicago: University of Chicago Press.

Kuncoro, Ari and Budy P. Resosudarmo (2005), "Understanding Indonesian Economic Reforms: 1983–2000," Global Development Network Understanding Reform Project, draft.

Kuo, Tai-Chun and Ramon H. Myers (no date), "Political Leadership, Institutional Reform and Economic Change in Taiwan, 1950–1960," Hoover Institution, Stanford University, available at http://www.miller-center.virginia.edu/pubs/misc_docs/china_conf/tai_chun_kuo_myers.pdf.

La Porta, Rafael, Florencio Lopez-de-Silanes, Andrei Shleifer, and Robert Vishny (1997), "Legal Determinants of External Finance," *Journal of Finance*, **52**, 1131–50.

—— (1998), "Law and Finance," *Journal of Political Economy*, **106**, 1113–55.

—— (1999), "The Quality of Government," *Journal of Law, Economics and Organization*, **15**(1), 222–82.

—— (2000), "Investor Protection and Corporate Governance," *Journal of Financial Economics*, **58**, 3–27.

Laffont, Jean-Jacques and Jean Tirole (1993), *A Theory of Incentives in Procurement and Regulation*, Cambridge, MA: MIT Press.

Lee, Chung H. (2005), "The Political Economy of Institutional Reform in Korea," *Journal of the Asia Pacific Economy*, **10**(3), 257–77.

Lee, Keun Lee, Byung-Kook Kim, Chung H. Lee, and Jaeyeol Yee (2005), "Visible Success and Invisible Failure in Post-Crisis Reform in Korea: Interplay of the Global Standards, Agents and Local Specificity," World Bank Policy Research Working Paper 3651, Washington, DC.

Levine, Ross (2005), "Law, Endowments, and Property Rights," *Journal of Economic Perspectives*, **19**(3), 61–88.

Levine, Ross and David Renelt (1992), "A Sensitivity Analysis of Cross-Country Growth Regressions," *American Economic Review*, **82**(4), 942–63.

Levy, Brian and Pablo T. Spiller (1994), *Regulations, Institutions, and Commitment: Comparative Studies of Telecommunications*, Cambridge and New York: Cambridge University Press.

Li, Cheng (2002), "After Hu, Who? China's Provincial Leaders Await Promotion," *China Leadership Monitor* 1 (Winter), available at www.chinaleadershipmonitor.org.

——(2004), "Bringing China's Best and Brightest Back Home: Regional Disparities and Political Tensions," *China Leadership Monitor*, 11 (Summer), available at www.chinaleadershipmonitor.org.

Lopez, J. Humberto (2004), "Pro-Poor Growth: A Review of What We Know (and of What We Don't)," World Bank, available at http://web.worldbank.org/WBSITE/EXTERNAL/TOPICS/EXTPOVERTY/EXTPGI/0,,contentMDK:20264272~menuPK:566333~pagePK:148956~piPK:216618~theSitePK:342771,00.html.

Lopez, Robert (1966), *The Birth of Europe*, New York: M. Evans and Company.

Lu, Susan Feng and Yang Yao (2003), "The Effectiveness of the Law, Financial Development, and Economic Growth in an Economy of Financial Depression: Evidence from China," Center for Research on Economic Development and Policy Reform, Stanford University, Palo Alto.

Lupia, Arthur and Mathew McCubbins (1998), *The Democratic Dilemma. Can Citizens Learn What They Need to Know?*, Cambridge: Cambridge University Press.

Mallaby, Sebastian (2004), *The World's Banker. A Story of Failed States, Financial Crises, and the Wealth and Poverty of Nations*, New York: The Penguin Press.

Mansuri, Ghazala and Vijayendra Rao (2003), "Evaluating Community-Based and Community-Driven Development: A Critical Review of the Evidence," World Bank Development Research Group Processed, Washington, DC.

Manzetti, Luigi (1993), *Institutions, Parties and Coalitions in Argentine Politics*, Pittsburg: University of Pittsburgh Press.

Martens, Bertin (2002), "Policy Conclusions Regarding Organizations Involved in Foreign Aid," in *The Institutional Economics of Foreign Aid*, Bertin Martens, Uwe Mummert, Peter Murrell and Paul Seabright (eds), Cambridge: Cambridge University Press, pp. 178–95.

Martens, Bertin, Uwe Mummert, Peter Murrell, and Paul Seabright (2002), *The Institutional Economics of Foreign Aid*, Cambridge: Cambridge University Press.

Ménard, Claude (2006), "Redesigning Public Utilities: The Key Role of Microinstitutions," paper presented at the annual meeting of the International Society for New Institutional Economics, Bolder, CO, 21–24 September.

Ménard, Claude and George R.G. Clarke (2002a), "Reforming Water Supply in Abidjan, Côte d'Ivoire: A Mild Reform in a Turbulent Environment," in *Thirsting for Efficiency: The Economics and Politics of Urban Water Sector Reform*, Mary M. Shirley (ed.), Oxford: Elsevier Science, pp. 233–72.

—— (2002b), "A Transitory Regime: Water Supply in Conakry, Guinea," in *Thirsting for Efficiency: The Economics and Politics of Urban Water Sector Reform*, Mary M. Shirley (ed.), Oxford: Elsevier Science, pp. 273–315.

Mèndez, Roberto (1990), "Opiniòn Publica y la Elecciòn Presidencial de 1989," *Estudios Públicos*, **38**, 68–97.

Millennium Challenge Corporation (2006), "Report on the Criteria and Methodology for Determining the Eligibility of Candidate Countries for Millennium Challenge Account Assistance in FY 2006,"

8 September, available at www.mca.gov/about_us/congressional_rep orts/FY07_Criteria_Methodology.pdf.

Mokyr, Joel (2002), "The Enduring Riddle of the European Miracle: The Enlightenment and the Industrial Revolution," draft notes presented to the Conference on Convergence and Divergence in Historical Perspective: The Origins of Wealth and Persistence of Poverty in the Modern World, Riverside, CA, 8–10 November, available at www.http://faculty.wcas.northwestern.edu/~jmokyr/papers.html.

—— (2006), "The Market for Ideas and the Origins of Economic Growth in Eighteenth Century Europe," Heineken Lecture, Groningen, Netherlands, 25 September, available at http://faculty.wcas.northwest-ern.edu/~jmokyr/papers.html.

Morck, Randall, Daniel Wolfenzon, and Bernard Yeung (2005), "Corporate Governance, Economic Entrenchment, and Growth," *Journal of Economic Literature*, **63** (September), 655–720.

Moroney, M.J. (1951), *Facts from Figures*, Harmondsworth, Middx: Penguin Books.

Mukherji, Joydeep (2002), "India's Slow Conversion to Market Economics," Center for Advanced Study of India, University of Pennsylvania, Working Paper 18.

Muller, Jerry Z. (2002), *The Mind and the Market. Capitalism in Modern European Thought*, New York: Alfred A. Knopf.

Mulreamy, John P., Sule Calikogul, Sonia Ruiz, and Jason W. Sapsin (2006), "Water Privatization and Public Health in Latin America," *Pan American Journal of Public Health*, **19**(1), 23–32, available at http://journal.paho.org/.

Munasinghe, Mohan (1992), *Water Supply and Environmental Management. Developing World Applications*, Boulder, CO: Westview Press.

Murrell, Peter (2005), "Institutions and Firms in Transitional Economies," in *Handbook of New Institutional Economics*, Claude Ménard and Mary M. Shirley (eds), Dordrecht, The Netherlands: Springer, pp. 667–99.

Noland, Marcus (2005), "From Player to Referee? The State and the South Korean Economy," Institute for International Economics, paper prepared for the conference, Toward the Second Miracle of Han River, Yonsei University, Seoul, South Korea, 12 October.

Noll, Roger (2002), "The Economics of Urban Water Systems," in *Thirsting for Efficiency: The Economics and Politics of Urban Water System Reform*, Mary M. Shirley (ed.), Oxford: Elsevier Science, pp. 43–63.

—— (2006), "Still Reforming Regulation," AEI-Brookings Joint Center for Regulatory Studies 2006 Distinguished Lecture, 14 November, Washington, DC.

Noll, Roger, Mary M. Shirley, and Simon Cowan (2000), "Reforming Urban Water Systems in Developing Countries," in, *Economic Policy Reform: The Second Stage*. Anne O. Krueger (ed.), Chicago: University of Chicago Press, pp. 243–91.

North, Douglass C. (1990), *Institutions, Institutional Change, and Economic Performance*, New York: Cambridge University Press.

—— (2005a), "Institutions and the Performance of Economies over Time," in *Handbook of New Institutional Economics*, Claude Ménard and Mary M. Shirley (eds) Dordrecht, The Netherlands: Springer, pp. 21–30.

—— (2005b), *Understanding the Process of Economic Change*, Princeton: Princeton University Press.

North, Douglass C. and Robert Paul Thomas (1973), *The Rise of the Western World: A New Economic History*, reprinted in 1999, Cambridge: Cambridge University Press.

North, Douglass C. and Barry R. Weingast (1989), "Constitutions and Commitment: The Evolution of Institutions Governing Public Choice in Seventeenth-Century England," *The Journal of Economic History*, **49**(4), 803–32.

North, Douglass C., John J. Wallis, and Barry R. Weingast (forthcoming), "A Conceptual Framework for Interpreting Recorded Human History," unpublished draft manuscript.

OECD (2003), "Philanthropic Foundations and Development Co-operation," *DAC Journal*, **4**(3), 350.

OECD, DAC (2006), "DAC Secretariat Simulations of Net ODA to 2006 and 2010," OECD, DAC, available at www.oecd.org/dac/stats/dac/.

—— (2007), "Statistical Appendix of the 2006 Development Cooperation Report," OECD, DAC, available at www.oecd.org/dac/stats/dac/.

Ohnesorge, John K.M. (2003), "China's Economic Transition and the New Legal Origins Literature," *China Economic Review*, **14**(4), 485–93, available at http://law.wisc.edu/facstaff/pubs.php?iID=68.

Oi, Jean C. (2000), "Bending without Breaking, the Adaptability of Chinese Political Institutions," Stanford University Center for Research on Economic Development and Policy Reform, Working Paper No. 61, available at http://scid.stanford.edu/pdf/credpr61.pdf.

Olson, Mancur (1965), *The Logic of Collective Action*, Cambridge, MA: Harvard University Press.

—— (1993), "Dictatorship, Democracy, and Development," *American Political Science Review*, **87**(3), 567–76.

O'Neil Trowbridge, Shannon (2001), "The Role of Ideas in Neoliberal Economic Reform: The Case of Argentina," paper presented at the Latin American Studies Association, Washington, DC, 5–9 September.

Ostrom, Elinor (2005), "Doing Institutional Analysis: Digging Deeper than Markets and Hierarchies," in *Handbook of New Institutional Economics*, Claude Ménard and Mary M. Shirley (eds), Dordrecht, The Netherlands: Springer, pp. 819–48.

Ostrom, Elinor, Clark Gibson, Sujai Shivakumar, and Krister Andersson (2002), "Aid, Incentives, and Sustainability: An Institutional Analysis of Development Cooperation," Swedish International Development Cooperation Agency (SIDA) Studies in Evaluation, Stockholm.

Papaioannou, Elias and Gregorios Siourounis (2004), "Democratization and Growth," London Business School, Economics Working Paper, November, available at SSRN, http://ssrn.com/abstract=564981.

Persson, Torsten and Torsten Tabellini (2006), "Democracy and Development: The Devil in the Details," NBER Working Paper No. 11993, January, available at http://www.nber.org/papers/w11993.

Pinera, Jose (1994), "Chile," in *The Political Economy of Policy Reform*, John Williamson (ed.), Washington, DC: Institute for International Economics, pp. 225–31.

Pistor, Katharina, Martin Raiser, and Stanislaw Gelfer (2000), "Law and Finance in Transition Economies," *Economics of Transition*, **8**(2), pp. 325–68.

Platteau, Jean-Philippe (2003), "Decentralized Development as a Strategy to Reduce Poverty," paper prepared for the Agence Française de Developpement (AFD) and the European Development Network (EUDN) conference, 13 November, Paris.

Porter, Roy (2000), *The Creation of the Modern World. The Untold Story of the British Enlightenment*, New York: W.W. Norton & Co.

Pratham (2006), *Annual Status of Education Report, 2005*, New Delhi: Partham.

Prichett, Lant (1996), "Where Has All the Education Gone?," World Bank, Policy Research Working Paper No. 1581, March, available at SSRN, http://ssrn.com/abstract=569239.

—— (2004), "Access to Education," in *Global Crises, Global Solutions*, Bjorn Lomborg (ed.), Cambridge: Cambridge University Press, pp. 175–234.

Prichett, Lant and Michael Woolcock (2004), "Solutions When the Solution is the Problem: Arraying the Disarray in Development," *World Development*, **32**(2), 191–212.

Przeworski, Adam and Fernando Limongi (1993), "Political Regimes and Economic Growth," *Journal of Economic Perspectives*, **7**(3), 51–70.

Przeworski, Adam, Michael E. Alvarez, Jose Antonio Cheibub, and Fernando Limongi (2000), *Democracy and Development: Political Institutions and Well-Being in the World, 1950–1990*, Cambridge: Cambridge University Press.

Public Broadcasting Television (PBS) (2002), Interview with Domingo Cavallo, conducted on 30 January, PBS, available at www.pbs.org/commandingheights.

Putnam, Robert (1993), *Making Democracy Work: Civil Traditions in Modern Italy*, Princeton: Princeton University Press.

Qian, Yingyi and Jinglian Wu (2003), "China's Transition to a Market Economy: How Far across the River?' in *How Far across the River? Chinese Policy Reform at the Millennium*, Nicholas C. Hope, Dennis Tao Yan and Mu Yang Li (eds), Stanford: Stanford University Press, pp. 31–64.

Rajan, Raghuram G. and Arvind Subramanian (2005), "Aid and Growth: What Does the Cross-Country Evidence Really Show?," International Monetary Fund, Research Department Working Paper WP/05/127, Washington, DC.

Rajan, Raghuram G. and Luigi Zingales (2003), "The Great Reversals: The Politics of Financial Development in the Twentieth Century," *Journal of Financial Economics*, **69**(1), pp. 5–50.

Reddy, Sanjay G. and Camelia Minoiu (2006), "Development Aid and Economic Growth: A Positive Long-Run Relationship," Working Paper Version 2.1, 11 July, available at SSRN, http://ssrn.com/abstract=903865.

Reinikka, Ritva and Jakob Svensson (2004), "Local Capture: Evidence from a Central Government Transfer Program in Uganda," *Quarterly Journal of Economics*, **119**(2) (May), 679–705.

Rigobón, Roberto and Dani Rodrik (2005), "Rule of Law, Democracy, Openness, and Income: Estimating the Interrelationships," *Economics of Transition / European Bank for Reconstruction and Development*, **13**(3), 533–64.

Rijsberman, Frank (2004), "Sanitation and Access to Clean Water," in *Global Crises, Global Solutions*, Bjorn Lomborg (ed.), Cambridge: Cambridge University Press, pp. 498–527.

Robinson, James A. (2002), "*States and Power in Africa* by Jeffrey I. Herbst: A Review Essay," *Journal of Economic Literature*, **XL**(2), 510–19.

Rodrik, Dani (2005), "Why We Learn Nothing from Regressing Economic Growth on Policies," unpublished paper, March, Harvard University, Kennedy School of Government, available at http://ksghome.harvard.edu/~drodrik/papers.html.

Rodrik, Dani and Romain Wacziarg (2005), "Do Democratic Transitions Produce Bad Economic Outcomes?," *American Economic Review*, **95**, 50–56.

Rodrik, Dani, Arvind Subramanian, and Francesco Trebbi (2002), "Institutions Rule: The Primacy of Institutions over Geography and Integration in Economic Development," Centre for Economic Policy Research.

Roe, Mark J. (2002), "Institutional Foundations for Securities Markets in the West," Washington, DC, draft prepared for the ASSA meeting, 3–5 January.

Roll, Richard and John Talbott (2001), "Why Many Developing Countries Just Aren't," Finance Working Paper No. 19-01, Anderson School, UCLA, 13 November, available at SSRN, http://ssrn.com/abstract=292140.

Roodman, David (2004), "The Anarchy of Numbers: Aid, Development, and Cross-Country Empirics," Center for Global Development, Washington, DC.

Rosenthal, Jean-Laurent (1998), "The Political Economy of Absolutism Reconsidered," in *Analytical Narratives*, Robert H. Bates, Avner Greif, Margaret Levi, Jean-Laurent Rosenthal and Barry R. Weingast (eds), Princeton: Princeton University Press, pp. 64–108.

Roth, Gabriel (1987), *The Private Provision of Public Services in Developing Countries*, New York: Oxford University Press.

Rubin, Paul H. (2005), "Legal Systems as Frameworks for Market Exchange," in *Handbook of New Institutional Economics*, Claude Ménard and Mary M. Shirley (eds), Dordrecht, The Netherlands: Springer, pp. 205–28.

Sachs, Jeffrey (2005), *The End of Poverty. Economic Possibilities for Our Time*, New York: Penguin Press.

Schama, Simon (1988), *The Embarrassment of Riches. An Interpretation of Dutch Culture in the Golden Age*, New York: Alfred A. Knopf.

Scully, Timothy R. (1995), "Reconstituting Party Politics in Chile," in *Building Democratic Institutions: Party Systems in Latin America*, Scott Mainwaring and Timothy R. Scully (eds), Stanford: Stanford University Press, pp. 100–137.

Seabright, Paul (2002), "Conflicts of Objectives and Task Allocation in Aid Agencies," in *The Institutional Economics of Foreign Aid*, Bertin Martens, Uwe Mummert, Peter Murrell and Paul Seabright (eds), Cambridge: Cambridge University Press, pp. 34–68.

Shepsle, Kenneth A. (2001), "A Comment on Institutional Change," *Journal of Theoretical Politics*, **13**, 321–5.

Shin, Doh Chull and Chong-min Park (2003), "The Mass Public and Democratic Politics in South Korea: Exploring the Subjective World of Democratization in Flux," Asian Barometer, Working Paper Series No. 15, available at http://www.asianbarometer.org/newenglish/publications/workingpapers/no.15.pdf.

Shiraishi, Takashi (2006), "Technocracy in Indonesia: A Preliminary Analysis," Research Institute of Economy, Trade, and Industry (RIETI) Discussion Paper Series 05-E-008, Tokyo, available at www.rieti.go.jp/publications/dp/06e008.pdf.

Shirk, Susan L. (1993), *The Political Logic of Economic Reform in China*, Berkeley and Los Angeles: University of California Press.

Shirley, Mary M. (1989), *The Reform of State-Owned Enterprises: Lessons from World Bank Lending*, Washington, DC: World Bank.

—— (1998), "Bureaucracy in Eastern Europe and the Former Soviet Union," in *The New Palgrave Dictionary of Economics and the Law*, Peter Newman (ed.), London: Macmillan.

—— (1999), "Bureaucrats in Business: The Roles of Privatization Versus Corporatization in State-Owned Enterprise Reform," *World Development*, **27**, 115–36.

—— (ed.) (2002), *Thirsting for Efficiency: The Economics and Politics of Urban Water System Reform*, Oxford: Elsevier Science.

—— (2005a), "Institutions and Development," in *Handbook of New Institutional Economics*, Claude Ménard and Mary M. Shirley (eds), Dordrecht, The Netherlands: Springer, pp. 611–38.

—— (2005b), "Why is Sector Reform so Unpopular in Latin America?" *Independent Review*, **10**(5), 195–207.

Shirley, Mary M. and Claude Ménard (2002), "Cities Awash: A Synthesis of the Country Cases," in *Thirsting for Efficiency: The Economics and Politics of Urban Water System Reform*, Mary M. Shirley (ed.), Oxford: Elsevier Science, pp. 1–41.

Shirley, Mary M. and John R. Nellis (1991), *Public Enterprise Reform: The Lessons of Experience*, Washington, DC: World Bank.

Shirley, Mary M. and Jessica Soto (2007), "The Role of Scholars and Scholarship in Institutional Change," working paper presented at the annual meeting of the International Society for New Institutional Economics, Reykjavik, Iceland, 21–23 June.

Shirley, Mary M. and L. Colin Xu (1998), "Information, Incentives and Commitment. An Empirical Analysis of Contracts between Government and State Enterprises," *Journal of Law, Economics and Organization*, **14**(2), 358–78.

—— (2001), "Empirical Effects of Performance Contracts: Evidence from China," *Journal of Law, Economics and Organization*, **17**(1), 168–200.

Shirley, Mary M., Colin L. Xu, and Ana Maria Zuluaga (2002), "Reforming Urban Water Supply: The Case of Chile," in *Thirsting for Efficiency: The Economics and Politics of Urban Water System Reform*, Mary M. Shirley (ed.), Oxford: Elsevier Science, pp. 189–231.

Shugart, Matthew S. and John M. Carey (1992), *Presidents and Assemblies: Constitutional Design and Electoral Dynamics*, New York: Cambridge University Press.

Siems, Mathias (2006), "Legal Origins," CBC Research Paper No. 0023, available at SSRN, http://ssrn.com/abstract=879720.

Silva, Eduardo (1993), "Capitalist Coalitions, the State, and Neoliberal Economic Restructuring: Chile, 1973–88," *World Politics*, **45**(4), 526–59.

Silva, Patricio (1992), "Technocrats and Politics in Chile: From the Chicago Boys to the CIEPLAN Monks," *Journal of Latin American Studies*, **23**(2), 385–410.

Sirtaine, Sophie, Maria Elena Pinglo, J. Luis Guasch, and Vivien Foster (2005), "How Profitable are Private Infrastructure Concessions in Latin America? Empirical Evidence and Regulatory Implications," *Quarterly Review of Economics and Finance*, **45**(2–3), 380–402.

Sokoloff, Kenneth L. and Stanley L. Engerman (2000), "Institutions, Factor Endowments, and Paths of Development in the New World," *Journal of Economic Perspectives*, **14**(3), 217–32.

Sokoloff, Kenneth L. and Eric M. Zolt (2005), "Inequality and the Evolution of Institutions of Taxation: Evidence from the Economic History of the Americas," working paper (April), available at http://www.yale.edu/leitner/zolt.pdf.

Spiller, Pablo T. and Mariano Tommasi (2000), "The Institutional Foundations of Public Policy: A Transactions Approach with Application to Argentina," presented at the annual meeting of the International Society for New Institutional Economics, Tübingen, Germany, 22–24 September.

Stokes, Susan (2001), *Mandates and Democracy: Neoliberalism by Surprise in Latin America*, Cambridge: Cambridge University Press.

Strang, David and Susan A. Soule (1998), "Diffusion in Organizations and Social Movements: From Hybrid Corn to Poison Pills," *Annual Review of Sociology*, **24**, 265–90.

Svensson, Jacob (2000), "The Cost of Doing Business: Firms' Experience with Corruption in Uganda," World Bank, Africa Region Working Paper No. 6, Washington, DC.

Taylor, Charles et al. (various), *World Handbook of Political and Social Indicators*, New Haven, CT: Yale University Press.

Temple, Jonathan (2003), "Growing into Trouble: Indonesia after 1966," in *In Search of Prosperity: Analytic Narratives on Economic Growth*, Dani Rodrik (ed.), Princeton: Princeton University Press; based on an August 2001 version of the chapter available at www.ksghome.harvard.edu/~drodrik/Growth%20volume/Temple-Indo.pdf.

Tendulkar, Suresh D. and T.A. Bhavani (2005), "Understanding the Post-1991 Indian Economic Policy Reforms," Global Development Network Understanding Reform Project, draft.

Tilly, Charles (1992), *Coercion, Capital, and European States*, Oxford: Blackwell Publishing.

Tiscali, Tiscali Reference Encyclopedia, http://www.tiscali.co.uk/reference/encyclopaedia/countryfacts/taiwan.html.

Troesken, Werner and Rick Geddes (2003), "Municipalizing American Waterworks, 1897–1915," *Journal of Law, Economics and Organization*, **19**(2), 373–400.

Tsai, Ming-Chang (2001), "Dependency, the State and Class in the Neoliberal Transition of Taiwan," *Third World Quarterly*, **22**(3), 359–79.

UN Millennium Project (2005a), *Health, Dignity, and Development: What Will It Take?* New York: United Nations Millennium Project.

—— (2005b), *Investing in Development: A Practical Plan to Achieve the Millennium Development Goals*, London: Earthscan, available at www.unmillenniumproject.org.

United Kingdom Department for International Development (2003), "Promoting Institutional and Organizational Development," 1–23, DFID, London.

US Government, Centers for Disease Control (1995), "Epidemic Cholera in the New World: Translating Field Epidemiology into New Prevention Strategies," *Emerging Infectious Diseases*, **1**(4) (October–December), available at http://www.cdc.gov/ncidod/eid/vol1no4/tauxe.htm.

Valdivia Ortiz de Zarate, Verònica (2001), "Estatismo Y Neoliberalismo: Un Contrapunto Militar Chile 1973–1979," *Historia (Santiago)*, **34**, 167–226, available at http://www.scielo.cl/scielo.php?script=sci_arttext&pid=S0717-71942001003400006&lng=es&nrm=iso.

Valenzeula, Arturo (1994), "Party Politics and the Crisis of Presidentialism in Chile: A Proposal for a Parliamentary Form of Government," in *The Failure of Presidential Democracy. Comparative Perspectives*, Juan J. Linz and Arturo Valenzeula (eds), Baltimore, MD: The Johns Hopkins University Press.

Velasco, Andres (1994), "The State and Economic Policy: Chile 1952–92," in *The Chilean Economy: Policy Lessons and Challenges*, Barry P. Bosworth, Rudiger Dornbusch and Raul Raul Laban (eds), Washington, DC: The Brookings Institution, pp. 379–429.

Volcker, Paul A., Gustavo Gaviria, John Githongo, Ben W. Jr Heineman, Walter Van Gerven, and John Vereker (2007), "Independent Panel Review of the World Bank Group Department of Institutional Integrity," World Bank, available at www.independentpanelreview.com.

Wane, Waly (2004), "The Quality of Foreign Aid. Country Selectivity or Donors Incentives?," World Bank Policy Research Working Paper 3325, Washington, DC.

Webb and Associates (1992), "Waterborne Diseases in Peru," World Bank, Background Paper for the *1992 World Development Report*, Washington, DC.

Weingast, Barry R. (1993), "Constitutions as Governance Structures: The Political Foundations of Secure Markets," *Journal of Institutional and Theoretical Economics*, **149**(1), 286–311.

—— (1995), "The Economic Role of Political Institutions: Market-Preserving Federalism and Economic Development," *Journal of Law, Economics and Organization*, **96**, 132–63.

—— (2005), "Self-Enforcing Constitutions: With an Application to Democratic Stability in America's First Century," working paper, Hoover Institution, Stanford University, November.

West, Mark (2002), "Legal Determinants of World Cup Success," available at SSRN, http://ssrn.com/abstract=318940.

Williamson, Oliver E. (1985), *The Economic Institutions of Capitalism*, New York: The Free Press.

Winston, Clifford (1993), "Economic Deregulation: Days of Reckoning for Microeconomists," *Journal of Economic Literature*, **31**(September), 1263–89.

Wonhyuk Lim, Philip (2003), "Path Dependence in Action: The Rise and Fall of the Korean Model of Economic Development," in *History Matters: Essays on Economic Growth, Technology, and Demographic Change*, Timothy W. Guinnane, William A. Sundstrom and Warren C. Whatley (eds), Stanford: Stanford University Press, pp. 142–62.

World Bank (1981), *World Development Report 1981: National and International Adjustment*, Washington, DC: The World Bank.

—— (1994), *World Development Report, 1994. Infrastructure for Development*, New York: Oxford University Press for the World Bank.

—— (1995), *Bureaucrats in Business: The Economics and Politics of State-Owned Enterprise Reform*, New York: Oxford University Press.

—— (1998), *Assessing Aid. A World Bank Policy Research Report*, New York: Oxford University Press.

World Bank (1999), "Indonesia Country Assistance Note," World Bank Operations Evaluation Department Report No. 19100, Washington, DC.

—— (2001), "Bolivia: Microeconomic Constraints and Opportunities for Higher Growth," World Bank: Washington, DC.

—— (2002), *World Development Report 2002: Building Institutions for Markets*, Washington, DC: Oxford University Press.

—— (2003a), *Toward Country-Led Development: A Multi-Partner Evaluation of the Comprehensive Development Framework*, Washington, DC: The World Bank, Operations Evaluation Department.

—— (2003b), *World Development Report 2003: Sustainable Development in a Dynamic World*, Washington, DC: The World Bank and Oxford University Press.

World Bank (2004a), "Books, Buildings, and Learning Outcomes: An Impact Evaluation of World Bank Support to Basic Education in Ghana," The World Bank, Operations Evaluation Department Report No. 28779, available at www.worldbank.org/ieg/ie/ghana_ie.html.

—— (2004b), *World Development Report 2004: Making Services Work for Poor People*, Washington, DC: The World Bank and Oxford University Press.

—— (2005a), "Annual Report 2005 Website: Organizational Information – Country Eligibility for Borrowing from the World Bank," available at www.worldbank.org/aboutus/annrep/.

—— (2005b), *Capacity Building in Africa. An OED Evaluation of World Bank Support*, Washington, DC: The World Bank, Operations Evaluation Department.

—— (2005c), "Country Policy and Institutional Assessments. 2005 Assessment Questionnaire," The World Bank, Operations Policy and Country Services, available at http://siteresources.worldbank.org/IDA/Resources/CPIA2005Questionnaire.pdf.

—— (2005d), *The Effectiveness of World Bank Support for Community-Based and -Driven Development. An OED Evaluation*, Washington, DC: The World Bank, Operations Evaluation Department, available at www.worldbank.org/ieg.

—— (2005e), "Ida 14 Replenishment Report, Annex 1."

—— (2005f), *World Development Report 2005. A Better Investment Climate for Everyone*, Washington, DC: The World Bank and Oxford University Press.

—— (2006a), "Doing Business 2007," The World Bank Group, available at Doing Business website at www.doingbusiness.org/methodologysurveys/startingbusiness.aspx.

—— (2006b), *Held by the Visible Hand. The Challenge of State-Owned Enterprise Corporate Governance for Emerging Markets*, Washington, DC: The World Bank, Corporate Governance.

—— (2006c), "How Ida Resources Are Allocated," available at http://web.worldbank.org/WBSITE/EXTERNAL/EXTABOUTUS/IDA/0,,contentMDK:20052347~menuPK:2607525~pagePK:51236175~piPK:437394~theSitePK:73154,00.html.

—— (2006d), "Impact Evaluation – the Experience of the Independent Evaluation Group of the World Bank," The World Bank, Independent Evaluation Group, available at www.worldbank.org/ieg/ie.

—— (2006e), *World Bank – Civil Society Engagement. Review of Fiscal Years 2005 and 2006*, Washington, DC: The World Bank, available at www.worldbank.org/civilsociety.

—— (2006f), "World Bank: Water Supply and Sanitation: Project Lending," http://www.worldbank.org/html/fpd/water/projectlending.html.

—— (2006g), *World Development Report 2006: Equity and Development*, Washington, DC: The World Bank.

—— (2006h), "World Development Indicators Database: GNI Per Capita 2005, Atlas Method and Ppp," World Bank, 1 July 2006, available at http://go.worldbank.org/K2CKM78CCO.

—— (various), "World Development Indicators," available at www.world bank.org/datastatistics/wdi.

World Bank, Independent Evaluation Group (2006), *From Schooling Access to Learning Outcomes: An Unfinished Agenda. An Evaluation of World Bank Support to Primary Education*, Washington, DC: The World Bank.

World Values Survey (various), "The Values Surveys," World Values Survey, available at www.worldvaluessurvey.org.

Wu, Jinglian, Xiochuan Zhou, Jiwei Lou et al. (1988), *Zhongguo Jingji Gaige De Zhengti Sheji [The Integrated Design of China's Economic Reform]*, Beijing: China Outlook Publishing House, in Chinese.

Wu, Yongping (2005), *A Political Explanation of Economic Growth: State Survival, Bureaucratic Politics, and Private Enterprise in the Making of Taiwan's Economy, 1950–1985*, Cambridge, MA: Harvard University Press.

Yu, Fu-Lai Tony (2006), "The Architect of Taiwan's Economic Miracle: Evolutionary Economics of Li Kuo-Ting," paper prepared for a seminar at the Department of Economics, Feng Chia University (Taiwan), 3 November.

Zanden, Jan Leiten van (2004), "Common Workmen, Philosophers, and the Birth of the European Knowledge Economy. About the Price and Production of Useful Knowledge in Europe 1350–1800," paper prepared for the GEHN Conference on Useful Knowledge, Leiden, the Netherlands, September, revised 12 October, available at http://www.iisg.nl/staff/jvz.php.

Zhou, Yuan and Richard S.J. Tol (2003), "Implications of Desalination to Water Resources in China – an Economic Perspective," Research Unit, Sustainability and Global Change, Center for Marine and Climate Research, Hamburg University, Working Paper FNU-22.

Zylbersztajn, Décio, Frederico Faccioli, Rodrigo F. Silveira, and Maristela F.P Leme (2004), "Business Environment in Brazil: Measuring Cost of Entrance in the Brazilian Garment Industry," The University of Sao Paulo School of Economics and Business, Brazil.

Index